MONEY

WITHOUT

MATRIMONY

MONEY

WITHOUT

MATRIMONY

THE UNMARRIED COUPLE'S GUIDE
TO FINANCIAL SECURITY

Sheryl Garrett, CFP®, and Debra A. Neiman, CFP®, MBA

Dearborn™
Trade Publishing
A **Kaplan Professional** Company

President, Dearborn Publishing: Roy Lipner
Vice President and Publisher: Cynthia A. Zigmund
Acquisitions Editor: Mary B. Good
Senior Managing Editor: Jack Kiburz
Interior Design: Lucy Jenkins
Cover Design: Design Literate
Typesetting: the dotted i

Published by Dearborn Trade Publishing
A Kaplan Professional Company

Printed in the United States of America

05 06 07   10 9 8 7 6 5 4 3 2 1

Library of Congress Cataloging-in-Publication Data

Garrett, Sheryl.
    Money without matrimony : the unmarried couple's guide to financial security / by Sheryl Garrett and Debra A. Neiman.
        p.   cm.
    Includes index.
    ISBN 1-4195-0688-9 (7.25x9 pbk.)
    1. Unmarried couples—United States—Finance, Personal. 2. Unmarried couples—Legal status, laws, etc.—United States.   I. Neiman, Debra A.
II. Title.
HG179.G38 2005
332.024′01′0865—dc22

                                                                                2005003102

Dearborn Trade books are available at special quantity discounts to use for sales promotions, employee premiums, or educational purposes. Please call our Special Sales Department to order or for more information at 800-621-9621, ext. 4444, e-mail trade@dearborn.com, or write to Dearborn Trade Publishing, 30 South Wacker Drive, Suite 2500, Chicago, IL 60606-7481.

PRAISE FOR *MONEY WITHOUT MATRIMONY*

"I love a book that feels like it was written with me in mind, and *Money Without Matrimony* is one of those books. It leads you step-by-step through the very complex issue of financial planning. And, unlike most books on the topic, it advises unmarried couples—gay or straight—about how to plan for living without the enormous financial advantages that marriage provides, such as Social Security survivor benefits."

Lisa Bennett, Director of the Human Rights Campaign Foundation's Family Project (http://www.hrc.org/family)

"The unfortunate (and sometimes tragic) truth in our society is that un-married couples of all genders and persuasions are routinely denied the more than 1,140 different legal protections afforded by the marriage cere-mony. In *Money Without Matrimony*, two highly respected members of the financial planning community give you a readable, personal guide to where the gaps are and how to address them, step-by-step, using real-world examples and offering real-world wisdom. At the end of the book, you won't feel quite so much like a second-class member of our marriage-centric economy."

Robert Veres, Publisher of *Inside Information* and Author of *The Cutting Edge in Financial Services*

"*Money Without Matrimony* addresses the unique financial planning needs of one of the fastest growing segments of our population. Unmarried couples who share emotional and financial commitments have to plan ahead to protect each other. Garrett and Neiman offer practical advice and use real-world examples to illustrate concepts. I highly recommend this book not only for all unmarried couples and but also for financial pro-fessionals who work with unmarried couples."

Dee Lee, Author of *Women and Money*

"This is a wonderful resource—concise, clearly expressed, and empowering. It skillfully integrates the essential elements of financial planning for couples: information, emotional intelligence, and inspiration!"

Frederick Hertz, Attorney and Coauthor of *Legal Guide for Lesbian & Gay Couples*

"Read this book for practical, easy-to-read, and essential financial advice for unmarried couples who recognize that rules and tools of everyday life don't always apply equally. The future really does belong to those who prepare for it. An important contribution."

Phyllis Bernstein, CPA, Coauthor of *Financial Planning for CPAs* and *Managing Client Expectations in an Uncertain Market*

"Sheryl Garrett is one of the true financial planning innovators. Along with coauthor Debra Neiman, she continues to break new ground with *Money Without Matrimony*. It is indispensable for unmarried couples. Amidst so much mass media financial noise, Garrett's book stands out with its rare common sense and clear explanations. Like Garrett and Neiman, this book is a trusted advisor for the way we live in the 21st century."

Richard J. Koreto, Editor-in-Chief, *Advising Boomers Magazine*

DEDICATION

To all unmarried couples who seek financial security and equality

Contents

Acknowledgments

We would like to express our sincerest appreciation to Cynthia A. Zigmund, vice president and publisher; Mary B. Good, acquisitions editor; and Al Martin, publicist, at Dearborn Trade Publishing for their vision and enthusiastic support of this book. Thank you for recognizing the enormous need of unmarried couples for qualified and practical financial advice.

We also owe a great deal of recognition to our collaborative writing partner, Susan J. Marks. Without Susan's steadfast devotion and sheer talent, this book might have been years in production.

We also wish to acknowledge the support and assistance of our professional organizations, Pride Planners™ and The Garrett Planning Network, Inc., whose members provided valuable assistance and input throughout the preparation of this book.

A huge debt of gratitude is owed to the staff of The Garrett Planning Network involved in this project, including Jamie Breeden and Justin Nichols, who spent a great deal of time researching, drafting, and verifying data used throughout this text, and Eva Brodzik for her passion and support and for her keen eye and fresh viewpoint during the planning, proposal, and editing stages.

Additionally, our appreciation extends to our attorney colleagues—Gail Horowitz, Stuart Hamilton, Laurie Israel, and Joyce Kauffman, and the great folks at Husch & Eppenberger, LLC—for their wisdom and guidance.

We wish to thank Jack and Barbara Garrett for continuously demonstrating that when true love and open communication exist, happiness and respect flourish. You're great role models. Happy 50th anniversary!

Finally, a special thank-you to Jack, Barbara, and Ellen Neiman and to Karen Nickel for their love, encouragement, and support.

Introduction

Financial planning is *not* just for married couples with loads of money. Anyone at any age, who is unmarried and living with or is considering living with a partner—or who owns property with that partner—needs to plan for their financial future. Planning is crucial for unmarried couples, whether they're together casually or committed, no matter their income or living situation. For a financially healthy present and a secure future, both partners need to understand where they're going and what it will take to get there.

Unmarried couples make up almost 5.5 million households in the United States. That's 11 million people, or more than 5 percent of the total U.S. adult population, who—for reasons ranging from financial to familial, personal, or otherwise—are coupled but not married. Yet these people aren't eligible for the basic legal protections afforded their married counterparts. Did you know that more than 1,140 federal laws apply to married couples but not to unmarried ones?

Financial planning is essential to ensure financial security and to protect these partners and individuals from legal and financial nightmares. Even casual companions should take steps to protect their financial and personal well-being.

Consider the following:

- If an unmarried couple buys a car jointly and one of them gets in an accident, the other individual could be held liable, and both could lose big.
- If an unmarried couple purchases a house together without ensuring that the property is titled correctly and additional documentation completed, if one of the partners dies or becomes disabled, the other could end up alone, homeless, and destitute.

Despite the horror stories, few unmarried couples of any age bother with financial planning. In fact, most of us—married or not—rarely get around to formal planning until we're overwhelmed by a money crisis or left holding an empty bag after a nasty ending to a relationship.

Solid tax-planning, estate-planning, and investment advice is readily available for married couples with money. But competent, affordable financial advice is tough to find if you're an unmarried middle-income couple.

Money Without Matrimony can change that situation. It's not an ordinary financial planning book that details how to budget, what to spend, and where to save and how much. Neither is it a book on investing. Investment advice is only one small part of financial planning. Instead, this book is a guide that helps couples plan for today, tomorrow, and well into the future. We take a holistic approach to financial planning. It encompasses money, relationships, lifestyles, health, family, and more. We address the simple issues, such as who picks up the tab for groceries this week, as well as the more complicated ones, such as coadoption for same-sex partners or compensating for lack of Social Security survivor's benefits.

This is the first book that actually combines financial advice with stories from the people—old and young—who have been there, who have struggled through the financial mazes unmarried couples face in a society that promotes marriage and children.

We recognize that being married isn't the lifestyle for everyone—that it isn't realistic for some and that it isn't legal for others. Not everyone stays married their entire life, either. Consider a few statistics:

- The average American spends the majority of their life unmarried. (Rose Krider and Jason Fields "Number, Timing and Duration of Marriages and Divorces: 1996," *Current Population Reports,* 2002)
- The number of unmarried couples living together increased 72 percent from 1990 to 2000. (U.S. Census Bureau)
- Forty-one percent of American women ages 15 to 44 have cohabitated at some point. In this study, *cohabitate* is defined as living with an unmarried, different-sex partner. (Centers for Disease Control and Prevention, "Cohabitation, Marriage, Divorce, and Remarriage in the United States." Vital Health and Statistics Series 23, Number 22, Department of Health and Human Services, 2002)
- 1.2 million Americans live with a same-sex partner—and these numbers could be significantly understated. That's 11 percent of the unmarried population in the United States. (U.S. Census Bureau, 2000)
- Fifty-three percent of women's first marriages are preceded by cohabitation. (Larry Bumpass and Hsien-Hen Lu, "Trends in Cohabitation and Implications for Children's Family Contexts in the United States," *Population Studies,* 54:29–41, 2000)

Whatever your age, sexuality, or lifestyle, we hope that *Money Without Matrimony* will open your eyes to the financial ramifications of coupling and help you—as an individual and a couple—learn what it takes to lead a happy, financially healthy life. If you're just starting out as a couple, this book will show you what to expect. If you already have financial and legal issues, this book will help you sort through, simplify, and resolve them. If things are going well financially, remember: there's always room for improvement.

For purposes of this book, we classify unmarried couples into three major categories:

1. Heterosexual men and women who choose to postpone marriage, who do not marry at all, or who are divorced and choose not to remarry. In this book, we'll call them *younger couples.*
2. Older heterosexual men and women eligible for Social Security benefits—including seniors, widows, and widowers—who are a

couple but opt not to marry or remarry for family, financial, or personal reasons. In this book, we will refer to them generally as *older couples.*

3. Same-sex individuals who are a couple and may be life partners but who cannot legally marry except, at the time of this book's publication, in the state of Massachusetts. We'll refer to them as *same-sex couples.*

Whichever category you and your partner fall into, *Money Without Matrimony* has the answers and will help both of you understand the financial ramifications (current and future) of coupling, what to expect, and, step-by-step, how to avoid the pitfalls of a system stacked against you. Then, instead of becoming victims of the system, you and your partner will be able to capitalize on the laws dealing with everything from credit and income taxes to property rights, inheritance, health and life insurance, death benefits, and more. As an unmarried couple you will learn how easy it is to be as well off—if not better off—than your married counterparts, instead of facing uncertainty and insecurity.

This book is about caring for your financial well-being and that of a partner. It's not about being politically correct or skirting the issues. It's designed to help you do what's right for you in the living situation of your choosing. That goes for older couples who choose not to marry, for same-sex couples who can't marry legally, and for younger, heterosexual couples who opt to remain unmarried or to postpone tying the knot.

We address the financial and legal nuances that couples encounter as well as the basics. Sometimes the latter represents the greater risk to unmarried couples because, all too often, the basics simply are overlooked with devastating results.

For instance, an older couple, both widowed and longtime companions, may have chosen the unmarried, coupled life specifically to preserve each other's Social Security survivor's benefits from prior spouses. But if they open a joint bank or investment account or buy property together, they risk incredible liability issues and face estate-planning nightmares.

Even scarier is the fact that two people—any couple, any age—who present themselves as a legal couple over a period of time, may, without realizing it, be deemed legally married under the common laws of their state (a limited number of states recognize common law marriage) and subject to the laws affecting married couples. That includes requirements for a formal divorce to dissolve their relationship, should it come to that.

Sheryl Garrett

Coauthor Sheryl Garrett, CFP®, is well qualified to help you make the right financial moves. She's a Kansas City–based Certified Financial Planner™ professional and recognized industry expert. As a financial planner for almost 20 years, she's helped countless couples, married and not, learn how to plan their financial lives so that their assets and resources work effectively and their dreams and goals can be achieved. She's also founder of The Garrett Planning Network, Inc., a nationwide network of more than 230 fee-only financial advisors who provide hourly, as-needed advice to people from all walks of life.

Garrett and her network of planning professionals have provided advice and commentary for major broadcast media outlets that include NBC *(Today Show)*, CNN/FN, Bloomberg TV, WGN, and PBS as well as print publications—the *Wall Street Journal, Money, Time,* and *Newsweek.*

For the past two years, Garrett has been on *Investment Advisor* magazine's list of the "Top 25 Most Influential People in Financial Planning." She's been named to *Mutual Funds* magazine's list of the nation's "Top 100 Financial Advisors," and she's on *Financial Planning* magazine's "Modern Masters" list. She's also been asked to testify before Congress on behalf of the planning industry and has served on the boards of various organizations, including the National Association of Personal Financial Advisors, the Financial Planning Association, International Association for Financial Planning, and Institute for Certified Financial Planners. She's also authored two other books, *Just Give Me the Answer$: Expert Advisors Address Your Most Pressing Financial Questions* (Dearborn Trade, 2004) and *Garrett's Guide to Financial Planning: How to Capture the Middle Market and Increase Your Profits* (National Underwriter, 2002).

Debra A. Neiman

Coauthor Debra A. Neiman, CFP®, MBA, is equally well qualified. A Certified Financial Planner™ professional based in Watertown, Massachusetts, she specializes in the investment, retirement, and tax-planning needs of unmarried couples and families. She understands the nuances of state laws that vary widely, and she provides a unique perspective on how to solve issues common among unmarried couples, with and without children.

Neiman is a frequent lecturer on the topic of financial planning for unmarried couples; assistant professor of financial planning at Bentley College in Waltham, Massachusetts; and chair of the Financial Planning Association of Massachusetts. She's also a founding member of Pride-Planners™, an organization of financial planners serving the gay and lesbian community. She has appeared on CNN/FN and National Public Radio's *Marketplace* and has been featured in numerous publications including *Business Week,* the *Advocate,* and *Kiplinger's Personal Finance.*

Together, Garrett and Neiman will help you plan for and navigate the pitfalls that unmarried couples face. You will find charts and pullouts throughout this book to pinpoint actions or strategies essential for a particular category of unmarried couples. The charts include the following icons to represent each group:

- Younger couples   **Y**
- Older or mature couples   **O**
- Same-sex couples   **SS**

Thorough definitions of many important terms are available in the glossary at the back of this book.

Throughout the book, we mention company names and products. That's not an endorsement of any company or its products. It's simply a means to provide you, our readers, with resources and examples to help you take the next step.

So let's get started clarifying, simplifying, and improving your financial life.

Sheryl Garrett, CFP®

Debra A. Neiman, CFP®, MBA

CHAPTER 1

Why Financial Planning Is Important for You and Your Partner

If something were to happen to you today, what would you want done with your "stuff"? Your stuff isn't limited to assets like stocks and bonds, condos or cars. What about your CD collection, jewelry, laptop, personal journals, artwork, pets, and other possessions? Who would you want to sort through those belongings and ultimately have them?

Every couple, unmarried or otherwise, should ask themselves these questions. If you're married and don't bother to answer the question, no sweat. The laws of the land have a plan for you—maybe not the plan you would like but a plan nonetheless. Without a will, your spouse automatically becomes your estate's executor. Your possessions automatically go to your next of kin, according to state law. Also, regardless of whether or not you have a will, married couples receive an unlimited marital transfer of property and avoid estate taxes on the first spouse's death.

But, if you're one of the more than five million unmarried couples in the United States and you want your partner or someone other than your parents or next of kin—no matter how distant a blood relationship—to sort through your possessions, inherit, or distribute your stuff, the situation is far more complicated. And it can have tragic consequences. It needn't, though, if you and your partner talk about and plan for your futures as individuals and as a couple.

Whether you're an older couple eligible for Social Security, a younger couple postponing or not interested in marriage, or same-sex partners who can't marry legally, it's imperative that you plan for the future.

WHY BOTHER?

Money affects almost every aspect of our lives, so it's just good sense to spend some time and energy on your financial goals, objectives, and plans both as individuals and as a couple. Beyond that, it's absolutely essential that unmarried couples talk about money and plan ahead. Legal protections afforded married couples simply don't cover unmarried ones, no matter their age, financial situation, or sexual orientation. As of this book's publication, a total of 1,143 federal laws apply to married couples but not to their unmarried counterparts. Those laws cover everything from cars to charge cards to homes, from liability to disability to after-death details.

Let's look a little closer at some of the most evident areas of discrimination against unmarried couples.

DISCRIMINATORY LAWS

Unmarried couples must deal with a legal deck stacked against them. A few of the areas in which inequities exist include:

- No unlimited marital deduction on transfer of property
- No Social Security survivor's benefits
- Taxes on domestic partner benefits like health insurance

Unlimited Marital Deduction/Gifting

Spouses can give each other anything—even $1 billion—without tax consequences. Tax laws allow married couples to defer estate taxes until after the second spouse dies. Unmarried couples, on the other hand, don't enjoy the same right. Unmarried partners are subject to potential gift tax consequences if gifts to each other exceed $11,000 a year or a $1 million lifetime maximum.

Also, any amount of a deceased individual's (as in unmarried partner's) assets that exceeds $1.5 million is subject to estate taxes assessed at rates ranging from 37 percent up to 47 percent.

Often, when a couple begins life together, they want to share assets. If the couple is married, their sharing is boundless. If unmarried, their sharing is restricted by gift tax laws.

Social Security Survivor's Benefits

All eligible workers pay into Social Security, but under the current system, only married couples are entitled to each other's benefits in the event a partner dies. Conversely, unmarried workers pay the same employment taxes as do their married counterparts, but a surviving partner of an unmarried couple isn't entitled to any survivor's benefits.

That means that a surviving spouse who has never paid a dime into Social Security can receive years of survivor's benefits after his or her spouse dies, but his or her unmarried counterpart isn't eligible for anything.

Domestic Partner Benefits Taxed

If domestic partners obtain health insurance through one partner's employer, the total cost of the premium paid by the employer for the domestic partner is considered phantom income—income that is not part of your salary but is taxed as if it were. A married couple, on the other hand, can get health insurance through either spouse's employer without incurring tax consequences. A married employee generally has to pay a premium for their spouse's coverage but can pay with pretax dollars.

The Consolidated Omnibus Budget Reconciliation Act of 1995 (COBRA) requires companies with 20 or more employees to continue medical benefits to spouses and dependent children in the event of divorce, reduction in hours, termination of employment, Medicare entitlement, change in dependent status, and death. Unmarried partners are not legally included.

That doesn't mean, however, that unmarried couples can't have most of the same or similar legal and financial protections as married couples. They can, but it takes a conscious, concerted effort by those couples to ensure that the protections are in place. The right kind of financial planning can make a world of difference both while you're alive and for your survivors after you die.

WHETHER CASUAL OR COMMITTED, ASK QUESTIONS

It doesn't matter if you and your partner are a casual couple or committed companions. Ask yourself these questions:

- Do you share finances and living space?
- Do you share an emotional and financial commitment?
- Do you buy anything—including groceries—together?
- Does one or do both of you have a child?
- Are you raising that child?
- Do you want to make sure you have a roof over your head?
- Are you concerned about your loved ones if something happens to you?

If you answered yes to any of these questions—if these issues matter to you as an individual and as an unmarried couple—you must talk about these matters and take specific steps to protect yourself, your partner, and your loved ones. Taking action will help you create a win-win situation for everyone. No one will feel slighted, cheated, or abandoned. An unmarried couple will be able to take advantage of legal tax breaks, buy and sell property easily, set up income protection plans, and establish a workable estate plan that carries out their wishes for the future.

Jim, 47, and April, 45, had lived together for several years in a home that Jim owned. Jim was the primary breadwinner, but he deferred buying disability insurance and visiting with an estate-planning attorney because, he reasoned, "I'm still young, healthy, and don't need it yet." Besides, the premiums and fees weren't cheap, and paying for them would have meant cutting back on something else.

Unfortunately, the insurance premiums and legal fees would have been money well spent. Jim unexpectedly was diagnosed as HIV-positive, a medical condition that made him uninsurable. Suddenly, it was too late to buy insurance. Jim was forced to quit working, and the couple's primary income evaporated. April struggled to make ends meet with her retail sales job. Eventually, however, as Jim's condition deteriorated and medical bills mounted, the mortgage company foreclosed on his house. Shortly after that, Jim's parents, who did not approve of his relationship with April, stepped in, took over, and whisked him away. April never saw Jim again.

This tragic scenario is all too common for unmarried couples of all ages and sexual orientation. Even though Jim and April had no intention of marrying, they did intend to stay together. Their outcome would have been very different if they had planned for the unexpected. Jim could have bought disability insurance, which would have provided income to replace his lost wages. He also could have obtained a power of attorney for health care that named April as his attorney-in-fact. She then would have been able to make the decisions for him. Instead, his parents had the legal right to do so. Financial planning is about preparing for any eventuality.

Communicate with Your Partner

If only April and Jim had communicated with each other and given a little thought to the future, their lives would be very different today. Do you and your partner talk about money? Or is the sum of your discussions simply to turn the other way or occasionally mumble under your breath, "We'll talk about it later."

Don't let denial rob you of your financial future. If you don't talk about money and discuss your attitudes and ambitions, financial needs and desires, and fears and concerns, you should. Without communicating about finances—as a couple and individually—you're asking for trouble, and you can't possibly chart an actionable financial plan.

Generally, neither our parents nor our educational system teach practical money-management skills or healthy ways to discuss financial issues with our partner and families. No one likes to argue, especially if the fight is over money. Unfortunately, too many couples fail to communicate in an open and healthy way about money. They have so little experience discussing finances that they don't know how to discuss finances reasonably. The subject is taboo—but it shouldn't be. Remember, it's healthy to talk about something that affects almost everything you do.

Cut to the Chase

Communication doesn't mean just talking about who pays for the groceries this week or who fills up the car with gas today. It means understanding a partner's attitudes toward and actions regarding the legal tender we use to live happy, healthy, comfortable lives. For most people, money habits were ingrained as a child. If your parents were frugal and handled money carefully, chances are that's why you clip coupons. If your mother's hobby was shopping, that's likely to be a favorite pastime for you, too. If your parents quibbled over every penny, you may avoid money issues altogether.

If you can't stand penny-pinchers and your partner is a cheapskate, talk about your differences. Discussing your "money personality" can be a catharsis, and subsequent financial planning is a good way to neutralize inborn differences. A couple's financial plan, for example, could give the tightwad permission to spend while reining in the partner addicted to "retail therapy."

If a Partner Isn't Interested

What happens if one partner says yes to communicating about money and financial planning, and the other initially rejects the idea, calling it "dumb" or "unnecessary"?

Try the Household Finance 101 approach. How much do you as a couple spend annually for groceries? Even running out to pick up "a few things" at the store can add up over time. Guesstimate what you both spend in a week, then multiply it by 52. The total won't be pocket change—guaranteed! But usually it will get a partner's attention.

If a partner still is unreceptive, go for bigger bucks. What's the annual cost of housing or health insurance? If a partner still turns a deaf ear, try talking about the cost of his or her favorite pastime like cable TV, music, golf, the health club membership, or sporting event tickets.

Whether money is no object or a couple struggles to make ends meet, sometimes the realization of just how many dollars are involved in running a household or pursuing an activity is enough to spark some interest in the subject. Also, recognizing how much money one or the other partner is, or isn't, spending on joint expenses opens the door to dis-

WHY EVERYONE NEEDS FINANCIAL PLANNING

Unmarried couples need financial planning for many reasons, including:

- To identify and understand the financial issues, obligations, and responsibilities inherent in a relationship.
- To protect yourself and/or your partner and your wishes in the event of disability or premature death.
- To capitalize on existing laws to minimize tax liabilities.
- To develop a legally binding framework for division of property and joint financial obligations in the event of dissolution of a relationship.

cussing inequities in the system. This is the perfect time to elicit a greater appreciation of contributions to the household if, for example, one partner doesn't work outside the home and his or her efforts are underappreciated. That, in turn, can help iron out related resentments that one partner or the other may harbor.

With communication and planning up front, financial inequities and potential disagreements can be averted before they get out of control, making the coupled life a lot easier.

THE BUSINESS OF COUPLING

It may not sound romantic, but an unmarried couple is a partnership very similar to a business partnership. Many of the partnership's domestic arrangements and financial controls are governed by business law. In a business partnership, an individual or company can prevent loss due to torts (intentional or unintentional harm to the person or property of another) by purchasing insurance. In a domestic partnership, this insurance is prudent financial planning with regard to wills, durable powers of attorney, medical issues, and more.

The Right Approach

Unmarried couples need to approach the economic commitments of their relationship as a business partnership. In theory, that approach isn't really so different from the legal commitment of marriage. Despite societal pressures and talk otherwise, the marriage pact, from a legal standpoint, is neither a spiritual, religious, nor personal commitment. In signing a marriage license, a couple agrees to uphold the laws that govern marriage, including property rights, tax liabilities, and what happens in the event of dissolution of the marriage or death.

Unmarried partners, on the other hand, have no such legal framework. They have no access to divorce courts or automatic property distributions. Such couples must set up their own rules with their own documentation and agreements. Couples must get beyond the fallacy that planning ahead, with documents in place as a contingency for the future, signifies a lack of love or trust. Married or unmarried, a couple must embrace financial planning and its attendant agreements while times are good. Otherwise, partners may find themselves squared off against each other in open court with a strange judge deciding their finances and futures and the fate of their loved ones.

You're Not Immune

If you believe you're too young or too uncommitted in a relationship to consider financial planning, think about the thousands of children left without a parent by the 9/11 terrorist attacks on the World Trade Center, the Pentagon, and United Airlines Flight 93. Consider, too, all the partners left alone by that day's tragic events. More than 3,000 people of all ages and walks of life unexpectedly were killed that day in September.

Still not convinced you need to make minimal contingency plans or chart a course for the future?

Mary and Samantha lived together as a couple and were business partners as well. Both were aware of the many legal issues they faced as same-sex domestic partners and had planned accordingly. They bought disability insurance to cover their financial needs should something unexpected happen to either one, and they had life insurance policies naming each other as beneficiary. Unfortunately, they hadn't planned quite as well as they thought.

As business partners, they purchased a 12,000-square-foot office building. Mary pitched in 70 percent of the multimillion-dollar price tag, and Samantha contributed 30 percent. Six months later, the domestic duo split up. Unfortunately, they had failed to put together a formal property agreement that addressed contingencies in the event of the dissolution of their domestic partnership. Among other things, the agreement would have detailed what would happen to their jointly held assets in the event that their domestic relationship ended. Fortunately, both partners were reasonable and civil people, and they were able to work out the differences relatively fairly.

But what if they hadn't agreed to cooperate and the courts had stepped in? Samantha couldn't have afforded to buy out Mary. The bigger bully, or the one with the bigger bank account, most likely would have walked away with almost everything, leaving the other shortchanged simply because unmarried couples—no matter how long they've been together—aren't protected by the property-distribution laws that cover married couples.

Contingency Planning

Even if you think you and your partner have covered your bases, think again. Are you prepared for *all* contingencies? As an unmarried couple, you had better be. Any planning should include a contingency for dissolution as part of a domestic-partnership agreement. In fact, that's the top consideration for unmarried partners. Even if you and your partner are casual companions, up front you need to write down provisions for what happens to each of your assets and obligations in the event that the partnership ends. No matter how infatuated, how committed, or how comfortable you are as a couple today, plan for tomorrow and a possible end to the relationship. Your relationship may last a lifetime; if not, it's far better to plan ahead while you both are happy and will be kind to each other. (See Chapter 8 for more information on breaking-up provisions.)

UNMARRIED FOR A REASON

The average American spends the majority of life as a single person, studies show. Whether a person is unmarried before a first marriage, in between marriages, as a widow or widower, as a personal preference, or out of necessity doesn't mean, however, that they don't couple and aren't committed to a partner. In fact, the number of unmarried couples living together increased 72 percent between 1990 and 2000, according to the latest U.S. census data (2000).

FIGURE 1.1 Unmarried Partner Households in the United States in 2000

Unmarried partner households total 5.2 percent of the 105,480,101 total U.S. households.

Type	Number of Unmarried Partner Households	% of total Unmarried Partner Households
Male/female partners	4,881,377	89.1%
Male partners	301,026	5.5
Female partners	293,365	5.4
Total	5,475,768	100.0%

Source: 2000 U.S. census

Some of Those Reasons

Keep in mind, too, that just because a couple isn't married doesn't mean the partners aren't committed to each other and their relationship. Coupling without matrimony occurs for many reasons, and most often it's done purposely.

It may not make sense financially for partners to marry. Widows or widowers, for example, may want to preserve Social Security or pension benefits from their deceased spouses. They also may want to make sure their children get their full inheritance. That can become a complicated and convoluted issue, especially given today's growing number of non-traditional and blended families.

Consider some recent U.S. census numbers:

- Children are included in more than 40 percent of the 5.4 million unmarried couple households in the United States. The share of unmarried partners who have children at home is not that much smaller than the share of married couples with children.
- Same-sex couples often have children living in their households. More than one-third of lesbian households (34 percent) and slightly

less than one-quarter (22 percent) of male gay households have children at home.

Jan, 37, is emphatic about not marrying her longtime companion, Tom. The reason: Matrimony would mean taking on his bad credit, and she's not interested in spoiling her perfect credit history with his bankruptcy blotch. It's not that Jan is any less committed and devoted than Tom. It just makes financial sense to her not to marry him.

Or consider the case of Jacob and Janice. The Massachusetts couple has been together 15 years. They have a son but never married, because they believe that marriage is a pact between two people and God and is none of the government's business. Remaining legally unmarried but spiritually committed is their personal choice.

Younger couples, who may not be ready for marriage anyway, may be in no hurry to get the legal system involved in their relationship, either. Most of us probably know couples like that. With more than half of all marriages today ending in divorce, opting out or postponing marriage may not be such a bad idea.

Same-sex couples still can't marry legally in most states. However, that likely will change. In 2004, the state of Massachusetts passed legislation allowing same-sex couples to marry, Vermont allows civil unions among

HOUSEHOLDS WITH CHILDREN UNDER 18*

Married couple households: 45.6%

Opposite-sex partners: 43.1%

Same-sex partners, male: 22.3%

Same-sex partners, female: 34.3%

* *Unmarried partners' children* refers to sons/daughters of the householder and to other children not related to the householder.

Source: 2000 U.S. census

same-sex partners, and several other states grant certain marriage-like rights to qualified domestic partners.

Couples of any age or sexual orientation also may choose not to marry to take advantage of tax breaks. Do you and your partner have more than one home and, perhaps, a big boat and maybe a time-share condo? If so, it's good to be unmarried. Two individuals can, in accordance with federal tax laws, own up to four homes as an unmarried couple and take the mortgage interest deductions on all of them. On the other hand, married couples only can deduct mortgage interest on one primary residence and one vacation home.

For most wage earners, there's virtually no marriage tax penalty anymore. However, for unmarried partners, if one partner itemizes and takes all the deductions while the other partner takes the standard deduction, there can be significant tax savings. (See Chapter 5 for more on taxes.)

Telling Numbers

Check out a few more statistics on unmarried couples:

- The majority of couples who get married today have lived with their future spouse first. (Larry Bumpass and Hsien-Hen Lu, "Trends in Cohabitation and Implications for Children's Family Contexts in the United States," Population Studies, 54: 29–41, 2000)
- Fifty-five percent of different-sex cohabitators get married within five years of moving in together, 40 percent break up within that same time, and 10 percent remain in an unmarried relationship five years or longer. (Pamela Smock, "Cohabitation in the United States," Annual Review of Sociology, 2000)
- 1.2 million Americans live with same-sex partners. (U.S. Census Bureau, 2000)

Several states—California, Hawaii, New Jersey, and Maine—and the District of Columbia have domestic partnership laws that grant certain rights to qualified domestic partners. Also, the state of Vermont licenses civil unions between same-sex partners. *Qualified partners* are same-sex couples and opposite-sex couples over the age of 62, although Maine and the District of Columbia include all domestic partners, no matter age or sexual orientation.

The catch to the California law (and laws in some other states), however, is that qualified domestic partners must be registered with the state for any of the associated rights to apply. Registration in California includes paying a nominal fee and filing a form with the office of California's secretary of state, with both partners' signatures notarized. California's law, Assembly Bill 205, passed in 2003 and effective January 1, 2005, stops short of sanctioning legal marriage between same-sex partners and does not allow them to file joint state income tax returns. It also defers to federal law on many federal and interstate issues and does not require formal court proceedings to dissolve such a relationship.

CATCH-22: COMMON LAW MARRIAGE

Watch out! Even if you and your partner think you're unmarried, you could be legally married. As incredible as it sounds, heterosexual couples could be married inadvertently. Eleven states and the District of Columbia recognize common law marriage between a man and a woman. Four other states—Georgia, Idaho, Ohio, and Pennsylvania—are phasing it out. Couples in those states who meet the common law marriage requirements by default could be subject to laws governing married couples. Even more important, if you and your partner split up, you must go through formal divorce proceedings. How scary is that for countless people who have lived with partners in the past? Also, note that federal law requires even those states that do not recognize common law marriage to consider as valid a common law marriage from a state that does recognize it.

COMMON LAW MARRIAGE

Common law marriage is legal in the following states and the District of Columbia, if specific conditions are met:

- Alabama
- Colorado
- District of Columbia
- Georgia (if begun before January 1, 1997)*
- Idaho (if begun before January 1, 1996)*
- Iowa
- Kansas
- Montana
- New Hampshire (for inheritance purposes only)
- Ohio (if begun before October 10, 1991)*
- Oklahoma
- Pennsylvania (if begun before September 1, 2003)*
- Rhode Island
- South Carolina
- Texas
- Utah

* Common law marriage laws being phased out in Pennsylvania, Georgia, Idaho, and Ohio.

Legal Requirements

Don't hit the panic button just yet, though. To qualify as being in a common law marriage, couples must satisfy very specific requirements. Just living together isn't enough to validate a common law marriage. The requirements vary by state, so check your individual state's laws.

REQUIREMENTS FOR COMMON LAW MARRIAGE

Every state has its own definition of common law marriage. But, in general, the following conditions must be met for a valid common law marriage to exist:

- Living together
- Being together for a significant period of time (which is not defined)
- Presenting yourselves as a married couple
- Intending to be married

Basically, if a couple truly wants to stay unmarried, they cannot present themselves as a married couple. Some ways of doing that include not using the same last name, not referring to each other as husband or wife, and not filing a joint tax return. However, avoiding common-law status is a bit more complicated in some states than others.

Just to be safe, a couple may want to draft, date, and sign with a notary as witness a Declaration Not to Be Common-Law Married.

DECLARATION NOT TO BE COMMON-LAW MARRIED

I, _____, and I, _____, hereby declare that, although we cohabitate and plan to cohabitate for the indefinite future, we have no intention of entering into any form of marriage.

Name:

Signature: Date:

Name:

Signature: Date:

Dying Intestate

If one partner dies without a will—known as dying intestate—the surviving common-law spouse is first in line to inherit a portion of the assets, with the remaining assets going to the next of kin. Partners shouldn't bank on a spouse's or family member's benevolence and good graces, either, when other people are involved. After a death, greed often rears its ugly head. The spouse or angry family members could come out of the woodwork and make the inheritance situation a nightmare for everyone.

That's one more reason why—as an unmarried couple and as an individual—paying attention to your financial life and planning ahead make perfect sense.

BOTTOM LINES

No matter their age, financial situation, or sexual orientation, unmarried couples across the board face virtually the same financial issues and must deal with them in much the same way.

Keep in mind, too, that life is ever changing, so financial plans should be dynamic. The reality of most financial plans is that they're static. Whatever way you and your partner decide to plan, forget the fancy, leatherbound version. Write your plan so it can be changed periodically as your situation and circumstances change.

As a couple and as an individual, if you do nothing else, at a minimum do the following:

- Recognize that unmarried couples of all ages and sexual preferences face virtually the same financial issues and can learn from each other's successes and mistakes. Discuss your personal ambitions and goals with your partner and work together to create a documented financial plan that focuses on achieving your individual and collective goals.
- Realize that a couple's financial plan, like life, needs to be dynamic and able to change, not chiseled in stone. The most important con-

cept in financial planning is to plan and protect yourself for the unexpected. That includes the unexpected death of a partner, disability, loss of a job, loss of health, unexpected inflation, and unexpected family responsibilities.

- Discover whether your state recognizes common law marriage. If it does and you and your partner don't want to be married, don't do anything that qualifies you as "married." Also, you might want to draft, sign, and have notarized a formal agreement stating that you and your partner do not want to be common-law married.

CHAPTER 2

The Starting Point

FINANCIAL GOALS AND OBJECTIVES

Stop reading for a few moments and, instead, think about what you really want out of life. What's important to you—as an individual and as a couple? Think about the long haul. Why do you work every day? Why do you accumulate possessions? What's it all for? What are your goals and objectives?

Forget the excuse that you have no goals. You do. Everyone does, consciously or otherwise. Even if you decide not to have goals, that's an objective itself. That solo Caribbean junket you're considering counts as a goal. So does buying a condo with your partner in a couple of years.

Your partner should consider these same questions, too, and come up with his or her own answers. This is the first step in the financial planning process.

OPERATIONAL DETAILS

Couples, unmarried or married, often don't bother to take the time to think about goals. That's a big mistake. If you know where you want to go individually and as a couple, it's possible to determine what it will take to get there *and* the roles each partner may or may not play in the process. Financial planning goes far beyond dollars and cents. For couples of any description and any financial standing, financial planning also means understanding what's fair and equitable in your relationship. The operational details are part of the responsibilities and obligations that you and your partner share.

Joint Process

Setting goals is a joint discovery process. As a couple, the solution isn't just to split all the bills down the middle, 50-50, and forget the details. That isn't always right or comfortable for the individuals involved. Each of you must understand the other's current financial behaviors and attitudes toward money, where those attitudes come from—including the financial behaviors you grew up with—and current and potential resources. Then you can strategize how best to set up household accounts in the most equitable way for each of you based on individual circumstances.

Pay attention to any differences between you and your partner and their potential for repercussions and pitfalls. Be totally honest with each other. For example, one person could be a strong personality and one more submissive, or one partner's income could be vastly greater than the other's. If one of you was brought up to be frugal and the other to be a spendthrift, throwing all your income into one pot may not work. The same could be true if one partner grew up in a household complete with the latest and greatest electronic gadgetry and a widescreen TV, while the other partner's family shunned TV and electronics as a waste of time and money. Or what about the couple in which one is a coupon clipper and the other a shopaholic?

All differences—whether social, physical, fiscal, or cultural—can create financial friction between partners, especially if talking about them isn't part of the goal-setting discovery process.

Fran and Alan split the cost of their household right down the middle. Each put the same amount into the pot. Together, they spent the entire household account every month. The problem was that Alan accounted for three-fourths of the household's total income yet pitched in only half of the household's total budget. Fran struggled every month to meet her commitment, spending 100 percent of her income on the household. She literally had nothing left over, while Alan easily put money aside. What would happen if the two split? Fran would walk away broke, while Alan would have a nice nest egg.

The income stream was even more lopsided for another couple, Ann and Erin. Ann brought in eight times the income Erin did. That's not a typo. Ann earned 800 percent more than Erin, yet both contributed equally to the household account. Can you imagine the animosity generated by the finances in that relationship? Think, too, what would happen to Erin if the couple split up. Chances are she would be out of luck. Unlike their married counterparts, unmarried couples have no recourse to property disposition laws.

FIGURE 2.1 Division of Expenses: Two Strategies

Here's a look at two different approaches to dividing expenses for unmarried couples.

Total income and expenses		Example: Expenses divided equally		Example: Expenses divided pro rata based on income	
		Partner 1	Partner 2	Partner 1	Partner 2
$60,000*		**$40,000**	**$20,000**	**$40,000**	**$20,000**
9,600	Mortgage payment	4,800	4,800	6,432	3,168
1,800	Taxes	900	900	1,206	594
1,000	Homeowners insurance	500	500	670	330
1,200	Maintenance	600	600	804	396
2,000	Vacation	1,000	1,000	1,340	660
5,000	Payment on 2 cars	2,500	2,500	3,350	1,650
3,500	Insurance	1,750	1,750	2,345	1,155
1,400	Leisure activities	700	700	938	462
$34,500	**Discretionary Cash Flow**	**$27,250**	**$7,250**	**$22,915**	**$11,585**

* $60,000 is net income for $75,000 gross.

When a couple with unequal incomes stays together, they can face significant issues as a result of their incomes. The higher wage earner may want to be in control, while the lower wage earner could have feelings of inadequacy.

Household Finance 101

The answer for these couples and others with varying incomes is household financial planning: Household Finance 101.

The course begins with both partners figuring out their individual goals and their goals as a couple. Then, together they must decide how to structure contributions to expenses so that their goals are achievable, affordable, and fair for both parties. Remember, no matter how unromantic it may sound, living together constitutes a partnership and needs to be structured as such. Most married couples would be a lot better off if they implemented Household Finance 101, too!

COMMUNICATION AND COLLABORATION

Communication is healthy. It's also a way for couples to recognize individual and partnered goals. When a relationship is collaborative, each partner feels as if he or she has a stake in it. It's a true partnership. Couples who understand and pay attention to each other's goals also are less likely to miss out on or overlook joint opportunities.

Roxanne and Steve had lived together in Massachusetts for nearly 20 years. Although they had a son together, they elected not to marry. Both had come from bad marriages and equally difficult divorces, and neither was in a hurry to tie the knot again. Besides, it didn't matter, they reasoned. They loved each other, they were comfortable, and that was what counted.

When Nick, their son, was born, everyone assumed that Steve and Roxanne were married, and the couple saw no reason to mention they weren't. In time, they essentially forgot about the issue.

However, Roxanne was rudely awakened to that not-so-minor detail after Steve died in an automobile accident. She was left with 12-year-old Nick and only a small life insurance policy. Because she and Steve never had married and they lived in a state that didn't recognize common law marriage, Roxanne was ineligible for Social Security survivor's benefits. Nick, as Steve's son, was eligible, but his benefits weren't enough to support both him and his mom. As a suddenly single mom, Roxanne was forced to find a job after a 20-year absence from the workforce. Steve had worked hard so that his family would be comfortable, yet the couple had failed to think through an important objective—financial support in the event something happened to the primary breadwinner.

Conversely, another Massachusetts couple had a bit happier financial ending to their life together. Paul and Pam, both professors, lived together in Cambridge for 25 years. They enjoyed their lifestyle and never married, although Pam had been married previously. Because Massachusetts does not recognize common law marriage, the partners remained unmarried in the eyes of the law despite their lengthy time together.

When Paul and Pam retired, they discussed their situation and made the decision to move to Rhode Island. Unfortunately, Paul died unexpectedly right after the move. Although the couple never had married officially, Pam applied for Social Security survivor's benefits and was approved. The couple had lived in Rhode Island for less than a year, but because the state recognizes common law marriages and Pam could prove her 25-year domestic partnership, she met that state's qualifications for benefits.

Don't Short-Change Yourself

The outcome could have been very different for Roxanne if, before it was too late, she and Steve had taken the time to talk about and plan their finances with goals and objectives in mind. Like any couple in a similar situation, they should have set financial goals together and, if necessary, met periodically with a financial planner to review how they were doing relative to those goals.

That CFP® could have helped them make the right financial choices and changes. They could have been guided to the right investments and savings that would have enabled them to retire early, perhaps to volunteer full-time or part-time for their favorite environmental cause. A CFP® also would have helped Steve realize the importance of setting up a 401(k) retirement savings plan through his employer, of having enough life insurance, and contributing as much as possible regularly. If Steve received a raise, his CFP®, in turn, probably would have suggested boosting contributions to that 401(k) or socking the additional money away in a tax-advantaged education savings plan like a 529 plan or Roth IRA to help pay for Nick's future college expenses. Both allow tax-free withdrawals for qualified education expenses, and the couple certainly had expected to have hefty college expenses, because they always had planned on Nick attending their alma mater, a prestigious, expensive college in upstate New York.

We have the benefit of hindsight. Think about your own situation and goals—individually and as a couple. Be honest and straightforward with yourself and each other. Only then will you be able to accomplish what truly matters to you.

Some questions that partners need to ask themselves and each other are quite basic and include:

- How much money will it cost this month or this year for your basic household living expenses like groceries, utilities, and more?
- How do you define *comfortable standard of living?*
- Do you want to purchase that condo or add on to the house?
- Do you want to take that vacation or buy a bigger car?

Other questions, however, may not be so easily answered. A few other questions you may consider in your own situation include:

- Are you satisfied with your current relationship and your role in it?
- Do you feel underappreciated or as if you don't have a stake in the relationship?
- What do you want to accomplish with your life?

- What are your dreams and ambitions for your career?
- Do you want to have children?
- If so and if possible, do you want a biological child?
- Are you open to adoption?
- If you could have or do anything in the world, what would it be?
- Where would you like to be one year, five years, and even further down the road?
- What would you do if a family member or loved one needed your financial or physical help?
- Do you want to marry?
- As a same-sex couple, do you want to legally marry? If so, are you willing to relocate to where that's an option?

Most important, partners never should lose themselves in a coupled relationship. After all, the relationship began with two individuals. Those individuals are the foundation of the coupling. Without that individuality, the foundation on which the relationship is built may shift and slide. Don't let mutual objectives and goals derail individual ones and vice versa. The right financial planning can help ensure that individual and mutual goals are achieved.

WARNING *Don't ever lose sight of yourself and your individual goals in any coupled relationship.*

Permanency of Relationship

Even a casual couple with no long-range plans for the future can set goals. Their goals individually and as a couple may differ from their more committed brethren's, but a relationship's relative lack of permanence doesn't negate the importance of the planning process. Couples still must buy groceries and figure out how best to divide the cost of rent or a mortgage and other household expenses.

Partners have individual goals and responsibilities that don't necessarily relate to each other, either. The unmarried, divorced dad partnered with someone other than his child's biological mother must meet monthly child support payments. The recent college graduate must pay off his or her college loan. The senior citizen, who made a deathbed promise to a sibling, feels obligated to pay the hefty expenses of a niece he rarely sees. The partner who is HIV-positive ponders her mortality and plans accordingly, while her partner has no such concerns personally.

BEYOND MONEY

Goals needn't be money oriented, either.

Liza was 72, widowed, and enjoying her golden years. Her current companion was Al, a widower. Neither one wanted to marry. Al wasn't quite as openly happy as Liza, because he wanted to do more volunteer work at a local hospital. But he was afraid to tell Liza, because he thought she would resent his taking time away from their relationship. It wasn't until the two sat down and discussed personal goals that Al learned that Liza wanted to do volunteer work, too. If the couple hadn't communicated honestly, Al's dilemma might not have had such a mutually happy resolution.

Amy and Ellen moved in together shortly after they met, when both were in their late 30s. Neither woman had children. The issue of parenting came up briefly once when Amy emphatically declared she didn't like kids because raising them costs a fortune, usually at the expense of your retirement savings. But that was the extent of the conversation.

The couple were very devoted to each other; they were comfortable financially and had planned well for the fiscal future. Their relationship seemed perfect. However, one problem was simmering. Ellen secretly wanted to have a biological child. She was afraid, though, that if Amy found out, she would leave her. So Ellen said nothing and suffered quietly. The years passed; so did the opportunity.

Less Can Mean Better

Unfortunately, many of us are forced into collaboration because our lifestyles have gotten so expensive that both partners must work. Even many retired seniors find themselves going back to work part-time as health care costs skyrocket and once-guaranteed benefits are slashed across corporate America. Pensions or retirement savings, too, have shrunk or disappeared altogether in the wake of financial crises and scandals at many of the nation's corporate giants. When a major company like Enron goes down, it takes the millions of dollars in savings of current and retired employees with it. Major airlines like United have threatened to cut off retiree benefits, as well.

No matter your age, use goal setting to reflect on whether you really can live that lavishly and still attain everything you want individually and as a couple. This kind of self-reflection is a part of successful financial planning.

Even though you've always had those two sets of season tickets to the local NFL team's games, perhaps you don't really need them and it's time to relinquish them. Or instead of fulfilling those weeknight volunteer obligations for four different organizations, maybe it would be better to cut back and spend more time at home.

And is it really so important to rack up all that overtime at work? Do you and your partner really *need* the money, or would that quality time with each other be more valuable?

Personal finance is not just a money issue. It's a lifestyle issue, too. It's about identifying and establishing goals and priorities and realigning them if it makes sense for you personally and as a couple. Even if you're very young, it's not a mistake to slow down or opt for more quiet times together. Stop the treadmill, get off it, and figure out what really matters in your life. That's what goal setting is all about.

Extended Family Issues

Beyond talking about strategic issues such as whether to have kids of their own, couples can't afford to overlook extended family issues, either.

A couple's relatives may pop up to haunt their unmarried lives. That means you must discuss with your partner the fact that you're the designated guardian of your sister's kids in the event something happens to her. It's always better to prepare a partner up front for any eventuality. Just as with domestic partnership agreements, it's far better to deal with the issue beforehand rather than after a purposely childless couple suddenly find themselves with a house full of kids.

The same is true if you're facing the prospect of reversing roles with your aging parents—whether supporting them from afar or having them move in with you at some point down the road. Talk about it with your partner up front. These issues could affect whether your partner takes a new job or if remodeling your condo becomes a higher priority.

Don't overlook that deadbeat brother or other relative who always has a hand out for money, either. If you're the kind of person who can't say no, your partner needs to know that up front.

Ellie and Debbie lived together quite happily at first. But after a while, Ellie got fed up with her "spendthrift" partner. Even though they both had great jobs that provided far more income than they needed, it seemed as though Debbie never had any money. The household account usually was running on empty, and Debbie frequently was asking Ellie for more money or a loan. The pair fought about it regularly, but Debbie usually just said, "I'm sorry. I can't help it."

The situation came to a head when Ellie said she was leaving Debbie for good because she was sick of Debbie frittering away all the couple's money. Finally, Debbie broke down and admitted the problem. It seems that her mother—who was relatively young, divorced, and unemployed—refused to relinquish the high standard of living she had grown accustomed to when married, even though she couldn't now afford it. She kept asking Debbie for money, instead. And Debbie, who couldn't say no to her mother, anted up the cash. Of course, giving her mom the money only perpetuated the problem and led to more demands for even more money.

Once Ellie learned about the problem, she was quick to give her partner the moral and emotional support she needed. Debbie at last was able to stand up to her mother. If the couple only had communicated sooner, they would have avoided needless stress and heartache.

Talk about such issues early and often with your partner. If you don't, they can end up dividing a couple, if not torpedoing the relationship altogether. Ellie and Debbie were lucky. Debbie confessed before it was too late. For many other couples, sadly, that's not the case.

MORE DETAILS

If unmarried couples take the right approach to financial planning, put in place the proper legal documentation, and capitalize on existing laws, it's possible to nearly equalize the inequities of a system geared toward married couples. In certain cases, unmarried partners even have greater tax advantages. For example, one partner can pay certain expenses and take the resulting deductions on his or her taxes, while the other partner takes the standard deduction. The result often can be significant tax savings. (See Chapter 5 for more information on tax strategies.)

For unmarried couples, ownership and titling of property, legal agreements, tax deductions, and life insurance literally make all the difference in the world.

To achieve financial success and security as a couple and as individuals requires recognition of and focus on goals and what it takes to achieve those goals. Beyond finances, it's about life planning and deciding what you want to do, where you want to do it, and when. Then, as long as you see progress toward your goals, stay on track. Money, after all, is the tool that makes possible so much of what we want to do.

A MORE PERFECT UNION?

When you and your partner set goals, remember that marriage is not necessarily a perfect solution, either. The marriage game plan has its flaws, too—whether the partners are heterosexual or same sex.

Rick and Michael lived in Massachusetts and had been together eight years. Well aware of the financial issues they faced as a same-sex couple, they had all the right documents carefully in place. (More on that in Chapter 8.) The couple was very committed to each other, so when Massachusetts legalized same-sex marriage, their friends assumed the pair would take advantage of this opportunity to marry legally.

But to their friends' surprise, Rick and Michael didn't run off to the courthouse. "I don't know. We're not so sure that marriage is the best thing for us," Rick explained. His reasoning: It would muck up all the legal documents the couple already had painstakingly put in place.

Other advantages for unmarried partners to remain so include:

- *Liability.* Unmarried couples can keep separate encumbrances like tax liens and debts. They don't risk loss of everything in the event of a lawsuit or other legal problems. That's not the case with married couples because, as spouses, you also marry your partner's debts.
- *Credit.* Unmarried partners don't have to merge credit woes. If one partner has bad credit, the other partner's credit can remain unscathed.
- *Inheritance.* If companions aren't married, partners aren't automatically entitled to any inheritance from each other. That can be advantageous, for example, to preserve an intact inheritance for a child from a previous marriage. That can be a big issue for older couples. Adult children often resent their widowed mom or dad taking up with another person, because they're afraid that person will take away their inheritance.
- *Social Security and pension survivor's benefits.* By remaining unmarried, partners who are widows and widowers remain eligible for these benefits that come from former spouses who now are deceased.
- *Financial aid for education.* A single parent may qualify his or her child for greater financial aid for education, whereas if the parent is married, the child may not be eligible.
- *Adoption.* Many countries outside the United States don't allow an openly gay or lesbian couple to adopt, so if a same-sex couple is considering adoption, marriage or civil union (in those states that recognize it) may only complicate, and in some cases even prevent, the adoption from going forward.

FIGURE 2.2 Why Not Get Married?

(The icons indicate which type of couple will benefit the most; SS in Massachusetts only.)

- *You don't need to.* Partners already are protected by the documents they have in place.

  `Y / O / SS` **(Massachusetts only)**

- *Liability risks.* Unmarried couples don't have to share a partner's tax troubles or legal woes.

  `Y / O / SS`

- *Credit concerns.* Unmarried partners can keep their credit separate.

  `Y / O / SS`

- *Inheritance issues.* If partners aren't married, in general they don't automatically inherit from each other unless specifically stated otherwise.

  `Y / O / SS`

- *Asset transfers.* Unmarried partners cannot give each other more than $11,000 per calendar year without triggering potential gift tax issues.

  `Y / O / SS`

- *Social Security and pension survivor's benefits.* Unmarried partners who are widows and widowers qualify for survivor's benefits from a previous spouse.

  `O`

- *Financial aid for education.* Unmarried partners are not both required to report income on the federal financial aid form.

  `Y / SS`

- *Health insurance benefits.* Unmarried partners aren't automatically granted domestic partner health insurance.

  `Y / SS`

- *Income tax planning.* Partners' aggregate tax liability may be lower if they're unmarried and plan properly.

  `Y / SS`

BOTTOM LINES

Forget the notion that you as an individual or as a couple have no goals worth documenting and working toward achieving. You do. Recognizing and prioritizing your goals requires that you and your partner both take the time and make the effort to think about what you do and do not want in life, then discuss it with each other. Life, after all, is a series of goals. Remaining unmarried is a goal, as a couple buying that living room sofa is a goal, figuring out who pays for what in your relationship is a goal, and taking that solo vacation is a goal, too.

As a couple and as an individual, if you do nothing else, at a minimum do the following:

- Communicate, communicate, communicate. Goal setting in financial planning is a joint discovery process.
- Don't lose sight of your partner's individual goals, either. After all, it was as individuals that you and your partner came together in a coupled relationship.
- Consider the advantages of being an unmarried couple and capitalize on them.

3

Yours, Mine, and Ours

ASSETS AND LIABILITIES

What you *own* individually and as a couple are assets. What you *owe* individually and as a couple are liabilities. For couples who don't plan, the lines between who owns or owes what can get rather blurred, and inequities in expenses and income become magnified.

The automatic reaction of many couples is to overlook or ignore the issues. Instead, such issues should provide the impetus to understand the ramifications of who owns what and why, and when to merge or comingle assets and liabilities and when not to.

THE EQUATION

As working adults, our single biggest asset is our ability to make money. Unfortunately, one of our biggest liabilities is the penchant to spend that money.

Few of us escaped unscathed the fast credit/fast spending mind-set of the 1980s and 1990s. Jobs were plentiful and raises automatic, as was the climb up the corporate ladder. Those of us in the workforce, or those who already had retired by that time, collected almost every kind of benefit imaginable—from free parking, bonuses, and stock options to life, disability, and health insurance, health club memberships, daycare, and senior care. Some employers even began to recognize the importance of domestic partner benefits. The long, hard work of gay and lesbian advocacy organizations finally began to pay off for all types of unmarried couples.

That was the upside. The downside was that, with society's instant gratification mind-set, people didn't plan ahead. Financial planning was for nerds. "I don't need it," so the reasoning went. After all, there always would be more money tomorrow. During that time, couples who partnered up procrastinated at coupling things, too, such as getting married, buying houses or life insurance, changing beneficiaries on assets, and, of course, retirement planning. They overspent and overplayed. Life was like sex before AIDS. So were attitudes toward money. "Easy money; easy credit." It was a recipe for disaster, and sure enough, disaster struck. The dot-com demise, coupled with the terrorism disasters of 9/11, left markets and the economy still limping toward recovery almost four years later.

How do intelligent people fall victim to the unending credit card sales pitches and incessant time-share schtick? It's a disease, and you're the victim. It's like being an alcoholic or a drug abuser. The buzz or the high creates a craving for a better buzz, a higher high. But the high can't last forever. In the case of finances, you know the old saying: If it sounds too good to be true, it probably is. Well, it *was* too good to be true back then, and it still *is* now, as many unmarried and in-debt couples discovered and keep finding out. After the Internet bubble collapse, we again realize we're lucky to have a job, and we're thrilled to get a small cost-of-living raise.

Financial planning—as in managing assets and liabilities—suddenly seems prudent, especially for unmarried couples trying to deal with the obligations and responsibilities that come with those assets and liabilities.

TO MERGE OR NOT TO MERGE

How does a couple decide who pays what bill and whether to manage their assets and liabilities collectively or concurrently? There is no one across-the-board answer. Concerns range from liability and psychological issues to tax consequences and more. The best course depends on the individual situation.

Two questions that all couples must ask first, however, are:

1. Is the relationship casual or committed?
2. Does the relationship include a financial commitment to each other?

If, as a couple, you're planning to buy something together like furniture or a car, you're making a commitment. Couples also need to pay attention to the psychological effects on a partner of merging or not merging assets and liabilities; how merging might affect potential liability for either partner; and merging's impact on federal, state, estate, and inheritance taxes.

Let's take a closer look.

Separate Entities

If partners aren't committed emotionally or financially to each other, it's best to keep assets separate. Don't blend anything, including bank accounts. The rent or mortgage can be paid with two separate checks; one partner can write the other a check for his or her share, or partners can alternate paying the obligation. Keep in mind, though, that owning a home together or sharing a lease *is* a financial commitment.

For those couples who decide that a joint checking account for mutual household expenses is just too convenient to pass up, that's OK. But there's absolutely no benefit to merging anything else. Casually committed couples should operate as two separate financial entities that happen to cohabitate. Generally, they should not merge any money or assets other than basic monthly household expenses like rent or mortgage, groceries, dining out, entertainment, and joint vacations. Most couples need to be sure that they have a domestic partnership agreement that includes a breaking-up provision stipulating the division of assets, liabilities, and obligations should the relationship end. Definitely don't design individual investment portfolios based on what the other partner is doing. There's no point in considering the asset allocation of your combined investment portfolio if you and your partner don't plan on being together over the long haul.

Nick and Lily spent all their free time together, so it was only natural that when Lily's roommate moved out, Nick should move in. First, however, the two sat down and talked at length about where each one was in life, what each thought they might want down the road, and how, as a pair, they would handle the finances of living together. Neither was interested in marriage or a long-term commitment to each other, so they agreed to keep their finances separate, except for setting up a joint household account. The couple agreed that each would fund the account equally and that household bills like rent, utilities, food, and joint entertainment would be paid for out of that account.

Nick and Lily also talked about what would happen to that joint account and to the household assets and liabilities if the couple split. It was tough to address those details, but the couple recently had watched some unmarried friends who split go through financial and emotional hell because they hadn't made contingency plans if their relationship ended.

Psychological Messages

Traditionally in America, society accepted and even assumed that married couples would merge most, if not all, of their money. With unmarried couples, however, keeping finances separate may be the very reason the partners preferred not to marry in the first place. Remember the woman who didn't want to marry her longtime companion because she didn't want his bankruptcy tarnishing her impeccable credit?

As living costs rise and more spouses—and unmarried partners—are forced into the workplace, and considering the fact that most of us have multiple significant relationships over our lifetimes, segregated finances are becoming more common for all couples.

Married or not, it's healthy for partners to have their own money. From a psychological viewpoint, it's satisfying for an individual to make his or her own money, have that money, and know that he or she can decide what to do with it, including spend it. After all, we are individuals first and couples second.

Also, keep in mind that the decision by a couple whether to merge their money sends a strong message to both partners in a relationship.

John, who wants eventually to marry and have a family, has dated Beth for two years. But he's not sure she's the one with whom he would like to spend the rest of his life. Besides, at 25, he's in no hurry to make a long-term commitment. That also means he's not ready to act as if he's married to Beth when it comes to all aspects of his financial life.

Still, John is tired of renting an apartment and eventually would like to own his own home and reap the tax savings that go with it. He suggests to Beth that they rent a condo together to save money, while keeping their personal finances separate. If things continue to go well, John says, eventually they could buy a place together and maybe someday get married. By taking that approach, John sends Beth an appropriate message that conveys his true feelings and doesn't get either of them in over their heads fiscally or emotionally.

On the other hand, what if John had suggested to Beth that the two merge their finances and buy a house together right away? The message to Beth would have been quite different. She may be thinking, "He's really interested in committing to me, and this is the first step of, potentially, a lifetime together."

Dollars and Sense

Whatever a couple's relationship or financial circumstances, the best approach to managing money in a household is to segregate it into three pots—Yours, Mine, and Ours. The Ours is the joint household account.

Short-term. If a couple's relationship is short term—casual or more serious—contributions to the Ours account should be split equally, no matter what an individual partner earns. The couple, after all, is not merging finances; they are sharing current costs and financial responsibilities, which include rent or mortgage, dining out, entertainment, and so on. A short-term couple's financial commitment to buy something like new furniture falls into that category, too. The household pot is not for paying off a partner's college loan, buying personal items like clothes, or funding a solo vacation with friends.

Long-term. In committed, long-term relationships, unmarried couples generally merge or comingle some of their assets. The question then becomes: To what degree are finances comingled? No matter how much is merged, though, partners almost always have their own money, too. Their joint pot should cover monthly expenses that also may be associated with more long-term purchases like life, disability, and health insurance policies; a vacation or retirement home if that's an option; funding home construction or remodeling; and paying for other long-term goals like their children's education.

Among the advantages of merging finances for long-term, committed couples:

- From a logistical standpoint, either partner can transact on the other's behalf.
- Partners are co-owners in a house, for example, and aren't paying rent to someone else.
- Partners feel equal. That's generally a feeling that comes more easily to married couples than unmarried ones.

Mark and Tom have been together 15 years. They're both nearing retirement and have monthly take-home income amounting to about $3,000 each. They each put $1,500 a month into the Ours, or joint, household pot. Their house is paid for, so the total $3,000 pot is plenty to cover monthly household operating expenses and other necessities like property taxes; life, disability, and health insurance premiums; and joint vacations. That leaves each partner with another $1,500 a month of his own money. The result is the partners having equal money and equal freedom, flexibility, and financial power.

Caveat: Beware of gift tax and liability issues that can be associated with a couple comingling finances. (See page 47 for more information on these issues.)

Investing. A long-term couple needs to approach each person's individual investment portfolio as if it were combined with their partner's to make sure they complement each other. Personal investments and retirement funds should be allocated so that the couple gets the best bang for their buck, whether in the form of earnings or tax advantages. For example, with younger couples, if one partner has great investment options in his or her tax-advantaged 401(k) retirement savings plan, and the other partner has investment options that aren't as attractive, develop an investment strategy for the couple's combined portfolio. If one partner is heavily invested in technology and energy, perhaps consider investing the other partner's 401(k) in less volatile sectors. Remember, investing as a couple is a partnership and a team effort.

Inequalities. Filling the household pot and having "mad" money left over for each partner generally isn't a problem when the partners' incomes are relatively equal. Problems often arise, however, when incomes are vastly different. Resentment, feelings of inadequacies, distrust, squabbles, and even breakups can result from the difference. All those issues are exacerbated if partners aren't honest with each other about how much they earn or need to save and about what's affordable based on that income and savings.

WARNING *Be honest with your partner when it comes to money. (Married couples could do with a dose of honesty, too!)*

One way to deal with the issue of unequal income is for both partners to contribute to the joint household pot on a percentage-of-income basis. Consider the following scenario as an example of this approach.

Joe and Jill are a couple in their late 40s who never have been married. Jill brings in $100,000, or two-thirds of the total household income, while

Joe brings in only $50,000, or one-third. They split expenses equally, each contributing the same amount to their Ours household pot. Together they spend 100 percent of that pot every month. But Jill's share of the pot amounts to only half of her monthly take-home pay. The rest she pockets, saves, spends, or uses to do whatever she wants. She's amassing quite a substantial investment portfolio. Joe, meanwhile, scrambles every month to come up with his share of the household pot. It takes 100 percent and sometimes even more of his somewhat modest teacher's salary. He has nothing left over and can't save. He's not building equity or assets, either. But Joe doesn't say anything. After all, as the man of the house, traditionally he's expected to be a good provider.

The serious inequity in the couple's financial relationship creates a stew of household tensions. The couple isn't married. Jill is saving thousands of dollars a year in her name, while Joe saves nothing. The bottom line is that Joe and Jill don't feel as though they are building a future together. Instead, they feel like roommates. Could it be that Jill doesn't trust Joe enough to commit all her income to the partnership? Or do one or both partners believe the relationship won't be long term? The situation isn't healthy for the relationship or for Joe.

The couple have three—actually four—options, if calling it quits counts as an option:

1. Lower their household spending level so neither Joe nor Jill has to contribute as much money to the joint pot. That would allow Joe to save money on his own.
2. Continue with the same 50-50 split in monthly household contributions but change the ownership and title of Jill's savings so it becomes the couple's savings.
3. Change the percentage of each partner's contribution to the household pot to reflect his or her contribution to the total household income. Joe would contribute one-third of the total pot, Jill two-thirds.
4. Forget their relationship and go their separate ways.

The options may sound relatively clear and simple, but they're not. Household financial inequities among unmarried—and married—couples are very common. Couples have trouble discussing such inequities, because the subject is sensitive. Often the differences create a wedge between partners that's impossible to remove. That's all the more reason to bring in an expert—a qualified financial planner—to help you and your partner deal with the important issues: financial, legal, and otherwise.

It's also more reason to plan your finances early and often. Work on differences before they get out of hand. Seek the advice of a competent third party when necessary. If Joe and Jill only had talked about their income differences in the beginning, Joe wouldn't have felt inadequate because he wasn't saving anything. We can't do anything about the fact that Jill makes more money than Joe. But if the household expenses were split based on income, Joe likely would feel better. He wasn't honest with Jill, and he wasn't open about his concerns. Instead, he wanted to impress her. Big mistake! The couple's differences ended up fracturing their otherwise happy relationship. Don't think such financial friction can't happen to you. It can and it does happen all the time to couples of all ages, sexual orientation, and financial situations. It's especially common with older couples, who over the years have become set in their financial ways and not easily swayed to change.

If you and your partner decide to work through your financial differences, keep in mind that the solutions must be mutually agreed on. That way, both partners will feel the decisions are fair and their wishes and needs are upheld.

Kelly and Michelle have been in a committed relationship with each other for four years. Though their incomes vary widely, the couple has devised an equitable way to share household expenses, while also saving individually and maintaining each other's financial independence. Each partner contributes to household expenses based on a percentage of her income, and then spends, saves, or invests the rest of her money as she chooses.

Bank Accounts

Yes, bank accounts *are* assets and should be treated like any other asset. The same issues that apply to other assets apply to them, as well. If a relationship is short term, as mentioned above, don't comingle bank accounts. There are few benefits in doing so.

However, certain psychological messages go along with this kind of independence. If a couple's relationship is more long-term, the partners might believe that unifying their assets is important. A word of warning: Be sure to proceed with caution and recognize exactly what the ramifications of comingling are. Other approaches to sharing assets with a partner may be able to provide many of the benefits without all of the drawbacks of comingling.

Partners never should merge or comingle any assets without first putting in place a domestic partnership—or living together—agreement that includes a breaking-up clause. That clause stipulates what will happen to joint assets in the event of the dissolution of a relationship. Remember, the agreement isn't about challenging or doubting a partner; it's merely an unmarried couple's version of a prenuptial agreement, cohabitation contract, and divorce decree combined.

Investments and Investing

Investments and investing for unmarried couples are not unique. What is different—and essential that couples get right—is how investments are owned or titled and the way in which related documents are structured.

How do couples approach and decide on Yours, Mine, or Ours when it comes to investing? Again, there's no easy answer. If one partner says, "I'll invest in all the bonds, and you take all the stocks," someone inevitably will come up short, because one partner is assuming more of the risk. If the couple decides to split up or one partner dies, one partner also gets shortchanged. If both partners in a relationship own individual retirement accounts, one partner could have far better investments than the other because of the plan offered by his or her employer.

Couples need to think about the total picture and understand up front the ramifications of their investment choices. That's especially important for younger couples who don't plan to marry.

In another scenario, both partners could be saving equally, but one might have a number of appreciated securities with capital gains built up, while the other has a stash of cash. That couple's domestic partnership agreement, with its breaking-up clause, would vary depending on the value and subsequent division of assets.

A better investment solution for an unmarried couple would be one that gives each partner a diversified portfolio that complements the other partner's portfolio. (See Chapter 7 for more information about partners and portfolios.)

LIABILITIES

This is one of the few areas in which unmarried couples can come out ahead.

For example, couples don't have to assume each other's debt. That means that you have no legal responsibility to pay off your partner's debt. No such luck for married couples! Capitalize on the opportunity.

WARNING *Beware of co-ownership of an asset or liability with someone else, including a parent, child, or partner. It's not about love. It's about risk and liability.*

Don't even think about merging assets with a partner without first looking at his or her liabilities. Do ask about prior credit history and credit rating. Even consider requesting copies of both of your credit reports, then reviewing them together. If your partner's finances are laden with huge liabilities or potential liabilities and credit issues, merging your finances can drag you down, too. Think twice before you put your name on your partner's debt.

Helping Out

If you're in a committed relationship, though, there are ways you can help a partner get out of debt without saddling yourself with additional liability. Don't simply pay off a debt for a partner without first finding out the reasons for it. Footing a bill for your partner may be OK, if the debt is the result of legitimate and necessary expenses, such as those related to an illness or a hostile divorce. But a partner also could have a chronic problem with spending money. If not forced to take responsibility for paying off his or her own debts, the lesson might never be learned. The same situation could recur again and again. Reality check: The average American's problem with money is that they spend more than they make. It's as complicated as that! Recognize the issue, and if that's your partner's problem, try to help him or her face up to it, understand it, and overcome it.

One way to help a partner manage debt is for *both* of you to take out a *joint* home equity line of credit to help pay off the debt. That gets the creditors off your backs and hopefully limits future credit problems. A word of caution, however: That joint line of credit *will* increase your liability exposure. Another approach to helping a partner is for you temporarily to cover some or all of the joint household expenses, like the mortgage and utilities, until a partner can pay off his or her creditors. Or you could lend your partner the money, as long as the loan is done through a formal agreement. (Check out CircleLending—800-805-2472, http://www.circlelending.com—for assistance in setting up and administering these loans.) Of course, you can lend the money interest-free, too. With these kinds of bailouts, you may wish to draft an agreement, stating that when or if the two of you decide to sell a joint asset like a home or car, you will receive a larger share of the profits as payback for the bailout.

The Risk

Liabilities aren't limited to credit cards, mortgages, and student loans. Is your partner in a high-risk occupation, such as physician? Is your partner a potential or active participant in a lawsuit? Has he or she been responsible for or involved in any recent accidents that resulted in personal injury or property damage? If you answered yes to any of those questions and the individual who alleges harm decides to sue, you and your partner could lose all your joint assets (more, in some cases) if the two of you have comingled your finances.

That's a lot of ifs, but is it worth it to risk everything? Usually not.

Here's something else for heterosexual couples to keep in mind. If one partner has credit problems and the couple lives in or is considering moving to a state that recognizes common law marriage, be careful that you don't present yourself as a married couple. As a married couple, common law or otherwise, you're limited by your spouse's credit problems. As we discussed in Chapter 1, avoiding common law marriage means that partners should not present themselves as a married couple in any way, shape, or form. To be completely sure they don't end up common law spouses, it probably would be a good idea to sign and have notarized a declaration not to enter into a common law marriage.

It's generally not a good idea for an older individual to comingle or have joint ownership of assets with an adult child, either. That exposes both individuals to major liability issues. Either party could lose his or her entire account balance if, for example, that child becomes involved in a lawsuit and loses.

Ed and Esther were widowed and in their late 70s. Both had older children who were not too pleased with the couple's relationship, so the companions opted not to marry. To further calm the inheritance worries of his somewhat difficult son, Ed included him jointly on the primary account that held his retirement funds. Horrible idea! Ed's son ran into some financial difficulties and ended up being sued for damages. The courts pursued Ed's retirement money, because it was in an account owned jointly by father and son. If a parent puts a child's name on one of his or her accounts, that parent's assets are potentially at risk if the child runs into legal problems such as tax liens, bankruptcy, divorce problems, business failures, and more. It's not a labor of love—or an act of appeasement. As in Ed's situation, it's one of liability.

Susan and Jodie splurged when the bought a luxury SUV. Though they both make good money, they knew the vehicle was an extravagance. But they rationalized that, because Susan would use it for her catering business, the expense was justified. Besides, the unmarried couple bought it jointly, so the payments weren't any problem. After all, Jodie is a pediatrician.

One day, as Susan was delivering trays of appetizers to a cocktail party in a typical Boston snowstorm, she was involved in a minor fender bender. No one was hurt, and both vehicles had only minor damage. The police came, and there appeared to be no problems. Susan exchanged information with the other driver, and away she went. About two weeks later, Susan and Jodie were notified that they both were named parties to a lawsuit filed by the other driver of the car that Susan hit. Perhaps once the driver—or his attorney—realized that a physician co-owned the car, the "previously unrealized" injuries mounted. In other words, the other driver saw the potential for dollars and jumped at the chance to sue.

Unmarried couples need to take potential liability issues very seriously. Susan should have owned the SUV individually. Other approaches to asset ownership are available as well. We'll talk more about them later.

Credit and Credit Cards

The lure of easy credit is tough to avoid these days. People often turn to spending as an outlet for boredom or depression or as a release for anger and resentment. Unfortunately, impulse buying seldom solves the real problem, and the resulting debt often outlasts the relationship.

Remember, one of the advantages of being an unmarried couple is that you don't have to intertwine credit ratings, credit cards, or most types of credit. That can be a big help to a partner who is trying to get back on the right credit track but lacks the credit rating or cash on hand to do so. This credit independence is an unmarried couple's big advantage. Your unmarried counterparts are envious—guaranteed!

Nix the car. Neither is it a good idea to share many debt commitments such as ownership of a car. Just as with Ed's putting his son's name on his retirement account, the risk associated with owning a car with a partner exposes both partners to unnecessary and potentially devastating risk.

Thirty-somethings Lou and Lisa had been together less than a year. Both adored each other but agreed neither was interested just yet in the commitment of marriage. They did, however, decide to buy a car together—an awesome red convertible, to be more specific. The payments were a breeze for the two professionals, because both earned a good living and lived in the home that Lisa's dad had given her outright several years earlier. Things went well until Lou was involved in an accident in the car. Lou figured that his insurance company would pick up the cost of everything, no problem. And even if the owner of the car that he hit decided to sue, Lou didn't have much anyway. The house was Lisa's. Her car was in her name. So what else was there?

Bad planning and poor assumptions on Lou's part: The awesome red sports car was owned by Lou and Lisa and titled under both their names, so all Lou's assets and the couple's jointly held assets were fair game. Luckily, however, the house was safe because Lisa was sole owner.

Gift Tax Implications

Giving money or assets to a partner or anyone else is known as "gifting." If the amount of the gift exceeds the tax-free maximum allowed by the federal government, it becomes the IRS's business, with potential tax consequences. As of 2005, the annual tax-free gift maximum is $11,000. Unmarried partners can't freely share assets with each other valued at more than $11,000 in a year without triggering potential gift tax ramifications. Married couples, on the other hand, automatically receive the unlimited marital property transfer and can give each other an unlimited amount of money, cars, homes, and more while living—and at death.

Unmarried couples still can share high-value assets, but the transfer must be done in a way that takes advantage of specific planning strategies. Keep in mind, too, that a gift has to be completed to have gift tax implications. An ultraconservative approach is to treat a gift, such as adding a partner's name to a bank account, as if it's complete when the partner's name is added to the account. The reasoning is that he or she then has complete access to the money. However, most tax experts agree that retitling is not enough. Instead, the gift has not been made—and therefore subject to potential gift tax implications—until the partner whose name was added to the account draws out the money. A gift of real estate, of course, is different. It's complete as soon as the recipient's name is added to a deed. (See page 61 for more on gifting.)

As an example of the most common approach to gifting and taxes, consider Eileen and Mark. They've been together as a couple for just more than a year and still maintain separate bank accounts. They don't even have a joint household account. However, Mark, who travels a great deal on business, decides that for convenience and in the event of emergency, he wants to add Eileen's name to his account. Once her name is on the account, though, the money becomes a gift only if and when Eileen withdraws any of it and uses it to buy something for herself other than basic necessities like food, clothing, and shelter. She could, perhaps, withdraw a chunk of it to pay for her upcoming trip to Europe. At that point, the money then becomes subject to gifting laws, and Mark subsequently has to file a gift tax return if the value of the gift exceeds the annual gift exemption, currently $11,000.

WARNING *Gifting, inadvertently or otherwise, has plenty of tax strings attached.*

OWNERSHIP STRATEGIES

This is a big decision for unmarried couples. How an asset is held or titled can make the difference between you, your partner, or your heirs being financially well off—even wealthy—or destitute and homeless. Ownership also is about control and freedom, risk and liability.

Here's a closer look at some ownership strategies and the ramifications of each.

Joint Tenancy

If an asset is held in joint tenancy, it's split *equally* between two or more partners. Joint tenancy also generally includes rights of survivorship. In the event of death, that partner's share of ownership, which is part of his or her estate, automatically transfers to the surviving partner or partners. The automatic transfer is not always assumed, so it's a good idea to ensure that any joint tenancy agreement also specifically stipulates right of survivorship. If you're buying a house or opening a brokerage account, confirm that something is held in joint tenancy *with* rights of survivorship (JTWROS). Sometimes, if a document reads, "joint owners or joint tenancy," it could really be tenants in common rather than joint tenants with rights of survivorship. In the absence of specifically declaring that the asset ownership is joint tenants with rights of survivorship, the default will be tenants in common.

Steve had sole ownership of the house he had lived in for a number of years with his partner, Bill. Steve died, and because Bill had no legal rights to the house, he ended up alone and homeless. If both men had held the home in joint tenancy with right of survivorship, Bill would have inherited the sole ownership of the couple's home. (See page 56 for more on joint ownership.)

One big caution for unmarried couples who opt to hold property this way: Pay attention to the order in which your and your partner's names are listed on the asset or account. Income and gains/losses will be reported under the Social Security number of the first name listed. If partners have an investment account at a brokerage firm, the brokerage will report that account's earnings under the Social Security number of the first individual listed. That can be advantageous from a tax-planning viewpoint: The partner with the lower income and, consequently, in the lower tax bracket may wish to be the first name listed on the bank or investment account. Conversely, the one in the higher tax bracket may want to have his or her name listed first on a deed and mortgage to claim the deductions.

Eve and Sally have a joint investment account at a large brokerage firm. Because Eve's income is significantly less than Sally's, the account lists Eve's name first and Sally's second. The company reports any earnings or losses that the couple's account incurs in Eve's name, because she is the lead account holder. Eve receives the IRS form 1099, then reports those earnings or losses on her individual income tax returns. In contrast, for a legally married couple, earnings and losses are filed on the couple's joint tax returns. (See Chapter 5 for more on the tax advantages available to unmarried couples.)

Tenants in Common

Holding an asset as tenants in common allows for ownership by multiple parties with *varying* percentages of ownership. It clearly does not carry rights of survivorship. When a tenant-in-common owner dies, his or her percentage of ownership becomes part of his or her estate, in turn passing to the heir(s) stipulated in the deceased's will. Without a will in place, the estate will be distributed in accordance with the laws in the deceased's state of residence.

Martha and Louise, for example, own a boat as tenants in common. Martha owns 60 percent, Louise the remaining 40 percent. Martha's will stipulates that, in the event of her death, her 60 percent ownership in the boat goes to her younger brother. Louise's will leaves her 40 percent share to Martha.

This is the only common method of co-ownership that allows a portion of the ownership to go to someone other than a partner. This makes sense when both parties' contributions to the purchase of an asset are not equal or when there could be potential estate tax issues if both partners are well off financially.

A couple of cautions when it comes to ownership strategies include:

1. Include an explanation of the ownership percentage split in your documentation.

2. Relying on a domestic partner to leave his or her portion of ownership to you can be risky. There's no guarantee a partner will do that. There's also no guarantee that if a co-owner designates his or her partner as heir, the co-owner subsequently won't change his or her mind and leave the portion of the asset to someone else.

Also, when choosing an heir to your assets, pay attention to how any potential heir might handle the situation if you died suddenly. That's especially relevant for same-sex partners considering leaving the bulk of assets to someone other than each other. How might that potential heir react if suddenly he or she is in control of the deceased partner's home, car, and other possessions? How might he or she deal with the surviving partner? Is he or she capable of accepting of the same-sex relationship, or could the surviving partner suddenly be rejected and homeless or, worse yet, dragged through courts out of the heir's greed or for some other inane and hurtful reason? That's not just a same-sex issue, either. It can happen with younger and older heterosexual couples, too. Once an individual is dead, pent-up emotions and greed of survivors often can boil to the surface. The issue no longer is one of care and compassion. It's dollars and cents.

Consider another potential problem. Jamie and Eric have been together for 12 years and are well off financially. They own two homes together as tenants in common—a condo in Manhattan and a beach house on Fire Island—and eventually would like to bequeath those homes to various charitable causes. But the couple also understands that, because they aren't married, if they do leave each other's percentage ownership in the homes to a charity, then when one partner dies, the surviving partner potentially could have problems. Consequently, they decide to will ownership of the homes to each other and name the charities as contingent beneficiaries. The charities eventually will end up with both homes after both partners' deaths.

Payable on Death or Transfer on Death

A Payable on Death (POD) or Transfer on Death (TOD) designation on an asset is a quick, easy, and cheap way to maintain control of an asset and to leave assets to a partner or other heir, while, at the same time, avoiding probate.

With POD/TOD, an asset is owned individually, but on death it transfers to the individual(s) specified without going through the probate process. The asset is part of an estate and still subject to inheritance and/or estate taxes. All the designated beneficiary must do is present the appropriate person with a certified copy of the asset owner's death certificate. POD/TOD also eliminates the liability exposure that would go along with holding an asset jointly outright.

Almost all states allow POD/TOD on assets generally sold at banks and brokerages, such as bank accounts, money market accounts, CDs, savings bonds, and investment accounts. But very few states allow this transfer for real assets like homes, cars, or boats. That's unfortunate because it's a great, inexpensive, asset transfer tool.

David and Chuck met while in their mid-30s and coupled almost immediately. At the time, Chuck was just beginning to pick himself up after a financially devastating illness. Because of the illness and related expenses, he had been forced into bankruptcy and had a lousy credit rating. Meanwhile, David had pristine credit and a substantial bank account. After the couple had been together several years and both clearly were committed long term to each other, their financial advisor suggested that David change the title on his bank account to Payable on Death with Chuck as the beneficiary. The reason: Chuck's credit troubles still blemished his record, and he had limited access to cash. Therefore, if David died suddenly and Chuck needed large amounts of money quickly to pay the mortgage and other bills, the POD account could provide that fast cash with a minimum of hassle. Setting up the account as POD also was a breeze. All David had to do was ask his bank for a form, then fill it out designating Chuck the POD beneficiary.

TOD also can be an excellent way for an unmarried couple to transfer ownership of a vehicle to one another in the event that one partner dies. It's quick and easy, because all you do is name the beneficiary of the vehicle right on its certificate of title. The beneficiary has no rights to or liability for the vehicle while the owner is alive, but ownership passes immediately to the beneficiary when the owner dies.

Those states that allow Transfer on Death of title to a vehicle include only California, Connecticut, Kansas, Missouri, and Ohio. Those states that allow TOD on real estate include Arizona, Colorado, Kansas, Missouri, Nevada, New Mexico, and Ohio.

To check if POD/TOD on personal property is legal in your state or locale, contact your county registry of deeds or motor vehicles department.

Revocable Living Trusts

A revocable living trust is yet another strategy for owning property. An individual or grantor places his or her assets in the trust and continues to control those assets by acting as trustee as long as he or she is living and cognizant. The living trust also spells out the legalese of what happens if

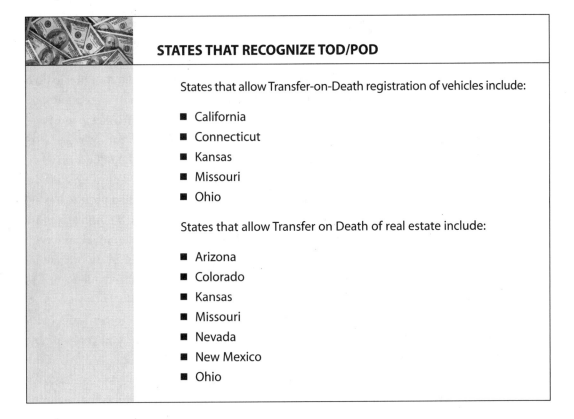

STATES THAT RECOGNIZE TOD/POD

States that allow Transfer-on-Death registration of vehicles include:

- California
- Connecticut
- Kansas
- Missouri
- Ohio

States that allow Transfer on Death of real estate include:

- Arizona
- Colorado
- Kansas
- Missouri
- Nevada
- New Mexico
- Ohio

the trustee—you—becomes disabled and can't transact on his or her own behalf, naming who will step in as the successor trustee to handle their financial affairs. An unmarried trustee, for example, could designate his or her partner as the successor trustee, allowing that partner to manage the couple's household affairs in the event that something happens to the original trustee.

Remember April and Jim, the unmarried couple in Chapter 1? Jim lapsed into a coma and was whisked away by his parents forever. Meanwhile, because Jim had no disability insurance to replace his income, or a health care directive that enabled April to make medical decisions for him, and April had no ownership of the home, she was left destitute and homeless after Jim's parents locked her out. (See Chapter 8 for more on health care directives.) If Jim had owned the home in a living trust with April designated the successor trustee and had a health care directive with April the designee to handle medical decisions, she could have had much more control over the situation. She would have been able to act on behalf of the incapacitated Jim with regard to the house and any other assets held by the trust.

A living trust also is a good option for an unmarried individual to hold property separately from his or her domestic partner without opening up either partner to the liability associated with owning an asset in joint tenancy. The individual owner (the grantor) has full control over the asset held in the trust until such time as he or she is not cognizant or dies, when the designated successor trustee steps in. Compare that approach with the riskier joint tenancy with right of survivorship, in which a partner has access to and control over everything from the beginning. If liquid assets are held in joint tenancy, a partner could get angry one day and walk out with all the couple's liquid assets. That happens frequently in divorce situations when an irate spouse empties a joint account, with the legal access to do so. Unmarried couples can and do clean out accounts as well.

If you own real property, like a vacation home in another state, holding title to the property in a revocable trust can save you considerable time and money on the death of the grantor of the trust.

Revocable living trusts do not require filing separate tax returns. (An irrevocable trust does.) From an operational standpoint, income or capital gains received on assets held in a revocable living trust are treated as assets of the grantor directly. That means the owner of the trust—the grantor—pays all income taxes on any income generated by the trust.

That's the good news. The bad news is that these trusts are costly to set up. In most markets, it costs at least $1,500 per person to have a revocable living trust designed and drafted. There's no annual fee, but the trust requires updating when situations change significantly.

Limited Liability Company/Revocable Trust Combined

Owning assets by combining a limited liability company with a revocable living trust is a sophisticated solution that unmarried couples with sizable assets may consider. It's also a costly option—$3,000 to $10,000 to set up, depending on the complexity of the situation and locale.

But this strategy may be necessary if the partners have many assets and need to create as many layers of protection as possible between a creditor and the assets. It might make sense, for example, if domestic partners own several rental properties. The limited liability company would own the properties and spell out each partner's responsibilities.

If couples think this strategy might be worth pursuing, it's best to discuss it extensively with a competent legal advisor.

Home Ownership

Home ownership often is an incredibly contentious issue between couples, especially unmarried ones. The controversies start early, including:

- Should we buy a home?
- If so, how much house can we afford?
- Should we contribute equally to the down payment?
- Who will own the home; that is, whose name will appear on the deed? How will the home be titled?
- Who will be responsible for the mortgage?
- Who will benefit from the home ownership in terms of the tax deduction for mortgage interest and taxes? How will that be determined?

FIGURE 3.1 Ownership Options

Here are a few ownership strategies that unmarried partners may want to consider:

- *Joint tenancy.* Asset ownership is split *equally* between two or more partners and generally includes rights of survivorship. After death, that partner's share of ownership automatically transfers to the surviving partner or partners, avoiding probate.

  Y / O / SS

- *Tenants in common.* Enables an asset to be held by multiple parties with varying percentages of ownership. Does not carry rights of survivorship. After death, that partner's share goes to the heir(s) named in the will or, if he or she died intestate, to the heirs designated by state.

  Y / O / SS

- *Payable on Death/Transfer on Death.* An asset is owned individually but, on death, transfers to a designated beneficiary, avoiding probate. This is a quick and cheap way to leave assets to a partner.

  Y / O / SS

- *Revocable living trust.* An individual places assets in the trust and continues to control those assets by acting as trustee as long as he or she is living and cognizant. The trust is revocable and provides contingencies in the event of disability by naming a successor trustee.

  Y / O / SS

- *Limited liability company with revocable trust.* Shares of a limited liability company, rather than being owned individually, are owned by a revocable trust that stipulates who will take over as controller of the trust in the event of the grantor's incapacitation or death. This setup adds a layer of protection between creditors and assets and allows for a smooth transition for the business in the event something happens to the grantor/limited liability company member.

  O / SS

- Who will control the capital, and who will provide the labor?
- Who will get the home if the couple breaks up?

With all those questions, why should an unmarried couple bother to jump into the fray? As we discussed earlier in this chapter, buying a property with a committed partner can be unifying, satisfying, and financially rewarding. The American dream of owning a home is a big attraction. It also provides tax breaks and the potential for capital appreciation. And, for those folks who choose not to marry or can't legally marry, often owning a home together represents both partners' commitment to each other.

The details. If you are a partner in an unmarried relationship and if you individually or jointly buy or plan to buy a home, pay attention to the documents and details. How an asset is titled or held, the kind of documents you put in place relative to your living situation, and the assets you have could affect you and your heirs for a lifetime.

First, look at your relationship. Are you financially committed to each other? If it's legally possible, do you plan eventually to marry this partner? Are credit or liability issues involved? Are extended families part of the picture? Do accompanying inheritance matters need to be considered? Do you want to provide for your partner in the event something happens to you? Do you or your partner have the necessary capital or access to the capital needed for a down payment on a home?

The answers to all these questions should figure into the decision on whether to buy a home individually or jointly, how to title it, how to pay for it, and how to maintain it.

Steve had bad credit, but he was able to buy a house, financing it through the seller at a high interest rate and with the stipulation that he would fix up the somewhat dilapidated home. Not long after that, Steve got into a long-term, committed relationship with Bill. Steve's poor credit still prevented the couple from refinancing the home conventionally. Even though the mortgage interest rate was high, Steve, Bill, and the seller/ mortgage holder got along well, so the couple assumed everything was fine. Meanwhile, they expended considerable time and effort on fixing up the house, which was located in a high-end neighborhood. The property's value skyrocketed.

The problem occurred when Steve died prematurely. Because of an exorbitant interest rate, the mortgage balance actually was higher than when Steve initially bought the home. Bill had impeccable credit but couldn't qualify for a mortgage large enough to let him refinance by himself and get out from under the stiff monthly payments. Steve had been HIV-positive, so he had not qualified for life insurance and had only Medicaid to cover health care costs. All this, plus ongoing medical bills from Steve while he still was alive left Bill financially crippled. The mortgage holder foreclosed, and Bill was evicted. Bill lost his partner and his home at the same time.

Simple solution. The sad thing is that Steve and Bill could have fixed the problem if they had attended to financial planning early on. They could have had protections in place, but they didn't recognize the potential downside of their situation:

- *First mistake.* The couple assumed that the mortgage holder—out of the goodness of his heart—simply would switch the mortgage and title on the home over to Bill, even though he had no legal obligation to do so.
- *Second mistake.* Steve should have added Bill's name to the deed and forced the refinance issue, especially because Bill had an excellent credit history. Someone would have given them a new mortgage, and it couldn't have been any more expensive than the one they already had.
- *Third mistake.* Steve didn't have legal documents in place that would have willed his home to Bill.

Don't be too critical of Bill and Steve's failure to plan. Most people fail to plan but never plan to fail. Always keep in mind that owning an asset is a business deal. It needs to be approached as such.

Deed details. Another caution with regard to titling a property: A homeowner should not decide suddenly to include his or her partner on the deed to their home, then run over to the office supply store, pick up a blank quit-claim deed, and fill it out. Doing so could be a major blunder with serious ramifications. In essence, if you do that, you give away half the asset, or half the home's equity, without the corresponding debt or mortgage. That's relinquishing half the collateral for the property's mortgage. As you can imagine, such a move probably wouldn't go over well with a mortgage company. That company could even foreclose on the property as a result of your action.

If you decide to split ownership of a property with your partner, generally you also must refinance the property so that both names appear on the deed or title and on the mortgage.

Also, remember that gifting more than $11,000 in a calendar year triggers gift tax implications. A way around that, however, is gifting over time. The retitling is done initially, but the gift and the actual transfer of ownership are completed over time. Additional documentation is needed stipulating that the gift is spread out over time. If the point is to gift the property over time, if it's done properly, it will not even show up on the giver's or the recipient's tax return.

Let's assume you have $100,000 equity in a home and want to retitle the property to joint ownership with right of survivorship with your partner. In essence, you want to give him or her $50,000 worth of equity in your home. In order not to incur any gift tax consequences, you must draw up separate documentation that stipulates the $50,000 gift is being made over five years. That keeps the annual gifts less than the current $11,000-a-year tax-free gifting maximum.

In another case, Robin bought her home five years ago for $200,000. She put down 20 percent, or $40,000, and assumed a mortgage for the balance ($160,000). Later, she met Carol Ann. After the pair had been together for several years, Robin decided to give Carol Ann half ownership in the house. By then, the home's value had climbed to $250,000, and Robin had paid down $10,000 of principal, so she now had $100,000 net equity in the property.

After talking about it with her Certified Financial Planner™ and attorney, Robin decided that, rather than make an outright gift of half the home, she would gift a portion of the home each year over time to Carol Ann, thus avoiding potential gift taxes. Of course, Carol Ann's name would be added to the home's deed, and the mortgage would be refinanced to reflect the joint ownership. Meanwhile, each partner would continue to pay half the mortgage and monthly upkeep.

Initially, the details of the transaction confused Robin. Here's how her planning team explained it. While the value of the house today is $250,000, the actual value of Robin's gift to Carol Ann is half of her net equity in the property, or $50,000. That's figured by taking the value of the house ($250,000), subtracting the remaining mortgage balance ($150,000), which equals $100,000, and dividing by 2.

With the intricacy of the arrangement, the safest ownership strategy is for both partners to own the home as tenants in common. That allows each to own varying percentages of the property as Carol Ann builds up her ownership stake through Robin's gifting over time. Once the deal is complete, it's often a good idea to make sure that the title is held in joint tenancy with rights of survivorship, which then would reflect the 50-50 ownership. (For a closer look at the numbers, see Figure 3.2.)

Let's look more closely. Assume that the value of the home remains constant at $250,000 and that the partners will split equally the amount of principal paid down on the new mortgage. With the current tax-free gift limit at $11,000 per calendar year, Robin's $50,000 in equity gift to Carol Ann will take approximately 4½ years to complete. Assuming that the gifting begins in 2005, Robin and Carol Ann will be equal owners by the end of 2009.

While this strategy is the safest tax-wise, it does require a new tenants-in-common agreement be drafted and recorded each year to reflect the new ownership percentages. Partners also can retitle a property as joint tenants with rights of survivorship up front. That's much easier. However, the couple also must have a legally binding side agreement in place—and make sure everyone knows about it—that spells out the gifting-over-time arrangement. The deed is public record, but the side agreement is not, so the IRS and creditors still could argue that both partners are 50-50 owners unless you prove the existence of the side agreement.

FIGURE 3.2 Gifting Over Time

Robin opted to gift half her home's net equity to her partner Carol Ann (who already pays half the monthly mortgage) over a five-year period ($11,000/year) to avoid potential gift tax issues. Here's how gifting over time works.

Home's Fair Market Value*	$250,000
Robin's Mortgage Balance	150,000
Robin's Current Net Equity	100,000
Initial Cost of House	200,000
Initial Mortgage	160,000
Down Payment	40,000

	2005	2006	2007	2008	2009
Assumed Market Value	$250,000	$250,000	$250,000	$250,000	$250,000
Mortgage Balance	150,000	148,200	146,300	144,200	142,000
Principal Paid Down	1,800	1,900	2,100	2,200	2,300
End of Year Equity	$101,800	$103,700	$105,800	$108,000	$110,300
Robin's Beginning Equity	$100,000	$89,900	$79,850	$69,900	$60,000
Gift to Carol Ann	11,000	11,000	11,000	11,000	6,000
Half of Principal Paid Down	900	950	1,050	1,100	1,150
Robin's Ending Equity	$89,900	$79,850	$69,900	$60,000	$55,150
Carol Ann's Beginning Equity	$0	$11,900	$23,850	$35,900	$48,000
Gift of Equity	11,000	11,000	11,000	11,000	6,000
Half of Principal Paid Down	900	950	1,050	1,100	1,150
Carol Ann's Ending Equity	$11,900	$23,850	$35,900	$48,000	$55,150
Robin's Ownership %	88%	77%	66%	56%	50%
Carol Ann's Ownership %	12%	23%	34%	44%	50%

*Based on the average of three appraisals

Pay attention to potential inequities in making changes to a home's deed. Sandy bought her home several years before she met Tom. The first time she saw him, she fell head over heels in love. Eventually, he moved in with her, and to make him feel more at home, the couple refinanced the house with a joint mortgage. But what about the deed to the home? No one bothered to change that, too. Suddenly Tom is saddled with half the debt on the home without legal ownership of any part of the corresponding asset. If his name is not on the deed, he has no legal rights to any part of the house.

If Sandy and Tom split, he still would be legally obligated to repay the entire mortgage if Sandy didn't pay any, and he would have no asset to back it up.

WARNING *Don't own property with a partner unless you also have a property agreement in place that details the responsibilities and obligations of all parties concerned.*

Don't own property with your partner unless you also have a property agreement up front that spells out the details of each partner's ownership, responsibilities, liabilities, and logistics. This agreement could be part of a domestic partnership agreement (see Chapter 8), but it doesn't have to be. Whatever its form, it should be in writing, signed, and notarized, and it must be detailed. Some of these details include:

- Who contributed what to the purchase price? If you and your partner split the cost 50/50, indicate that. If partner A loaned partner B 20 percent of his or her 50 percent share, spell that out, too, along with how the money will be repaid, in what time frame, and so on.
- Who takes care of what and when as far as maintenance, utilities, and upkeep?
- Who is responsible for ensuring that any legal documents and/or tax returns related to a property are completed and filed on time?
- Who pays the bills, how, and when?

- In the event of disability or death, how will the property be maintained, sold, or split? How will heirs receive their share and in what time frame?
- If disputes arise, what methods will be used to resolve them, when, and in what time period?

Tax details. Don't forget to include details about which partner will get the mortgage interest tax deduction and which the property tax deduction. Remember, unmarried partners must file individual tax returns, so it can make financial sense as an unmarried couple to bunch deductions with one partner if your tax brackets differ. A word to the wise, however: Legally, whoever pays the mortgage is entitled to take the deduction. So be careful and be aware of that when drafting a property agreement. Whether it concerns a 50-story office building or a 3-room bungalow, a property agreement is a business contract between domestic partners and, therefore, critical and legally binding. Make it work for you.

Breaking-up contingencies. Another ingredient critical to the property agreement is a detailed explanation of what happens in the event of dissolution of the relationship. Who has first right to buy out the other partner's share of ownership in the property, under what circumstances, at what price, and in what time frame? A fair price, for example, could be the average of two independent market appraisals of the property. This provision also could state that, in the event of dissolution of the relationship, the property ownership (and title) changes from joint tenancy with rights of survivorship to tenants in common.

Emily and Tim found out the hard way what happens when a property agreement doesn't specify those details. The pair built the home of their dreams in the perfect setting. Shortly afterward, they split up. Neither wanted to sell his or her share to the other. The case ended up in court, where a judge ordered the two to sell the house to a third party to resolve the situation. They had to sell at a fire-sale price, and neither Emily nor Tim ended up with their dream home. If they had drawn up the right kind of property agreement, the scenario could have been vastly different. (See Chapter 8 for more information on how to deal with breaking up.)

FINAL CAVEATS

Committed or casual, short-term or long-term, couples should draft and sign contingency agreements and other important documentation when they're in love, because, if they break up, their arguments won't be about love—they'll be about money.

Unfortunately, the efforts required to initiate many of these legal agreements may take some of the bloom off the romance. That's a downside of trying to create a workable legal structure for an unmarried couple. But remember, unmarried couples don't have the option of divorce courts and related legal precedents. The courts have a formula for married couples. Unmarried couples have no formula without drafting their own agreements that specify rights, obligations, and responsibilities as well as account for the what-ifs in the relationship.

The upside is that, with the agreements in place, you and your partner are protected by a legal framework similar to that available to married couples.

Also, in the event you break up, don't forget about your designated beneficiaries on various assets. Depending on your arrangements with that now former partner, you may wish to change your beneficiaries. That includes IRAs and other retirement accounts, bank accounts of all kinds, savings bonds, brokerage accounts, and even that freebie $1,000 life insurance policy you may have signed up for through your credit union. Otherwise, in the event something happens to you, that *former* partner could waltz off with the goods.

BOTTOM LINES

Unmarried couples need to pay attention to how they own assets. Unlike the situation for their married counterparts, it's not a simple matter of buying a major asset and then forgetting about it. Unmarried partners must put in place legal protections via ownership strategies and written agreements, or they open themselves up to all kinds of risks and liabilities.

However, with proper financial planning, unmarried partners can have many of the same legal protections that come with asset ownership by married couples.

As a couple and as an individual, if you do nothing else, at minimum do the following:

- Don't automatically split assets and liabilities 50-50. Look at the pros and cons of your options. How you and your partner decide to handle your assets and liabilities can have tremendous, far-reaching ramifications for life.
- Realize that asset and liability decisions should not be based on emotion. They should be sound financial decisions.
- Consider and then capitalize on the advantages you have as an unmarried couple.
- Don't own property jointly or take on liabilities jointly without also putting in place a property agreement that spells out the related rights, obligations, and responsibilities of each partner.

4

Insurance

Insurance is protection—all kinds of it. If you, a partner, or family member are seriously ill, health insurance covers the majority of medical bills. In the event that you become disabled and can't work, disability insurance is the safety net that provides income to pay the bills. If you die, life insurance replaces lost income for your partner and family left behind, creates wealth for your heirs without gift tax consequences, and can offset hefty inheritance and estate tax issues relatively painlessly.

Insurance is especially important for unmarried couples because—as mentioned repeatedly throughout this book—unmarried partners aren't allowed many of the legal protections afforded their married counterparts. Most employers do not provide unmarried partners with health or life insurance. Also, unmarried partners generally are ineligible for income replacement through surviving spouse benefits from Social Security or through a deceased partner's pension plan.

Domestic partner benefits *are* gaining acceptance, and their availability is rising, but not fast enough to keep pace with the growing numbers of unmarried partners and nontraditional families. The number of unmarried couples living together increased 72 percent from 1990 to 2000, according to the U.S. census. As of 2004, only 34 percent of employers offered some type of domestic partner benefits to opposite-sex partners and 27 percent to same-sex partners, according to the Society of Human Resource Management.

Unmarried partners generally aren't protected by inheritance tax laws, either. (Exception: In New Jersey, registered domestic partners are exempt from inheritance taxes.) When an individual dies and their partner is the primary beneficiary of the estate, the assets are subject to inheritance tax in most states that impose it because that partner is not a legal spouse. That's a state tax of up to about 15 percent, depending on the individual tax rates of the state and if the value of the assets exceeds an allowable maximum, which also varies by state. Some states allow no exemption, so inheritance tax is due on every dollar that a nonspouse inherits from their partner. State inheritance taxes are different from federal

STATES WITH INHERITANCE TAX

The following states assess inheritance tax. Rates vary by state and estate amount, as do the exemption amounts:

- Kansas (inheritance tax due on estates with gross value of $850,000 and up)
- New Jersey ($500 exemption)
- Oregon ($850,000 exemption)
- Utah ($1.5 million exemption)
- Nebraska (taxed at the county level; $500 exemption)
- Iowa (no exemption)
- Tennessee ($850,000 exemption)
- Indiana ($100 exemption)
- Kentucky ($500 exemption)
- Pennsylvania (no exemption)
- Connecticut ($200,000 exemption through year-end 2004; gradual phase out of inheritance tax through 2007)
- Maryland ($1,000 exemption)

estate taxes and subject to different rates. (See Chapter 6 for more information on taxes and estate planning.)

The state of Maryland, for example, exempts from inheritance tax $1,000 in assets of a deceased individual passed on to a nonspouse or lineal descendant. Assets exceeding that threshold are taxed at 10 percent.

Let's say your partner died, leaving you his Chevy Chase brownstone, valued at $700,000. That's a 10 percent tax on $699,000 (the difference between the $1,000 exemption and the home's $700,000 value). Do you have $69,900 in ready cash to foot the tax bill? As heir, you are given nine months from the date of death to produce the cash. What if you don't have the money at your fingertips and must take out a loan to pay the taxes? Don't forget that, if the house you inherited has a mortgage, it must be refinanced right away because you're the new owner. By the way, the inheritance tax is over and above any estate taxes that also may be due. (Estate tax is levied on the estate of the deceased and imposed before assets are distributed to heirs. An inheritance tax is generally levied on a nonspouse who receives assets by the deceased.)

Don't feel too confused or alone in your confusion. Many other people are bewildered by inheritance taxes and how they work, too. But the solution is simple: life insurance and planning. Inheritance and estate taxes aren't as frightening if partners have life insurance policies on each other that are large enough to cover the estate and inheritance taxes, if any, and, of course, name each other as the policy beneficiary. The policy then will pay the beneficiary directly and not be subject to probate.

WARNING *If you're not legally married, any recipient of assets after your death could be subject to inheritance tax.*

LIFE INSURANCE

Life insurance literally is a financial lifesaver. It's a painless, simple way for unmarried couples to transfer liquid assets to each other income-tax-free after one partner dies. The designated beneficiary simply provides a certified copy of the death certificate to the insurer or its representative, and in a short time, the check is delivered with no strings attached. Certified copies of a death certificate are available from the vital statistics office or county health office in the county in which the individual died. The funeral home often will do the legwork for you, too, providing as many copies of the death certificate as needed.

> **WARNING** *If unmarried partners don't provide for each other in case one dies, the other is on their own. Only spouses are eligible to receive Social Security survivor's benefits and pensions, with certain exceptions that include state pension benefits for employees of California, New Jersey, Vermont, and Massachusetts.*

Forget Inheritance Tax Exclusions

If you think you and your partner don't need life insurance on each other, think again. Do you currently need both of your incomes to support your lifestyle? If you die, how will your partner make up the lost income? Keep in mind, too, that neither of you is eligible for the most common income streams afforded married couples—Social Security survivor's benefits and, occasionally, pensions.

Consider this nightmare in which a surviving partner with a modest income faces the daunting task of coughing up $300,000 in cash to pay an inheritance and estate tax bill. Longtime couple Michael and Sherri lived in an upscale beach community where they earned adequate, though modest, wages. Michael died suddenly, leaving a $2 million estate, with Sherri the primary beneficiary. It sounds like a mass of assets—even Sherri was amazed at the dollar amount. But it isn't that much, considering that the couple jointly owned two homes. Sherri originally had owned the condo at a Colorado ski resort, and Michael had inherited the beach home from his mother years earlier. Because of their locations, both homes' values had skyrocketed over the years. Together, Michael and Sherri also owned a boat and two vehicles (both SUVs).

Because the couple had never married, in accordance with federal estate transfer laws, 100 percent of the value of their joint investments was included in the estate of the first partner to die—in this case, Michael. However, if Sherri could prove she contributed to the assets before Michael died, that portion would be excluded from Michael's estate. (The burden of proof is on Sherri, and she'll need property agreements and canceled checks as well as any other related documentation to prove that she contributed more than 50 percent to the Colorado property.) If these assets had been held as joint tenants with rights of survivorship and Sherri holds the assets until she dies, they would be counted as part of her estate, too, unless she convinced the IRS otherwise. (See Chapter 6 for more information on estates and taxes.) That wouldn't be the case for a married couple, because spouses automatically receive unlimited marital transfers without gift or transfer tax consequences. This double whammy is just one more way the laws are geared toward married couples.

Federal law also allows the first $1.5 million in assets held by any *U.S. citizen* to be exempt from estate transfer taxes. Therefore, only $500,000 of Michael's $2 million estate is subject to federal estate tax. In this case, the state inheritance tax rate is 10 percent on the entire inheritance. Because Sherri is inheriting the entire estate, she owes about $200,000 in state inheritance taxes. Add to that the federal estate tax of almost 50 percent in Michael's bracket, and Sherri now owes another $250,000 for a whopping total tax bill of $450,000! That's certainly not pocket change for Sherri. Could you raise that kind of cash? Sherri can't, so she's facing some tough decisions. Because the vast majority of the $2 million in assets is tied up in the couple's two homes, she may be forced to sell one at a fire-sale price or try to borrow money to pay the taxes. It's not a burden that Michael would have wished on his longtime companion—and all in the shadow of his death. If Michael had purchased adequate life insurance, it could have paid the tax bill and replaced his lost income, providing for Sherri when she needed help the most.

Short-Term Couples

Even if partners are coupled casually with no long-range plans to-gether, life insurance makes sense if the two rely on each other's income.

Beneficiaries can be changed as often as desired—with a change of partner, for example.

Life insurance allows any partners at any age to provide for and protect each other. A small policy can pay burial costs, final medical expenses, and a few bills. It also can replace the income stream, which helps the surviving partner maintain the lifestyle he or she is accustomed to or buy the stay-at-home partner time to reenter the workforce without the pressure of mounting bills.

Al and Barbara bought a condo together, even though neither felt emotionally committed to each other for their lifetimes. They titled the property as tenants in common. Each had an equal percentage of ownership, and both worked and contributed equally to household expenses. Together they earned just enough to make ends meet every month. Not long after buying the condo, Al died unexpectedly. He had no life insurance. Because the couple had not held the condo as joint tenants with rights of survivorship, and because Barbara couldn't afford to buy out Al's share of ownership from his heirs, she was forced to sell the condo. Life insurance would have provided Barbara the cash to buy out Al's heirs, and she would have been able to keep her home.

If partners are financially committed—if they enter into any kind of substantial purchase together—it's a must that both partners buy life insurance policies as protection for their financial interests in the event something happens to either one. Consider the cost of the policies as part of the asset's purchase price.

Questions Partners Need to Ask

Even if Al had owned the condo individually, and even if he had wanted Barbara to have it, that might not have been possible legally unless he had specifically bequeathed it to her. That's where financial planning can help. All unmarried partners need to discuss and subsequently address the what-ifs that could occur if one or the other died. Life insurance is a viable safety net that can protect each individual's interests and security. It could be money well spent.

Some more questions to ask yourself and each other include:

- Do you feel responsible for what happens to your partner after you die?
- Will either of you have the necessary financial wherewithal to buy out the deceased partner's interest from any heirs?
- Could you qualify to refinance the property on your own if your partner died?
- What happens if your deceased partner was the sole owner of the property?
- Can either of you continue to support yourself without the other's income?
- Would your lifestyle have to change if your partner died?

"Dying wishes" aside, legal documentation and life insurance are necessary to ensure that a partner is taken care of and an individual's wishes carried out. Purchasing a life insurance policy for a domestic partner isn't a declaration of eternal love or commitment. It's just smart planning.

Remember Mary and Samantha, the domestic and business partners who owned the multimillion-dollar office building? If Mary had died before she and Samantha split up, her 70 percent share of the building would have gone to an estranged sister with whom neither partner got along. Samantha would have ended up in an involuntary partnership with Mary's sister, because she couldn't have afforded to buy out Mary's 70 percent share in the property. Samantha would have had to sell her own share, probably not for its full value, if the pair had not had life insurance to cover this hypothetical dilemma.

In another instance, an older couple, Terry and Ellyse, are committed to each other but unmarried. Terry owns the home the couple share, and his heirs know that if anything happens to him, he wants Ellyse to have the house. But absolutely nothing guarantees that will happen without proper planning. Legal documentation and life insurance or cash would be needed to ensure that Ellyse can buy Terry's family's share of the home.

A Caveat: Insurable Interest

Adding to the complications, unmarried partners may hit yet another snag with insurance companies when attempting to designate a domestic partner as beneficiary. That snag is known as "insurable interest." An insurer may question whether a nonfamily member has an economic interest in the life of the insured. In other words, would the beneficiary incur financial hardship at the death of the insured?

Insurable interest is not the roadblock it once was, but it can be a nuisance. In the past, companies refused to issue a policy if the beneficiary was not a relative, a business partner, or a spouse. Same-sex partners circumvented the dilemma by taking out a policy and naming a brother, sister, or other family member as the beneficiary. Then, as soon as the policy was issued, the insured filed a change-of-beneficiary form, designating his or her partner as the beneficiary.

Today, such maneuvers usually aren't necessary. But just in case your company clings to the past, it's worth the effort to double-check that an insurance company is, indeed, in step with the times.

The issue of insurable interest also may arise if the dollar amount of an applied-for policy exceeds a certain threshold. That's what happened when Carol applied for a $1 million life insurance policy through USAA, the financial services giant specializing in providing services to active and retired members of the U.S. military and their families. She wanted to name her partner, Katherine, as beneficiary of the policy, because Carol owned the couple's $800,000 home. If something happened to her, Katherine wouldn't have the financial ability to buy out Carol's heirs. USAA wanted to know why Carol needed such a large policy with a beneficiary who was not a family member. The company was questioning Katherine's insurable interest. Carol showed the insurer that Katherine was her domestic partner and that, as her partner, if Carol died, she would need liquidity to buy the house from Carol's heirs. Knowing that, USAA issued the policy.

Even though companies recognize that domestic partners may have an insurable interest, don't be surprised if an insurer asks you about it anyway. A requirement to prove insurable interest likely won't deny you coverage, but it's one more step in the application process that forces unmarried partners to jump through more hoops than their married counterparts.

How Much Is Enough?

Determining the amount of life insurance to buy involves far more than picking an arbitrary number. For the insurance to serve its intended purpose, partners must ask themselves—and, if possible, potential beneficiaries—several questions and make some fairly extensive calculations:

- What do you want life insurance to do for you? Is it to pay final expenses and/or inheritance taxes, to act as interim income, to replace income for life, to build wealth for your heirs, or to make charitable gifts? Any or all of these reasons or others could apply.
- Do you feel responsible for what happens to your partner after your death?
- Does your partner plan to work if you die prematurely?
- Are you the primary breadwinner?
- How extensive are your and your partner's debts, including your mortgage if you have one?
- Do you have young children? If so, you must consider future costs of raising them, too. (More on that in Chapter 9.)
- Does anyone else, like an elderly parent or someone else, rely on you financially now, or might they in the future?
- Would you like to leave money to your alma mater or to any charities?

Life expenses. The dollar amount of insurance that a partner—unmarried or otherwise—buys must reflect individual assets and liabilities as well as the assets and liabilities of the couple. If a partner is the primary breadwinner in a committed relationship, he or she generally wants to provide enough life insurance to ensure that his or her partner and family, if applicable, will have enough money to maintain their lifestyle.

Estimate your and your partner's annual expenses, then multiply that by the number of years a payout must cover. For example, if you're a male, 45, and your partner is a 40-year-old female, you'll need to calculate the amount needed to take care of her—and any children in your relationship—for the rest of her life. The average female life expectancy as of 2001 is 79.8, according to the Centers for Disease Control's National Center for Health Statistics, so you will need to replace ordinary living expenses plus any foreseeable extras for at least 40 more years.

Of course, income on investments made with the life insurance payout will count when you're figuring the total. But that could be offset by inflation increases. The point is that if unmarried partners want to take care of each other, they likely need sizable amounts of life insurance. Remember, too, that unmarried partners don't get the benefit of Social Security survivor's benefits as do their married counterparts. It takes a lot of assets or life insurance to replace income. For those who aren't insurable, annuities are an option.

Many older unmarried couples may want to consider buying life insurance as a replacement for Social Security income in the event of one partner's death. Otto and Rebecca both lost their spouses around the same time. They met at a church social shortly afterward and immediately were attracted to each other. The two eventually moved in together. From a financial standpoint, pooling Otto's Social Security and Rebecca's Social Security survivor's benefits from her deceased spouse (it was a bigger benefit than the one she qualified for based on her own workplace experience) worked out well. The couple decided against marriage, because their adult children were having a hard enough time dealing with their relationship.

Otto, however, was worried about what would happen to Rebecca if he died first and feared she might have to cut back on her lifestyle. His financial planner suggested that he purchase a life insurance policy that would provide Rebecca the income to replace his Social Security in the event he preceded her in death.

Casual or new relationships. As already mentioned, if partners aren't committed to each other for the long term, or the relationship is new, instead of your family having to pick up your final expenses, the right insurance could be just enough to cover funeral and death costs with a little left over—$10,000 to $20,000. Or the amount could be sufficient to help a partner through a transition period—perhaps $200,000 or so to take care of final expenses and provide supplemental cash flow for a period of time. What if, for example, you and your partner combine your incomes to take out a three-year lease on a condo in Manhattan, and then you die? A small life insurance policy with your partner as beneficiary could provide the cash to keep him or her from being forced to sublet the condo or even have to declare bankruptcy if not able to afford to the payments.

Another option is that a partner may buy a much larger policy, continue to fund it over the years, and simply change beneficiaries or the percentage going to each beneficiary as appropriate. Changing a policy's beneficiary is as easy as filling out a simple form and filing it with an insurer. A word to the wise concerning this strategy, though: Don't forget to change the beneficiary if you change partners. Otherwise, a girlfriend or boyfriend from years past could end up with an unexpected inheritance!

Stay-at-home Partners

Don't overlook buying life insurance for stay-at-home partners, either. Consider a $250,000 term life insurance policy the minimum. A partner who doesn't work outside the home may not contribute dollars to the household account, but he or she has tremendous value, especially if children are involved. How much would you have to pay someone to perform that partner's duties if he or she died? If that partner's role involves handling the household affairs, that's equivalent to a chief operating officer. If the duties also include raising a child or providing childcare, you'd better raise that policy amount. Forget the old attitudes that a stay-at-home, "nonworking" partner doesn't play an important role. Today's couples—married or not, young or old—are a collaborative partnership, and each brings tremendous assets—tangible or not—to the relationship. Plan for all contingencies.

FIGURE 4.1 Life Insurance Costs

(Approximate lowest premium; assumes nonsmoker in good health)

Male Premiums: $250,000 Policy

Age	10 Year	Co.	20 Year	Co.
25	$ 118	FK	$ 155	WC
35	118	FK	160	WC
45	213	LN	363	WC
55	490	LN	820	AF
65	1,243	PR	2,518	PR
75	4,035	WC	8,010	FK

Male Premiums: $1,000,000 Policy

Age	10 Yr.	Co.	20 Yr.	Co.
25	$ 300	AG	$ 470	AM
35	300	AG	490	AM
45	640	LN	1,255	PR
55	1,700	LN	3,055	AF
65	4,715	PR	9,815	PR
75	15,700	WC	31,860	FK

Female Premiums: $250,000 Policy

Age	10 Year	Co.	20 Year	Co.
25	$ 103	WC	$ 135	WC
35	103	WC	135	WC
45	178	LN	273	WC
55	348	LN	580	AF
65	800	FK	1,710	PR
75	2,538	FK	5,675	FK

Female Premiums: $1,000,000 Policy

Age	10 Yr.	Co.	20 Yr.	Co.
25	$ 250	AG	$ 370	AM
35	250	AG	410	FC
45	530	LN	900	AM
55	1,210	WC	2,085	AF
65	2,940	WC	6,200	AM
75	9,010	ML	22,520	FK

*Revised 11/10/04

Companies:

- AF=AMERICAN FIDELITY
- AG=AMERICAN GEN.
- AM=AMERICOM L & A
- FC=FIRST COLONY
- FK=FEDERAL KEMPER

- LN=LINCOLN NAT'L
- ML=MONY LIFE
- PR=PRUCO LIFE
- WC=WEST COAST

Source: Courtesy Insure.com

Wealth Building and Taxes

Life insurance provides readily available cash after your death for your heirs and can create wealth for them, as well. But the cash and the wealth may not come tax free. Life insurance payouts escape gift and income taxes, but if the policy was owned by the insured, it is considered part of the deceased individual's estate and is subject to state inheritance and federal estate taxes. It's easy to see how the value of an estate can climb quickly when life insurance policies are added to the pot. One solution to this dilemma could be for partners to take out life insurance policies on each other—in other words, own each other's life insurance policies. That means the value of the death benefit is excluded from the estate, and the proceeds from the life insurance policy are free of income tax, regardless of who owned the policy.

Nonetheless, life insurance is a far more tax-efficient way than outright gifting to transfer large sums of money to a partner. Federal gift tax laws currently stipulate that, basically, anyone can give anyone else gifts equal to up to $11,000 a year without incurring gift tax obligations, and up to a total $1 million over a lifetime. Anything in excess of that amount triggers hefty gift taxes—47 percent in 2005, dropping to 46 percent in 2006, and 45 percent in 2007. (The $1 million lifetime gifting threshold is separate from the amount of assets that Uncle Sam allows us to transfer tax free when we die. Every U.S. citizen can transfer up to $1.5 million in assets at death to heirs tax free, according to federal estate tax laws.) Life insurance basically avoids the gift tax issue, because death benefits are not a gift.

HEALTH INSURANCE

Health insurance is everybody's headache these days. Low-wage earners, the self-employed, and part-timers worry about where to get it and how they can afford it. Full-time employees wonder how much extra their employer will withhold to pay for it. And retirees fret that former employers will drop the coverage they already have and were "guaranteed" at retirement.

Domestic Partner Benefits

The health insurance playing field for unmarried couples poses all those woes plus a few more. Although more companies are recognizing the importance of domestic partner benefits, a smaller number offer the benefit to same-sex couples compared with opposite-sex partners. Almost three-fourths of U.S. companies provide no domestic partner benefits to unmarried partners no matter their sexual orientation, according to a recent study by the Society of Human Resource Management (SHRM).

Employers that do offer the benefits—primarily health care—may extract more than just money from employees who opt for domestic partner benefits. Same-sex partners, for example, could be subject to the ridicule of fellow employees. Other unmarried partners also could face insinuations, innuendos, and more just because of their lifestyles.

Here are more 2004 numbers from the SHRM study:

- Overall, regardless of company size, 34 percent of the companies in the study offer domestic partner benefits for opposite-sex couples, and only 27 percent for same-sex couples.
- Forty-four percent of large companies (500 or more employees) offer domestic partner benefits for opposite-sex couples. That compares with 36 percent that offer it to same-sex couples.
- Thirty-one percent of small companies (fewer than 100 employees) offer the benefits to opposite-sex couples, and only 22 percent to same-sex couples.

FIGURE 4.2 Domestic Partner Benefits

More employers are offering benefits to domestic partners regardless of sexual orientation, according to the Society of Human Resource Management's 2004 Benefits Survey. These numbers are broken down by partner sexual orientation.

Year	2001	2002	2003	2004
Opposite-sex partners	26%	31%	31%	34%
Same-sex partners	16%	23%	23%	27%

Source: Society of Human Resource Management

Benefits Taxed

As mentioned earlier, the amount your employer pays for health care premiums for your domestic partner is taxed as ordinary income to you. It shows up embedded in your wages (Box 1) on your W-2 form.

Output without input. With the cost of health care premiums so high these days, that extra or "phantom" income can adversely affect an unmarried couple's finances. Stacey received domestic partner health care benefits through the employer of Chris, her partner. That added almost $3,000 a year to Chris's taxable income, throwing him into a higher tax bracket, which meant he was paying a lot more in taxes without actually seeing any extra income.

Unmarried couples "lucky" enough to have access to domestic partner benefits actually pay Uncle Sam for the right to provide a partner with health insurance through an employer. But remember, the tax you pay on the health insurance premium is still only a fraction of the total cost of the insurance, so it's better than nothing. The cost of health insurance premiums for spouses, on the other hand, is *not* taxed. So much for equity when it comes to health insurance! If you are trying to decide whether to apply for domestic partner benefits through your employer or to obtain an individual policy for your partner, don't forget the real cost of the domestic partner benefit equals your premiums *plus* the amount of taxes on the employer's share of the cost.

Covering children. Fortunately, the cost of health care premiums for your dependent child is not taxed. An employee can claim a partner's child as a dependent if the child legally is so by adoption or if the child satisfies the dependency test—he or she lives with the employee the entire year, and the employee pays more than 50 percent of support. If the child is not a legal dependent, the employee will be taxed on any premium that an employer pays for the child's health insurance. There's that phantom income again! That income will show up on a W-2 form as ordinary income in the Wages or Box 1.

Domestic Partner Registration

Another catch-22 in the health insurance realm and elsewhere as we mentioned earlier, is that, in some locales, unmarried partners can get domestic partner benefits through an employer only if the couple is "registered" as domestic partners or if the couple signs an affidavit attesting the same. It doesn't matter if the couple is same-sex or heterosexual. Laws on the books in various municipalities actually stipulate that municipal employers can't discriminate against domestic partners, including gays and lesbians, if the partners register as such. More than 50 cities and counties across the country have domestic partnership registries. Those municipal areas range from Albany, New York; Ashland, Oregon; and Atlanta, Georgia; to Travis County, Texas; Tucson, Arizona; and St. Louis, Missouri.

But unmarried couples shouldn't automatically sign up in these registries or fill out the affidavits without first sitting down to talk about it and discuss the options. Weigh the pros and cons carefully before labeling yourselves *domestic partners*. That's good advice for couples no matter their age, financial situation, or sexual orientation.

Once again, it's time to ask each other and yourselves some questions:

- How do you and your partner feel about registering your relationship?
- What are the cost advantages of registering or filling out an affidavit?
- Are any savings significant enough to warrant doing so?
- Is this an important symbolic gesture that overrides the financial costs?
- Will an employer possibly provide a domestic partner benefit without your registering or signing an affidavit?
- Are you willing to make your relationship publicly known?
- For heterosexual couples, if possible, would it be preferable to get married?
- Do you want your employer to know your personal living situation?

For many couples, domestic partner benefits are not worth the trouble of registering or declaring via an affidavit. They balk at signing, either on principle or for privacy concerns. Obtaining domestic partner health insurance benefits also may not be as cost effective as you initially might think. Remember the additional costs in the phantom income and tax ramifications? When considering the pros and cons of whether to get domestic partner health insurance benefits through an employer, be sure you're comparing apples with apples.

Privacy

Beyond privacy issues related to a government record of your living situation, many couples prefer to keep their relationships private. It's not a matter of shame. It's one of privacy. Your personal living situation is no one's business but your own.

No matter how liberal or conservative your boss is, would you prefer that fellow workers and supervisors not know you're living with your partner? That can be an especially pertinent question if partners are in a same-sex relationship. But it's not *just* a same-sex couple's issue. If your employer's benefits director is a blabbermouth, do you want everyone in your company to know with whom you're living? Even if the director of human resources is discreet, how many employees have access to the HR files? What about the half-dozen people responsible for payroll? Do you want all of them to know your circumstances, too?

For many, the answer is a resounding no. It doesn't matter how much money can be saved by tapping domestic partner health benefits at work.

Rachel worked at a small, conservative, family-owned construction company. A very private person, she kept to herself her relationship with her longtime partner, Anna. Even though the company offered domestic partner benefits, Rachel did not claim them for Anna, because she didn't want her sexual orientation known in the office. In her pursuit of privacy, she didn't even name Anna as a beneficiary on the company-sponsored life insurance policy. Rachel reasoned that sometimes self-preservation and privacy take precedence over saving some money. On their own, the couple bought life insurance to protect Anna in the event of Rachel's premature death.

Same-sex couples in situations like Rachel's, as well as older and younger heterosexual couples in search of privacy, have an even greater need for insurance to fill the income gaps in the event of problems. Private health insurance as well as life and disability insurance are available from many excellent providers. These policies may cost more than similar ones issued through your employer, but your privacy remains intact. Meanwhile, take the free life insurance offered at work, name an inconspicuous beneficiary or a trust as beneficiary, and take care of your additional financial planning matters privately.

Cost Details

For those couples who prefer or need private health insurance, costs vary drastically. The best advice is to shop around and compare coverage and costs from a number of reputable providers. Organizations like Quotesmith.com and its subsidiary, Insure.com (http://www.insure.com), for example, are excellent sources of information and comparison tools for all kinds of insurance from many different providers.

Here are some considerations to keep in mind when you're shopping around:

- The cost of a family health plan for two or more people may be greater than buying two individual policies.
- Don't overlook industry associations and other organizations as possible sources of health insurance. Often these organizations will negotiate with providers to offer members lower group rates. Whether either partner currently belongs to the organization or not, any membership dues may be well worth the expense if its health insurance rates are reasonable.

DISABILITY INSURANCE

Virtually everyone is underinsured when it comes to disability insurance. A preretirement individual's single greatest asset usually isn't a home or retirement plan but their earning capacity. Couples must be prepared in case something happens to the earning capacity of either partner.

As a general rule, unmarried couples aren't eligible for their partner's Social Security disability benefits, either, creating an even more crucial need for disability insurance as an income replacement.

Incapacity

Even those couples who consider disability insurance often overlook a key part of the contingency planning equation—What happens to your assets and your partner if you become totally incapacitated? Remember Jim and April, the couple in Chapter 1? Even though he was the couple's primary breadwinner and owned the couple's home, Jim didn't buy disability insurance because he figured, at age 47, he had plenty of time. Jim suddenly contracted a horrible disease, became incognizant, and his parents took him away. April ended up homeless and helpless in the matter, because in the eyes of the law, she had no legal status with Jim and no financial control over the unmarried couple's home or finances. (The couple lived in a common law marriage state, but they never represented themselves as married.)

Jim should have sprung for the cost of disability insurance. That would have helped replace income for the couple until the benefits ran out at age 65, as generally happens, when Social Security retirement benefits kick in. As sole owner of the couple's house, he also had other options he could have exercised with his partner's welfare in mind. He could have owned his home in a revocable living trust, which would have let him stipulate that April should have the house if he became incapacitated. Also, if he had put in place financial and health care powers of attorney, April would have been the one making the decisions on Jim's health care as well as his finances.

The situation actually could have been worse. At least with Jim and April, Jim's parents acted together decisively to come in and take Jim away. Both parents made a collective decision and followed through on it. What happens if, instead of two parents deciding what to do, it's two or three or four or more adult children and their spouses? In the case of older couples who might have children from various marriages, a disability situation becomes an even bigger nightmare. With several adult children, each likely has their own agenda, spouses may enter the fray too, and no one is in control. The entire family could melt down and possibly never recover. Meanwhile, dad or mom is incapacitated somewhere and would be horrified if they were aware of what was happening. Plan ahead for contingencies, and give yourself and your partner peace of mind in the process.

Cost

How do you know how much disability insurance to buy? That's easy. Buy as much as you can afford. Companies generally only will sell you a policy that provides 60 to 70 percent of your monthly income in case of disability. The real questions—those that boost the premiums—deal with under what circumstances will the benefits be paid, when a disability benefit kicks in, and the duration of the payments. The more liberal the definition of *disability*, the more expensive the policy. The shorter the waiting period, the more quickly the benefits begin, and the more the policy will cost. The longer the period of time that you are eligible to receive the benefits also adds to the cost of the policy.

If supporting your lifestyle takes all of your current paycheck, buy as much disability insurance as you can qualify for and afford. Keep in mind that, if you pay the premiums, your benefits will be income tax free. If your employer pays the premiums, the benefits are taxable income to you. Therefore, if you pay the premiums, the 60 to 70 percent tax-free maximum allowable coverage through most insurers actually will come very close to a full replacement of your current wages in the event of disability. If your employer pays the premiums and the benefits are taxable, you may fall short and should consider purchasing a supplemental disability policy.

More Issues

- *Self-insure for the first 6 to 12 months of disability.* You can do that by keeping reserves set aside in a savings account or money market fund to cover what you would need in the event of disability. Many people call this reserve an "emergency fund."

- *Secure coverage until at least age 65.* If that kind of coverage is cost prohibitive, obtain all that you'll need in the event of disability for at least five years, and then accept a lesser benefit—perhaps 70 percent of your need—until age 65. That will give you a phase-in period to adjust to a reduced income. Unfortunately, however, at age 65 your only income may be Social Security retirement benefits, which could be substantially less than what you'll need to sustain the standard of living to which you're accustomed.

- *Make sure that any disability policy factors automatic cost-of-living adjustments (COLA) into the benefit.* COLA is essential. Get the maximum COLA available in a policy.

- *Pay attention to a policy's definition of* disability. Purchase "own occupation" coverage. This type of policy defines *disability* relative to whether or not you can perform your own job. Some policies—"any occupation" policies—won't provide disability benefits if you're still able to perform any gainful occupation. Still others define *disability* based on "modified any occupation," which means you are unable to perform any occupation for which you are reasonably trained and suited. If own occupation coverage is cost prohibitive, many policies will cover the insured's own occupation for two to five years, then any occupation for which you are reasonably trained and suited for the remainder of the coverage period. This type of policy can buy you time for retraining if possible and necessary.

- *Be sure any insurer is of high quality and rated A+ or A++ by rating agencies like A.M. Best or Moody's Investor Services.*

Questions to Ask Yourself

A disability can be more financially devastating than death. It's one of those double whammies. Not only does it stop your income stream, but generally expenses increase also. Don't count on Social Security or some other public welfare program to take care of you. In most cases, it won't, and even if the government offers some assistance, you'll need supplemental private insurance or a lot of assets, too.

When you're trying to figure out what kind of disability insurance policy is best for your needs, here are a few questions you may want to ask yourself:

- What would happen financially to you and your family if you suffered either a short-term or long-term disability?
- If your employer offers disability insurance, can the policy be converted to an individual policy? That's important if you anticipate frequent job changes or are concerned that you may develop a med-

---

FIGURE 4.3 Charting the Best Course in Case of Disability

- If you're 60 years old, do you need disability insurance? Chances are you may not need it if you already have plenty of income or assets. Check with an advisor.

  O

- At any age, you may not need disability insurance if you have a stay-at-home partner who could go to work in the event you became disabled. An essential question, however, is whether that person can bring in enough money to replace your lost income.

  Y / O / SS

- If you're older and planning to retire in a few years, disability insurance may not be worth its high cost, because most policies pay only until the policyholder is 65 or for five years, whichever is longer. In this case, self-insuring makes sense.

  O / SS

- For younger individuals, your most valuable asset is your ability to earn money, so you better have disability insurance.

  Y / SS

- If you or your partner works full-time, you both must have disability insurance, unless your individual salaries more than cover your household expenses and/or you have sufficient assets to self-insure.

  Y / SS

ical condition that makes you uninsurable or ineligible for future coverage.

- If your employer does have disability insurance, are the policy benefits enough? You may want to buy additional individual insurance.
- If you need to purchase a supplemental policy, are you a member of an industry organization or group that offers disability policies?
- Is a policy noncancelable? If so, that guarantees the insured the right to renew the policy for a certain number of years at a guaranteed premium. A policy that's "guaranteed renewable" is not the same thing. It allows renewal, but with premium adjustments.

Long-term Care

By 2013, health care spending in the United States is expected to reach $3.4 trillion, or 18.4 percent of the nation's gross domestic product. That's an average 7.3 percent increase every year from 2002 through 2013, according to projections from the U.S. Department of Health and Human Services. Out-of-pocket costs for health care will climb, too, as employers continue to shift health care costs to employees. And almost every other

DISABILITY INSURANCE PROVIDERS

A few disability insurance providers include:

- MetLife, Inc. (http://www.metlife.com, 800-638-5433)
- Assurity Life Insurance Company (http://www.assurity.com, 800-869-0355)
- Unum Provident Corporation (http://www.unum.com, 877-322-7222); includes The Paul Revere Life Insurance Company subsidiary (http://www.paulrevere.com)
- Northwestern Mutual Financial Network (http://www.nmfn.com, 414-271-1444)

aspect of health care costs continues to climb, too. The average annual cost of nursing home care is upward of $75,000 in many areas. Meanwhile, the average life expectancy of men has climbed to just over age 74. For women, it's almost 80 years. The moral of the statistics: It takes a chunk of change to deal with health issues today and likely will take much more in the not-so-distant future.

That's where long-term care insurance can help. It offers a way to protect yourself in the event you need nursing home or skilled in-home care. Long-term care insurance also gives an individual more choice in terms of facilities and quality of care.

Can anyone afford *not* to buy long-term care insurance to handle the cost of extended skilled and custodial care outside the hospital? Perhaps the very wealthy can afford to self-insure—in other words, gamble that they'll have enough money to cover their needs. But that approach may not make solid financial sense even for them.

For the vast majority of Americans, buying long-term care insurance isn't an option—it's a necessity. If you're an unmarried younger couple, who will take care of you if something goes terribly wrong? If you're an older or elderly couple with children, do you really want the burden of your care to fall on your children? Medicaid will take care of you only if you're basically broke. If you own the home that you and your partner live in, you'll have to give it up. However, if the home is owned jointly, one partner will have to buy out the ill partner's share of ownership to satisfy the lien that Medicaid places on the home. In turn, that ill partner must use up those assets by paying for their long-term care before Medicaid will pick up the tab for care. And Medicaid won't cover all the costs.

Consider the case of Bill and Steve, domestic partners who had been together many years before Steve died after a long illness. Unfortunately, Steve had owned the couple's home. Bill lost the house after Steve's death because, among other things, he couldn't afford to pay Steve's exorbitant medical bills or the financially crippling mortgage on the home. At least part of the problem was that Steve didn't buy health insurance or long-term care insurance before he was diagnosed with cancer. After that diagnosis, he couldn't buy health insurance or qualify for long-term care insurance. As a result, before he died, he spent two years in and out of the county hospital because he couldn't pay for the full-time, in-home care that he needed. To further complicate the situation, although Steve and Bill lived in a major metropolitan area of two million people, only one of the area's seven hospitals would take him because he was on Medicaid.

Steve made a good living and could have afforded long-term care insurance. But he was young, always had been strong, and felt invincible before he contracted cancer. If he only had the appropriate insurance policies in place, it would have made his illness easier on himself and Bill.

Can either you or your partner afford to foot the bills for long-term care that easily can climb into the hundreds of thousands, if not millions, of dollars? Most likely not!

The answer, of course, is that individuals and couples should buy long-term care insurance. Buy it when you're in your late 40s or early 50s, when the premiums are lower, and make sure that any policy you buy has provisions for inflation in the cost of care.

Julie and Doris have been together as a couple for almost 20 years. For almost as long, they've watched Julie's once-vibrant grandmother suffer with Alzheimer's disease. About five years ago, the couple took over as her primary caregivers, and though the responsibility has taken an emotional toll on each of them, it's also strengthened their resolve to plan for the future should something happen to either of them. Whatever the situation, both agree they don't want to burden the other as a full-time caregiver, so they decided to buy long-term care insurance to cover the cost of nursing home or skilled in-home care for each other in the event either needs it.

Their financial planner referred them to a long-term care insurance agent experienced in dealing with unmarried couples. The agent found policies that meet their needs with a company that offers discounts to domestic partners. Julie and Doris now live each day knowing that, if the worst should occur, they are adequately prepared.

WARNING *Buy long-term care insurance long before you think you'll need it, because when and if you do need it, you won't be able to get it.*

The Details

Several companies offer multiple policy discounts to domestic partners, so shopping around is worthwhile. The cost of a policy has many variables, including age, current health, location, features, and the benefit. An unmarried couple can save up to 20 percent on premiums when both partners buy coverage, according to MAGA Limited, a Deerfield, Illinois–based insurance agency that focuses exclusively on long-term care insurance. (MAGA also has offices in Phoenix, Arizona, and San Diego, California.)

If you truly can't afford the cost of the premiums and already have trouble making ends meet every month, buying long-term care insurance may not be for you. The same is true if you have the financial wherewithal to self-insure.

LONG-TERM CARE INSURANCE

Several companies that offer long-term care policies include:

- John Hancock Financial Services Incorporated (http://www.johnhancock.com)
- Genworth Financial Incorporated (http://www.genworth.com, 888-436-9678)
- CNA Financial Corporation (http://www.cna.com, 800-775-1541)
- MAGA Limited (http://www.magaltc.com, 800-533-6242)
- MetLife Incorporated (http://www.metlife.com, 800-638-5433)
- Lincoln Benefit, part of Allstate (800-525-9287, http://www.lincolnbenefit.com)
- State Life Insurance Company (http://www.statelife.com, 800-428-2316)

Choosing the Right Policy

Shop around for the policy that fits your needs and preferences. Some questions and issues to consider include:

- *What kind of care do you want and where do you want to get that care?* Many policies provide for care in a variety of places, including a nursing home, assisted-living facility, Alzheimer facility, adult day-care, or in-home care.
- *How much money do you want or need as a daily benefit?* Nursing home daily costs generally are covered 100 percent up to the daily benefit amount, but other care may not be. If a policy instead pays the "prevailing cost" for a service up to the daily benefit amount, be aware that it may not cover the total cost of care. In that case, you may want to purchase an indemnity benefit that pays the full daily benefit regardless of costs.
- *How long a waiting period is acceptable before benefits kick in?* This is the equivalent of an insurance deductible. The longer before the benefits begin, the lower the cost of the premium.
- *What kind of inflation adjustment will you accept on a policy?* Keep in mind that health care costs generally increase faster than the rate of inflation. Buy as much inflation protection as you can.
- *How long do you want the benefit period to last?* Common options include three, four, and five years or up to a lifetime. For the most security, buy the lifetime benefit.

AUTOMOBILE INSURANCE

The issue of liability and lack of legal protections haunts unmarried couples when it comes to automobile insurance.

In the last chapter, we discussed the dangers and tremendous vulnerability of unmarried couples concerning liability issues related to co-ownership of cars and vehicles. Please pay attention to the warning. If you and your partner co-own a vehicle and either of you gets in an accident, whether you think you're at fault or not, both of you could risk everything if you're sued. So why risk mucking up the works by having joint owners on a vehicle? Besides, many of us turn over vehicles often enough, that our relationships tend to outlast our cars.

Truth or Consequences

It is OK, however, for you and your partner to drive each other's cars frequently *if* both of you are on each other's insurance policies. Some insurers refer to that practice as disclosing "occasional" drivers. Forget about not disclosing or lying about that. Couples absolutely need to disclose if they drive each other's vehicles. Your premium may increase because of the disclosure; nonetheless, do it. And do it even at the risk of much higher premiums if your partner has a poor driving record. It's well worth the protection if and when it's needed.

The other option for couples is not to drive each other's cars ever, and that's not necessarily practical. You do not want to give an insurer any reason whatsoever not to pay a claim. If the company discovers that someone—your partner—has lived with you a long time, drives your car regularly, and is not disclosed as a driver on your policy, you could lose big time.

You also may be asking for trouble to declare a partner an occasional driver of your car if he or she really drives it regularly. The insurer may investigate and, one way or another, discover the truth. A caveat: Make sure you understand your insurer's definition of *occasional.* Generally, insurers define an occasional driver as the person who is not the primary or principal driver of a vehicle. Talk to your agent or company to be sure you and your partner are covered.

Renting a Car

How often do you wonder what to do regarding insurance and liability when renting a car? Do you hesitate to initial those boxes that supposedly absolve the rental car company of liability? More important, where in the world does your partner—who also plans to drive the car—fit into the equation? He or she isn't a "spouse," and there certainly isn't an appropriate box to check or line to fill out on the rental agreement.

Back to our society and its discrimination against unmarried couples. Did you know that if you and your partner want to rent a car, some rental car companies charge extra for an unmarried second driver or require membership in the company's premier renters' club to avoid the charges? Not so for married couples. With many companies, spouses automatically can drive a vehicle rented by either partner—at no extra cost.

WHO CHARGES EXTRA?

Some rental car companies charge additional-driver fees for a renter's domestic partner. Here's a broad look at some of the major companies. (Additions, exclusions, and other requirements figure into whether a driver is authorized or not.)

- *Alamo.* An additional driver fee is required at most locations.
- *Avis.* Renter's spouse or life partner may drive without additional fees; must be at least 25 years of age and have a valid driver's license.
- *Dollar.* Additional authorized driver may be required to pay a fee, but varies by location.
- *Enterprise.* A fee may be charged for each additional driver.
- *Hertz.* No charge for a domestic partner as a driver if renter is Hertz Number One Club Gold or Platinum member or an AAA or AARP member.
- *National.* Renter must be Emerald Club member for common law spouse or same-gender domestic partner to drive a vehicle without additional charges.
- *Thrifty.* A daily charge may apply for any other individuals who are listed on the contract as additional renters.

A word of advice: If you and your partner maintain separate auto insurance policies, you should disclose that fact to the car rental agent. Before renting a car, check with your insurance agent to find out about your coverage. It may not make financial sense to purchase the optional extra coverage that the rental car company offers.

PROPERTY/HOMEOWNERS INSURANCE

Just as when insuring vehicles, both partners' names should be included on property insurance policies, too. Even if partners don't disclose their living situation, an insurer invariably will find out nonetheless, and the deception will come back to haunt you.

Xenia owned an upscale loft in Manhattan that she shared with her longtime partner, Tom. The couple wasn't married. Although they had lived in the condo for 4½ years, Xenia never bothered to tell the insurance company that she shared it with Tom. She paid her premiums on time, so she didn't think it mattered or that it was anyone's business that she shared her home or with whom. One day, while Xenia was out of town on business, Tom was cooking dinner and accidentally started a fire that destroyed the condo's kitchen. Subsequently, the insurer investigated and ultimately denied the claim because it had no knowledge that Tom lived there. Be honest with those insurers!

The Catch-22

An unmarried couple sets out to buy insurance jointly on the home they own jointly. It sounds so simple, but, once again, it may not be. The big catch-22: An insurer could require special documentation or set limits on who can file claims or make changes to a policy.

Nate and Austin jointly own a vacation home. Because Austin is a member of USAA, the financial services giant, they insure the vacation home through USAA. The company does offer domestic-partner coverage, but you have to ask for it. Nate's property within the home is insured through USAA and, regardless of the catastrophe, the policy kicks in. But it's not what one would consider a simple, ordinary property and casualty policy. Nate's name is on the policy, and it's also on the home's deed. But Nate can't make changes to the policy, file a claim, or even call customer service about it, because he's not a USAA member—nor is he allowed to be. That's something to keep in mind if you have your insurance through an organization. If Nate comes home and finds the house burglarized, he must wait for Austin, who's the only one who can file the claim. But, if Nate and Austin were to marry—they live in Massachusetts, a state that allows same-sex marriage—Nate automatically would become a USAA member.

If one partner owns a home individually, the other needs to be named somehow on the policy. That's done sometimes with a rider that stipulates the partner as an additional occupant of the home. In the case of USAA, the member homeowner must fill out a cohabitant form for a partner to be covered under the same homeowner's policy. That could be another psychological blow for an unmarried partner's self-esteem. If an insurer doesn't allow a rider or coinsured, the partner not on the policy technically is considered a renter and needs to take out a renter's insurance policy on his or her contents in the home. In general, insurers write homeowner policies the same way the home or residence is titled, but some insurers will add a nonowner's name to a policy. In that case, all claim checks will be made payable to both partners. You may wish to think about the nature and longevity of your relationship before listing a partner as coinsured.

If both partners' names are not on the home's deed, another option is for both to get individual policies. Come "out of the closet" about your living situation, or it may come back to bite you.

Nate and Austin have another property insurance issue that illustrates yet another problem for unmarried couples—the importance of coordinating various insurance policies. Nate individually owns the couple's primary residence. Austin does not appear on that policy. He has a separate renter's policy through his insurer. If Nate takes something from the primary residence up to the vacation home, and that vacation home subsequently is burglarized and Nate's property stolen, which insurance company is responsible for the claim? Nate didn't tell his insurer about the vacation home or the USAA policy. Why should he?

Do you and your partner have both your insurance policies with the same company? Ideally, you should. You both could save money by way of multiple-policy discounts. But sometimes logistics get in the way, as in the case of Nate and Austin. In the above instance, Nate's property, no matter where in the world it is, would be covered by his homeowners policy. One caveat, however: If the personal property is extremely valuable, Nate's policy might only provide limited coverage.

Consider buying an umbrella liability insurance policy, too. It provides an individual with a level of protection over and above home and auto (it includes boats, too), and makes lots of sense in today's litigious society. Let's say that someone living in a condominium starts a fire that spreads to other units in the building. That person's homeowners policy may not have enough liability coverage to cover the damage to the other units. Or what if someone gets into an auto accident and injures a physician resident at the local hospital. The resident then sues, not only for lost wages but also future wages as a practicing physician.

Umbrella liability also covers slander and liable. Relatively inexpensive for the coverage, polices can be purchased in $1 million increments. The minimum is $1 million.

If partners rent a condo or apartment, each will have to buy individual renter's insurance, although some providers may allow a joint renters' policy. Again, check with your individual insurer.

Riders and Valuables

Also, don't overlook the importance of telling your insurer if you or your partner has antiques, art work, jewelry, collectibles, or other high-value items. An insurer may require you to purchase a rider or addendum to your general policy to cover those items based on an independent, written appraisal by a qualified expert of certain items.

Replacement Cost

Be sure that any property insurance policy calls for *replacement cost* reimbursement in the event of a loss. That's not automatic, and often couples find out the hard way that the policy they purchased reimburses them for only a fraction of the cost to replace something lost, stolen, or destroyed. The difference in the cost of the premium—factoring in replacement cost versus depreciated value of property—is relatively small and well worth it. Don't even think about not getting the replacement cost insurance!

Certain insurers also offer specialized coverage for period or historical homes. These insurance policies actually provide for replacement of items down to the architectural details on the home. Suppose, for example, you and your partner own a Queen Anne–style home from the 19th century with a period slate roof. If the roof is damaged—perhaps by hail—these special policies will pay for its replacement with like-kind materials.

But don't assume your insurer will do that. Always ask questions. Of course, these policies come at a cost premium. But before you opt for the lowest-cost policy, consider the home's value. If you opt for the more expensive policy that provides specialized coverage for period homes, in

INSURANCE RESOURCES

Options and solutions to property/casualty needs vary by carrier, so it's important that consumers shop around for the provider and the policy that best fits their needs as individuals and as couples. Here are a few places to start:

- A.M. Best Company (908-439-2200, http://www.ambest.com) is a worldwide insurance-rating and information agency.
- Comparison Market, Inc. (877-605-7707, http://www.comparisonmarket.com) is a clearinghouse (online and off) that works with a number of automobile insurance providers to link consumers with competitively priced auto insurance.

INSURANCE RESOURCES, continued

- Independent Insurance Agents and Brokers of America (http://www.iiaa.org) is the nation's largest national association of independent insurance agents and brokers with more than 300,000 members. The Web site includes an insurance agent database.
- Insure.com (800-556-9393, http://www.insure.com) is a comprehensive online consumer insurance information service. Instant policy quotes are available from more than 200 insurers.
- InsWeb Insurance Services (916-853-3300, http://www.InsWeb.com) is an online insurance marketplace offering a variety of insurance products.
- Moody's Investors Services (212-553-0300, http://moodys.com) is a global source for corporate credit ratings, research, and risk analysis.
- National Association of Insurance Commissioners (816-842-3600, http://www.naic.org) is a national organization of state insurance regulators. Visit its Consumer Information Source (http://www.naic.org/consumer).
- PrimeQuote (888-600-3600, http://www.primequote.com) is an insurance marketplace that provides information, resources, and personalized quotes on insurance products.
- Standard & Poor's (212-438-2400, www.2standardandpoors.com) is an independent analyst company that includes a rating service.
- United Underwriters Incorporated (http://www.uuinc.com) is an Exeter, New Hampshire–based national organization catering to insurance brokers. It also provides a wealth of insurance information available to anyone online. Check out an insurance company's rating and more at (http://nettrac.ipipeline.com/link.asp?cin=10&npt=14).
- Weiss Ratings, Inc. (800-289-9222, http://weissratings.com) tracks ratings of thousands of insurers as well as banks, savings and loans, stocks, and mutual funds.

essence you could be preserving your home's historical and financial worth.

BOTTOM LINES

Be sure that you're insured against the perils that you can't afford to weather. Insurance, after all, is protection against catastrophe. Also, make sure that you and your partner assess your resources and determine your insurance needs. Don't be leery of seeking the advice of insurance agents, either. They know the policy provisions, have access to the most current information, and their time spent talking with you about the various available policies should be free.

Honesty is the best policy on long-term care insurance, health insurance, disability insurance, and any other insurance. Disclose your health or medical issues and if your partner lives with you. If your partner drives your car, disclose that, too. If a partner is getting ready to lose his or her driver's license because of a lead foot, don't ever let that partner drive your car and don't add him or her to your insurance policy. If you choose to coinsure with your lead-foot partner, the premiums may be higher. But not having insurance and being forced to pay home, health, or auto claims out of pocket could wipe out you and your partner financially.

Claims on any insurance policy can be hefty, so an insurance company is extremely motivated to fight a claim. Unmarried partners—married ones, too—shouldn't offer these companies any opportunity to back out. Come out up front and often. It's hard to beat the insurance companies.

Insurance of all kinds is about protecting you and your partner. As a couple and as an individual, if you do nothing else, at a minimum do the following:

- *Obtain adequate coverage from quality companies for auto, home, liability, life, health, disability, and possibly long-term care insurance.*
- *Be honest and open with your insurer.* Full disclosure is the only way to ensure full coverage. You don't want to give an insurer the slightest excuse not to pay a claim.

- *Don't overlook multiple-policy discounts from insurers.* If you insure your auto(s) and home with the same insurer, you usually receive a multiple-policy discount.
- *Know what features and benefits you want from an insurance policy.* Check out some of the great resources on the Web or at least consult with an independent insurance agent, who most likely represent all of the lines of coverage that you need.

CHAPTER 5

Taxes

ISSUES, OPPORTUNITIES, AND PITFALLS

With the right kind of financial planning, taxes are one area in which unmarried couples actually can come out ahead of their married counterparts—and not because of any legal protections afforded them by the system. To the contrary, tax laws are stacked against unmarried couples, who must learn how to make the system work for them. If the paper trail leads to the right person, tax issues like medical and miscellaneous deductions provide fertile ground for potential savings.

Making the utmost of a legitimate tax advantage is not unethical or dishonest; it's simply good common sense. Keep in mind that financial planning is designed to work within the system and get the most from it.

To capitalize on their potential tax advantages, unmarried couples first must become aware of them and then plan how to leverage them. Don't be scared off by the prospect of planning or making decisive financial moves. Do be conscious of what is required to maximize whatever tax advantages and deductions are due you.

MAXIMIZING DEDUCTIONS

First, for those unmarried couples who have comingled or merged any part of their finances, income tax season is the time to go back and "unmerge" finances between partners. The reason: As part of an unmarried couple, each partner must file an individual federal tax return. Ditto for filing state income taxes. Unmarried couples can't file joint returns.

If partners share a bank account or have purchased a home, opened a joint investment account, made charitable deductions as a couple, or bought mutual funds together, all those transactions must be separated into Yours and Mine for you or anyone else to prepare your taxes. Doing that can be simplified a bit by taking three folders—even three shoeboxes—and designating one for each partner's taxes and the third for joint tax information. Throughout the year, as statements like annual mortgage interest payments or monthly brokerage accounts arrive, put them in the appropriate folder or box. Also, remember that, for purposes of your paper trail, an individual can take a deduction only for the expenses they actually paid.

Also make sure that your tax preparer is familiar with your and your partner's situation and knows how the joint assets and liabilities will be split.

Effective Tax Rates

Savings strategies start with each partner determining his or her effective tax rate. That's the tax rate levied by the U.S. government on earned income, and it varies depending on the amount of income. If an individual has a 20 percent effective tax rate, for example, that means for every $1 he or she earns, 20 cents goes to the federal government for taxes. Your effective tax rate—the percentage of your income actually paid out in taxes—will be less than your tax bracket. (Don't forget to add your effective state tax to your effective federal tax to calculate your total tax rate.) Most states have income taxes generally ranging from 4 to 10 percent.

FIGURE 5.1 Income Tax Rates

2004

Single Filers

Taxable income range			Tax
$0	to	$7,150	10% of taxable income
$7,151	to	$29,050	$715 plus 15% of the excess over $7,150
$29,051	to	$70,350	$4,000 plus 25% of the excess over $29,050
$70,351	to	$146,750	$14,325 plus 28% of the excess over $70,350
$146,751	to	$319,100	$35,717 plus 33% of the excess over $146,750
$319,101+			$92,592.50 plus 35% of the excess over $319,100

Head of Household

Taxable income range			Tax
$0	to	$10,200	10% of taxable income
$10,201	to	$38,900	$1,020 plus 15% of the excess over $10,200
$38,901	to	$100,500	$5,325 plus 25% of the excess over $38,900
$100,501	to	$162,700	$20,725 plus 28% of the excess over $100,500
$162,701	to	$319,100	$38,141 plus 33% of the excess over $162,700
$319,101+			$89,753 plus 35% of the excess over $319,100

2005 (Projected)

Single Filers

Taxable income range			Tax
$0	to	$7,300	10% of taxable income
$7,301	to	$29,700	$730 plus 15% of the excess over $7,300
$29,701	to	$71,950	$4,090 plus 25% of the excess over $29,700
$79,951	to	$150,150	$14,652 plus 28% of the excess over $71,950
$150,151	to	$326,450	$36,548.50 plus 33% of the excess over $150,150
$326,451+			$94,727.50 plus 35% of the excess over $326,450

Head of Household

Taxable income range			Tax
$0	to	$10,450	10% of taxable income
$10,451	to	$39,800	$1,045 plus 15% of the excess over $10,450
$39,801	to	$102,800	$5,447.50 plus 25% of the excess over $39,800
$102,801	to	$166,450	$21,197.50 plus 28% of the excess over $102,800
$166,451	to	$326,450	$39,019.50 plus 33% of the excess over $166,450
$326,451+			$91,819.50 plus 35% of the excess over $326,450

If partners' incomes and, therefore, effective tax rates are the same or similar, fewer tax-saving strategies are available. But for unmarried partners with a considerable disparity in income—and tax brackets—a little planning can be your ticket to significant savings.

To find your individual effective tax rate, ask your tax preparer. Alternatively, you can determine your adjusted gross income (total income minus business expenses and other deductions, such as alimony paid and IRA contributions) by looking at a copy of your prior year's Form 1040 (Line 35), or you can annualize it based on the year-to-date information from a pay stub or your records. If a partner gets domestic partner benefits, don't forget to add the *taxable* cost of domestic partner benefits to the income of the partner whose employer provides the benefits. (See page 118 for more information on domestic partner benefits.)

Another option is to determine your effective tax rate by dividing last year's tax liability, which is line 60 of your 1040 return, by your taxable income, line 40.

Then check online at the IRS Web site (http://www.irs.gov) or in a current tax booklet to match your income with the current tax rate. Make sure the chart you use is current.

Lumping Deductions

There's a silver lining to all the effort. Once you and your partner know where you stand relative to Yours and Mine, it's much easier to determine how best to maximize your deductions as a couple. One effective strategy calls for lumping tax *deductions* on the higher-income taxpayer's return, because he or she has a higher tax rate, and then lumping taxable *earnings* on the lower-bracket partner's return because of his or her lower tax rate. That effectively lowers the total taxes paid by an unmarried couple.

Another strategy involves assigning medical or miscellaneous expenses to the lower-income partner. Medical deductions, for example, are not allowed unless they exceed 7.5 percent of a taxpayer's adjusted gross income. One silver lining for couples who take domestic partner benefits through an employer: As with married couples, the cost of the health insurance premium *is* tax deductible. Miscellaneous deductions must exceed 2 percent of the taxpayer's adjusted gross income. Miscellaneous deductions include things like tax preparation fees, IRA custodial fees, investment research, safe deposit boxes, and unreimbursed employee expenses. The smaller the income, the easier it is to reach that deduction threshold.

Ownership Issues

One point of this effective-tax-rate exercise is to underscore that the way in which an asset is titled or owned—even if it's owned jointly with a partner—can make a significant difference in an unmarried couple's total tax liability. This is one of the major tax advantages that unmarried couples have over their married counterparts.

Here's how it works. As we discussed in Chapter 3, any earnings or losses on joint accounts and jointly held investments will be reported to the IRS under the Social Security number listed first on the account or asset's title. The person listed first then receives the 1099 in his or her name. It doesn't matter whether or not partners contribute equally to an account. The issue is decided strictly by the order in which the names appear on the account.

If you and your partner are in different tax brackets, the partner in the lower bracket should be listed first on any joint accounts. That, in turn, means the earnings will be reported to the IRS under the Social Security number of the partner who is in the lower tax bracket, resulting in a smaller tax liability due on earnings in those accounts. It doesn't diminish a partner's legal rights to the joint account; it merely indicates to whom the IRS will send the 1099.

If, for example, one partner is in the 25 percent tax bracket and the other is in the 35 percent bracket, a couple can save 10 percent on the taxes on their investment earnings simply by having the partner in the lower bracket claim the income.

If you already have an account that lists the partner in the higher tax bracket first, don't fret. Instead, when you and your partner file your taxes, both of you could list the account on your tax returns, then indicate that income for the account is being reported by the lower tax–bracket partner and include his or her name and Social Security number. You also could talk to the brokerage about changing the ownership on the account.

Conversely, as long as a paper trail exists showing proof of contributions and payments, that same couple could lump their deductions under the partner who is in the higher tax bracket, thus lowering that partner's taxable income and, as a result, his or her tax liability. If you and your partner already have a property agreement in place that spells out who contributes what, be sure your deductions correspond.

Jeanne and Julie are a perfect example of a couple who capitalized on this tax strategy (see Figure 5.2). Jeanne, a Realtor, makes considerably more money than Julie, a graphic artist. Jeanne is in the 33 percent tax bracket and Julie the 25 percent bracket. Because of that disparity, even though the couple splits expenses, Jeanne pays the mortgage every month. She also makes all the couple's donations to various charities and nonprofits from her own checking account. At the end of the year, Jeanne deducts the mortgage interest and the charitable contributions on her tax return, and Julie takes the standard deduction. At the same time, the couple shares a joint investment account at a major brokerage. Julie's name is listed first on the account; the brokerage reports the account's earnings under her name, and she, in turn, pays the taxes—assessed at her 25 percent rate—on any earnings.

Let's look at another approach to lumping deductions, which is to capitalize on the allowance for medical expenses if they exceed 7.5 percent of a taxpayer's adjusted gross income (AGI). Gina has an AGI of about $25,000 a year as a part-time dental hygienist. The AGI of her partner, Bart, an advertising executive, is around $75,000 a year. If the couple lumped all their medical deductions on Gina's tax return, they would need only $1,875 to reach 7.5 percent of her AGI. That goal is considerably more attainable than the $5,626 required if the expenses were deducted on Bart's return. But to take advantage of this and other tax strategies, couples must plan ahead.

For Gina to take the deduction, she must pay all the couple's medical expenses. Therefore, Gina and Bart must plan accordingly so that Gina

FIGURE 5.2 Bunching Saves Partners on Taxes

Jeanne and Julie save almost $1,300 in taxes by bunching deductions and income.*

	Bunching Deductions (Julie Reports Joint Interest)		Splitting Deductions Equally (Split Joint Interest)	
	Jeanne	**Julie**	**Jeanne**	**Julie**
Income:				
Wages	$200,000	$60,000	$200,000	$60,000
Interest and Dividends	0	2,000	1,000	1,000
Total Income	200,000	62,000	201,000	61,000
Total Adjustments	0	0	0	0
Adjusted Gross Income	**200,000**	**62,000**	**201,000**	**61,000**
Personal Exemptions	1,674	3,100	1,612	3,100
Itemized Deductions:				
Charitable Contributions	2,000	0	1,000	1,000
Taxes**	15,425	3,111	12,978	5,558
Mortgage Interest Expense	12,000	0	6,000	6,000
3% AGI Floor	−1,719	0	−1,749	0
Total Itemized	27,706	3,111	18,229	12,558
Standard Deduction	4,850	4,850	4,850	4,850
Total Deductions from AGI	29,380	7,950	19,841	15,658
Taxable Income	**170,620**	**54,050**	**181,159**	**45,342**
Net Federal Tax Due	43,594	10,256	47,072	8,069
Resident State Tax	10,425	3,111	10,478	3,058
Net Resident State Tax Due	10,425	3,111	10,478	3,058
Total Net Tax Due	**$54,019**	**$13,367**	**$57,550**	**$11,127**
Marginal Nominal Federal Rate	33%	25%	33%	25%
Marginal Federal Rate with Phaseouts	35	25	35	25
Marginal Resident State Rate	5	5	5	5

Total taxes paid if couple bunches deductions and Julie reports interest: $67,386

Total taxes paid if couple splits deductions and interest: $68,677

Difference: **−$1,291**

* Assumptions: Massachusetts residents; wages are net of 401(k) contributions; Julie's exemption and itemized deductions phased out due to her adjusted gross income.

** Includes $5,000 in real estate taxes.

writes the checks for these expenses. Because Bart earns considerably more money than Gina, he could, in effect, spend the money he'd otherwise put toward medical bills on other items.

Charitable Giving

The IRS defines a charitable donation as voluntary and made without expecting or getting anything of value in return. Whether you and/or your partner give cash or goods to qualified charities while you're alive, or bequeath to them when you die, the advantages are twofold. Your donation helps others, and if it's to a qualified organization, it brings significant tax advantages. The fair market value of the donation can be deducted from your gross income up to certain limitations. Also, if made at death, charitable contributions are deductible dollar for dollar directly from the gross value of an estate before any tax liability is assessed.

To take the full deduction of a donation, however, the receiving organization must qualify as a 501(c)(3) under IRS rules. Qualified organizations include nonprofits that are religious, charitable, educational, scientific, or literary, and have various purposes and missions. Political organizations do not qualify.

Your total deduction in general is limited to 50 percent of your adjusted gross income. But other limits also may apply, so be sure to check with your tax advisor. To find out if an organization is eligible to receive tax-deductible charitable contributions, ask them or check out IRS Publication 78, Cumulative List of Organizations described in Section 170(c) of the Internal Revenue Code of 1986, online at http://www.IRS.gov.

Gifting securities that have appreciated in value to qualified organizations is another financial planning strategy that you and your partner may want to consider. It not only enables you to deduct the full market value of the security, but if the gifting is done properly, you also can avoid paying capital gains taxes on the securities. This holds true for property as well.

Making donations at death is a simple process. In your IRA, will, trust, life insurance contract, retirement plan, or any TOD/POD investment, you name the qualified charity—in other words, the 501(c)(3)—as beneficiary. You retain control of the asset and can access it while you're alive; then, after you die, it goes to the organization.

Madgie, a widower, had no surviving children and worked long and hard for years cleaning houses for others. She lived modestly, but when she died, she had amassed almost $1 million in securities, which she left to a hospital in her hometown. That hospital had worked hard to help her successfully overcome breast cancer years earlier. Because Madgie decided to donate all the securities to the nonprofit hospital, a 501(c)(3) organization, she escaped having to pay any capital gains tax on the appreciation of her securities. Plus, her estate got a tax deduction for the full fair market value of the stock as of the date of the donation.

Some other ways to donate appreciated securities include:

- *Charitable remainder unitrust.* Al wanted more income from his investments but didn't want to pay capital gains taxes if he sold his stock, so he gifted a portion of his stock holdings into a charitable remainder unitrust in his name. As a result, no one paid capital gains. Al received an immediate charitable deduction, and the unitrust pays him 7.5 percent interest on the value of the trust assets for the rest of his life.
- *Gift annuity or charitable remainder annuity trust.* Deborah, 90, had appreciated stock and needed income, but she didn't want to pay capital gains taxes that would be due if she sold the stock. By setting up a charitable remainder annuity trust, she receives a set income from the trust for the rest of her life, she gets a tax deduction, and her chosen charity is funded in perpetuity.
- *Gift of life insurance.* An older couple, William and Alex, are avid financial supporters of several charities in their small community. They both were concerned that when either of them dies, the charities would suffer. Both are comfortable financially, so William, with his financial advisor's help, bought a large life insurance policy and designated a community foundation as the owner and beneficiary of the policy. The life insurance premiums are tax deductible, because the charity is the owner and beneficiary. William structured the pol-

icy so it will be paid up when he dies. At that time, the policy will be paid to his endowment fund at the community foundation. That fund in turn, in accordance with William's wishes, will help fund his favorite charities from the earnings on its investments.

Here are a few more things to keep in mind when it comes to charitable giving:

- A number of software packages are available to help you determine the fair market value of donated goods. Two include H&R Block's DeductionPro (http://www.deductionpro.com) and Intuit's ItsDeductible (http://www.itsdeductible.com). A note of caution: Be careful if you donate a car. Beginning in 2005, generally you only can deduct the actual amount of money that the charity receives from the sale of the car.
- You can't deduct the cost of your time spent doing volunteer work, but you can deduct expenses related to the volunteering such as mileage incurred from traveling to and from the volunteer site.
- Be sure to get documentation from the receiving organization detailing the gift you donated and verification of mileage, if applicable. Such documentation is required with any gift of more than $250, but it's generally a good idea to have the documentation on any gifts.

Whatever you and your partner decide to do, be sure to talk with your financial advisor to ensure that the charitable giving is done in the smartest way possible and in the right time frame to allow maximum tax advantages.

IF YOU PARTNER . . .

Many unmarried couples feel that they want to split everything equally, including tax deductions. Tax experts are divided on whether or not that makes sense from a tax liability standpoint.

Keep in mind, too, that splitting a deduction also dilutes its size and dollar amount, which could negate any value or tax savings the deduction could offer if one partner took the entire deduction and the other took the standard deduction.

Nonetheless, if you and your partner decide to split deductions, here's one approach. The partner whose names appears first on the 1098 mortgage interest statement should indicate on Schedule A, line 10, the amount of interest paid; the other partner then lists on Line 11 his or her portion. Use language like, "Split with taxpayer John D. Public, Social Security number 123-45-6789.

Always ask your tax advisor's opinion, then decide what's best for you. Keep copious records, including any canceled checks. If you are challenged for a deduction, the IRS will demand proof that, for example, you do indeed own half the house and make equal contributions to it or that you made 100 percent of the payments on a family-owned home.

Taking a partner as a dependent. Gray area. Red flag. Proceed with caution. The IRS enforces its stated rules addressing the citizenship, income, marital status, and support required for an individual to be considered a "dependent."

The IRS defines *dependent* as "a person, other than the taxpayer or the taxpayer's spouse, for whom an exemption can be claimed." That means generally that you can claim an exemption for a dependent if the dependent

- lives with you in your household for the entire year or is related to you.
- is a U.S. citizen, a U.S. resident, or a resident of Canada or Mexico.
- does not file a joint or individual return.
- does not have $3,100 or more of gross (total) income in 2005. (This rule does not apply to your child if they are under age 19 or they are a student under age 24.)
- is supported (more than 50 percent) by you.

Also, the relationship cannot be in violation of local law; for example, if you live in a city or state that enforces a law that prohibits cohabitation or relations between same-sex partners.

Some people take the rules literally and may try to claim a domestic partner as a dependent on a tax return. Because several issues are involved, consult with a qualified tax advisor first.

Same-sex dilemma. Partners of the same sex encounter even more shades of gray when it comes to filing and signing a federal tax return. What should a legally married same-sex couple in Massachusetts do when filling out and signing federal tax returns? The couple files a joint or married-filing-separately Massachusetts return but cannot, by law, file federal taxes jointly. Each partner must file an individual federal return and then—on pain and penalty of perjury—sign his or her tax return, attesting to his or her "single" status.

Until the issue of same-sex marriage shakes out through our nation's legal system, a couple can do little more than go ahead and file individual returns for Uncle Sam. But, to protect yourselves, same-sex couples should send an addendum or cover letter with their federal tax returns that states each partner is legally married under Massachusetts law. The disclosure will explain the discrepancies between the partners' federal and state tax returns. This is necessary when applying for a mortgage or other loans.

CAVEATS

Whoever would benefit most from taking a specific deduction should write the checks related to that deduction. Whoever will be impacted the least should be listed first on joint investment and savings accounts. Consider having a tax-planning meeting with your tax preparer up front. Have them run the numbers different ways to determine what strategy works best for you. Then, based on the results, decide what's more advantageous for both of you. Remember, too, that both of you—most importantly—and your tax preparer, if you have one, must be comfortable with the tax strategies you choose.

FIGURE 5.3 Addendum/Disclosure to 2004 Federal Income Tax Return

Here's a sample addendum that same-sex spouses in Massachusetts may want to include with their federal tax return.

Jane Q. Public
123 Main Street
Anytown, MA 02135
SSN: 123-45-6789

April 15, 2005

Internal Revenue Service
Andover, MA 05501

Dear Sir/Madam,

I am enclosing this cover letter with my 2004 federal income tax return because of my tax filing status. On May 20, 2004, I was legally married in the Commonwealth of Massachusetts to Susan B. Doe (Social Security Number: 987-65-4321), and, consequently, filed a joint Massachusetts tax return for 2004. Due to the Defense of Marriage Act (DOMA), I am forced to choose a single filing status and have prepared my tax return accordingly.

Respectfully,
Jane Q. Public

Enclosure (optional): Commonwealth of Massachusetts Marriage Certificate

---

In many cases, however, it may make sense to bunch deductions and earnings because the tax savings can be in the hundreds—if not thousands—of dollars. Unmarried couples face so many disadvantages and expenses associated with buying and setting up various legal instruments, you may want to let the tax system offset the additional expense as much as possible.

WARNING *Make sure your documentation matches your tax strategies. If a partner plans to claim a deduction, he or she should write the check for it.*

Documentation

No matter what tax strategies a couple chooses, make sure the paper trail matches the strategy. In other words, if Jeanne takes the deduction for mortgage interest paid, she should be the partner who writes the mortgage check every month. Jeanne also makes the deductible contributions to the Red Cross, the American Heart Association, and the local Boys and Girls Club. She pays the couple's church tithe and anything else that can be deducted, as well. Her partner, Julie, in turn, writes the checks to the brokerage to buy the mutual fund and the stocks that generate taxable dividend income for the couple. By being able to produce the signed and canceled checks, Jeanne and Julie are more likely to be able to prove their case, if necessary, with the IRS.

To get the most from this tax strategy, the difference between the partners' incomes needs to be fairly significant. What's "significant"? Again, that's up to you and your partner, but partners should be in different tax brackets. If your marginal tax brackets are only 3 to 5 percent apart, bunching may not be worth the effort. You will save some tax money, but you may have estate tax and inheritance tax problems associated with having to substantiate contributions in the event of a partner's death. If the disparity isn't large enough to make a significant difference in tax liabilities, consider splitting all the couple's income evenly as long as it's paid evenly.

However, have your tax advisor run the numbers before you decide. Even if you and your partner are in the same marginal tax bracket, your combined tax bill could be lower if one of you bunches deductions while the other takes the standard deduction. In some instances, the partner who itemizes may even end up in a lower marginal tax bracket.

Whatever the strategy, keep copious records. If the IRS decides to challenge you, it will demand that you produce all the details.

INADVERTENT GIFTING

Are you giving away all or part of an asset without even realizing it? That's not a far-fetched scenario and, in fact, happens all the time among unmarried couples. It could happen to you, too. Without advance planning, the wrong people may end up with your or your partner's money—with neither of you discovering the situation until it's too late.

Caleb and Allison were older and had been together for about six years. Caleb had grown children from a previous marriage who disapproved of his relationship with Allison. Also, Allison, who was much younger than Caleb, had an income ten times his. Because of these issues, the couple intended to keep their finances separate.

The couple lived in the home (valued at $700,000) that Caleb had owned for 25 years. The problem surfaced when they decided to remodel their house and wanted to use the equity in the home to foot the bill. Caleb had a ton of equity in the house, but Allison had the majority of the income. The couple needed to put the home in joint ownership because Caleb, with his $20,000 a year retirement income, couldn't qualify for the $400,000 mortgage. The only way the couple was able to refinance was by applying jointly for a mortgage, and the only way Allison agreed to assume the mortgage was if her name was added to the deed. That caused big problems.

No one died, no one got sick, but Caleb—by refinancing the mortgage with Allison and retitling the property in joint ownership to correspond with the mortgage—just gave her 50 percent of his $300,000 equity in the home. He committed a major financial blunder. Consider the tax implications of this inadvertent gift. Not only has Caleb's "gift" exceeded the $11,000 annual tax-free gift threshold, he's just given away $139,000 (which is the $150,000 minus the $11,000 gift tax exclusion) or a big chunk of his lifetime gift tax exclusion. When Caleb dies, his estate will have lost that amount of the exclusion, and Allison—or Caleb's heirs if Allison dies first—likely would face a hefty tax bill. Remember, unmarried partners don't qualify for the unlimited marital property transfer between spouses. Also, Caleb's grown children might be resentful that their father replaced their mother and shared his bed with a "younger woman" who "stole" the family home. Adding insult to their perceived injury, Caleb's children also lost part of their inheritance to pay a hefty tax bill—all because no proper financial planning was done when their father put Allison's name on the deed to the property.

Gift tax return. The other issue is that if Caleb were to gift $139,000—inadvertently or not—to Allison, he's required by law to notify the IRS by filing a gift tax return. Worse still, if he doesn't even realize he's given the gift, no one else may discover the blunder, either, possibly for decades. If Caleb and Allison hadn't wanted to remodel and refinance, Caleb simply might have added Allison's name to the deed on the home, and no one would have discovered that for years—most likely not until Caleb died and Allison was prepared to inherit the home. Adding to the problem, the gift would not be considered a completed gift because the gift tax return was not filed, and, as a result, the entire value of the house would be included in Caleb's estate. And chances are the home's value will have appreciated by then, so his estate would face a bigger tax bill.

Another approach. Ed wanted his partner, Judy, to have half of the $110,000 equity in his home, so he decided to refinance the house jointly with her. To avoid incurring gift tax liability on the $44,000 ($55,000—half the equity—minus the $11,000 allowed tax free) that Ed was giving Judy, the couple also had a side agreement drawn up that stipulated Judy would make all the mortgage payments on the home until she had "purchased" her share of the property. She then would become technical and legal half-owner of the property—and so the couple would neatly sidestep the gifting issue. The side agreement is legally binding because it's a business agreement. Remember, the courts view properly drafted and executed domestic partnerships as business partnerships.

Consider what could happen if Ed simply had added Judy's name on the deed as a tenant in common because it seemed like the right thing to do. Ed would still "own" the house, or so he would think. Let's assume that three years later the couple split up and several more years pass. Judy's name never gets removed from the deed, because she's not interested in a word Ed has to say, let alone willing to cooperate with him on anything. (Such a scenario is even more impetus for couples to sign all the right documents while they're in love and not when a relationship has deteriorated into distrust or even hatred.)

Meanwhile, neither ex-partner recognizes the significance of what's happened. Ed dies suddenly without a will. Judy, who's been out of the picture for years, owns half the house. Never mind about Ed's current partner, who had been with him longer than Judy ever was and is now homeless. Judy now is faced with a pair of prospects, if Ed's heirs are willing to cooperate. Either she can immediately sell the property to pay off those heirs for Ed's share of the property, or else she can come up with the cash some other way to buy out the heirs and own the property outright. It's an accidental nightmare caused by the fact that neither ex-partner paid attention to keeping finances current or bothered with any financial planning.

DOMESTIC PARTNER BENEFIT

Don't overlook the fact that if your partner receives domestic partner health benefits through your employer, the amount of the employer-paid portion of the premium is added to your income. For tax purposes, it either shows up as additional wages on your W-2 form or may be reported on a separate 1099, and it's subject to Social Security taxes.

With the high costs of health care today, that phantom income shuffle can throw someone into a higher tax bracket, especially if it's not expected. So, if your employer finally recognizes and provides domestic partner benefits, just remember it's a taxable benefit but a benefit nonetheless. Taking the benefit could boost your income into a higher tax bracket. And for those married same-sex couples who live in Massachusetts, the benefit is taxable only on your federal tax returns, because the federal government doesn't recognize your marriage.

Chad and Tommy were thrilled when Tommy's employer offered domestic partner benefits. As a young couple struggling to make ends meet, they jumped at the chance to get health insurance for Chad, who had none. The added cost of coverage for Chad was minimal. Things went well until Tommy received his W-2. His employer had added almost $3,000 in phantom income to his annual salary. That extra income was the cost of health care premiums that the company had paid for Chad. Suddenly, Tommy faced an additional tax levy of about $750, which, combined with the few dollars a month extra, still is well worth paying for a year of health insurance. If the couple could have married legally, no phantom income would have been added (or taxed) for the cost of a spouse's premium. If a similar scenario occurred in Massachusetts, for example, and Chad and Tommy chose to marry legally, Tommy would not face added state tax for the cost of the premiums, but the phantom income would count when figuring his federal taxes.

BURDEN OF PROOF

When it comes to taxes and the IRS, the burden of proof is on you, period. Unmarried couples need to keep meticulous records, especially when it comes to joint ownership of a home and other assets. If the IRS senses something amiss about anything you've done, it *will* come calling. That doesn't mean you are wrong and they are right. It just means you had better be able to support what you've done with more than simply a canceled check.

Red Flags and Audits

If an unmarried couple reports everything accurately, they have no greater chance of an audit than anyone else. The IRS, after all, relies initially on Social Security numbers, not names or marital status.

Historically, however, certain deductions or actions can trigger closer scrutiny or an audit by the IRS. Some tax advisors even suggest avoiding certain deductions unless they net substantial tax savings, because such deductions wave a red flag at the IRS. Others insist that taxpayers should take all the deductions they are entitled to receive. It's up to you—as an individual taxpayer and as a couple—to determine whether a deduction is worth it. Don't, however, be paranoid about standing up to the IRS. Only about 1 percent of taxpayers are audited. If you're owed a deduction, take it. Pay every bit of tax you're required to but nothing more.

If any type of cohabitation violates federal law, it could draw IRS attention. It doesn't matter if the law is antiquated or even laughable. Some municipalities or counties, for example, allow only one name or a married couple's name on a residential deed as a way to prevent cohabitation. Another example involves same-sex occupants in a home. Certain laws— some written more than a century ago—prohibit more than a certain number of people of the same sex occupying a certain amount of space without separate bedrooms for each. Years ago, these laws were designed to prevent brothels, but they now mean that if three sisters and two of their girlfriends wanted to share a two-bedroom condo, they technically would be violating that law.

BOTTOM LINES

Instead of sitting back and waiting for Uncle Sam to decide what he wants from you or hoping the IRS won't pounce on you for questionable tax strategies, be proactive and act within the law.

Check out the IRS's Web site to learn more of the details on various laws and how they might relate to you and your partner. Tons of brochures as well as tax forms are available online to help you.

As a couple and as an individual, if you do nothing else, at a minimum do the following:

- Figure out your effective tax rates.
- If appropriate, consider shifting deductions and lumping them under the partner's name that will provide the greatest tax advantage. Do

the math and determine which type of shifting works for you as a couple.

- Whatever you do, make sure your documentation matches your tax strategy. If partner A deducts the mortgage interest paid, make sure that partner A writes the mortgage check.

- Utilize smart charitable giving strategies to maximize your deductions.

- Use the same tax advisor or tax preparer your partner uses. This advisor should have experience helping unmarried couples minimize their combined tax liability.

- If you prepare your own tax returns using a software package like TurboTax, keep in mind that TurboTax, like most other tax preparation software, doesn't account for unmarried partners—it doesn't know that you and your partner share assets and liabilities. It's up to you to account properly for income and deductions. You'll have to research and, in turn, understand federal and state tax rules, then make sure that your tax returns make sense. While no one tax guide exists for unmarried couples, the IRS and individual states have various free publications and guides available on their Web sites.

- Start your tax planning at the first of the year as opposed to trying to re-create the past year at tax time.

CHAPTER 6

Estate Planning
ISSUES, OPPORTUNITIES, AND CONCERNS

"The only certainties in life are death and taxes." We've talked about the latter; now consider the other inevitability, death.

The U.S. government has done a pretty good job of ensuring that everyone prepares for and pays income taxes. Unfortunately, it hasn't been as successful at getting Americans to prepare financially for death. Estate planning enables you to do that with your loved ones and heirs in mind. If you don't, Uncle Sam has his own estate plan for you. And, generally, it's not what any of us would have intended.

In the last chapter, we discussed the importance of tax planning and the nightmares that can result without it. Estate planning is no different. Without it, an individual can end up struggling to make ends meet in what are supposed to be those golden retirement years. After death, loved ones—especially unmarried partners—can become mired in a financial and emotional mess—destitute and homeless—all while trying to cope with the loss of a partner.

None of that is an exaggeration, either. Without the right kind of planning, life for you and your partner—and the aftereffects of your death on surviving loved ones—can be a nightmare.

Let's take a closer look.

THE PLAYING FIELD

Existing estate and inheritance laws are designed to protect spouses and biological family members. Uncle Sam gives married U.S. citizens an unlimited, tax-free asset transfer to the survivor upon the death of a spouse. Every U.S. citizen also gets a $1.5 million estate tax exemption. Every U.S. citizen can go to the grave knowing that $1.5 million worth of their assets will pass to their heirs free of federal estate tax. Any assets that exceed $1.5 million face estate taxes that, as of 2005, begin at a hefty 39 percent and rise to 47 percent for the largest estates. That means at least 39 cents of every dollar over and above an estate's tax-free asset threshold goes to pay federal estate taxes.

It doesn't matter if a couple has been together three months or 30 years. If they're unmarried, they're out of luck, maybe out of a home, and maybe even out of money if they don't plan ahead. That planning includes setting up documentation and keeping affairs up to date. Yes, at minimum, estate planning should include a will, but a will alone is hardly sufficient for unmarried couples to ensure that their wishes are carried out and their loved ones taken care of.

Casual or new couples need estate planning, too, because it's really designed to protect each individual and his or her heirs. Planning is important regardless of whether someone wants to leave everything to a partner or other loved ones. It's not how much money you have that determines your need for financial planning, either. Regardless of the size of your estate, you must attend to the standard details and then deal with the more complex issues, if necessary. Those standard issues include disposition of your personal journals and artwork as well as what happens to your pets. Complexities can include a business that you want to keep going or property that can't be transferred easily or immediately.

One general rule that unmarried couples need to bear in mind regarding estate planning: Consider hiring separate attorneys, especially if significant assets are involved and family members potentially could be hostile. If only one attorney draws up the estate planning documents for both of you, family members could argue that an individual signed his or her will under duress or pressure from the other.

Let's look more closely at the options and opportunities.

SURVIVOR WITHOUT BENEFITS

Social Security provides a $255 token death benefit for *everyone* as long as he or she qualifies for Social Security benefits of any kind. The dollar amount is small because it originally was meant to cover the expense of a burial. That was then. This is now. The benefit isn't indexed for inflation, so today it probably won't even cover the cost of just a cremation or a stripped-down casket.

Social Security does, however, add one small qualification for an individual to be eligible for this paltry benefit. It's available only to a surviving spouse or dependent child. All you unmarried couples out there—more than 11 million people—are out of luck. (Of course, if you're widowed and receiving Social Security survivor's benefits it's a different story.)

The vast majority of unmarried couples don't qualify for joint or survivor Social Security benefits or pension benefits, either. The exception, of course, is an "unmarried" couple who in reality are common law husband and wife. Remember Paul and Pam, the couple from Chapter 2 who lived together for many years in Massachusetts, a state that does not recognize common law marriage? The couple retired and then moved to Rhode Island, a state that does recognize such marriages. After Paul's death, Pam petitioned Social Security for survivor's benefits even though the couple never officially married. She was granted the benefits on the grounds that the couple's joint history in Massachusetts met the qualifications for common law marriage in Rhode Island. Luckily for Pam, they had held themselves out as a married couple. As a widow, Pam will retain her survivor's benefits as long as she does not remarry. The same is true for widowers and surviving divorced spouses (provided the marriage lasted at least ten years).

Arnold and Bea met shortly after both their spouses died. They dated for several years and eventually moved in with each other. They've been together so many years they've lost count, or so they like to say. Although there's no question of their commitment and devotion to each other, they never married. The reason: As widow and widower, both Bea and Arnold are entitled to Social Security survivor's benefits through their deceased spouses. Their individual health insurance also comes from those spouses' pension plans. The couple counts on all that to fund their comfortable lifestyle. If they married, they would lose their survivor's benefits, and they can't afford to let that happen.

Willy and Heather are registered domestic partners in California, a state that allows domestic partners to receive survivor's state pension benefits (after January 1, 2005). Heather never has held a wage-earning job and has relied on Willy to take care of her financially for the past 20 years. Both partners are nearing retirement age and are confident that Willy's substantial pension will provide for them in their golden years. It's a perfect scenario, especially because the unmarried couple live in a state that allows Heather to receive state pension survivor's benefits. If that wasn't the case and Willy died, then Heather would find herself dumped into the workforce after 20 years away from it, or on welfare, and most likely facing a very different future.

STILL BLEAKER OUTLOOK

Few surviving partners succeed in their battles for recognition in the form of benefits or cash. Dan and Marty had lived together for 24 years when Marty died unexpectedly of a brain hemorrhage. Marty had worked for a firm that, like most companies, had adhered to a long-standing policy of paying pension benefits to spousal beneficiaries only. However, the company was particularly progressive. Just two weeks before Marty died, it amended its pension plan to allow a distinction for unmarried partners. An unmarried partner, however, needed to file a form that designated a (nonspouse) partner as beneficiary or else forfeit the benefits. Marty had picked up the form from the company's human resources office, but he hadn't bothered to fill it out and file it with human resources. First of all, he wasn't planning to die just yet; and, second, only a week before his death, he had received a clean bill of health from his doctor.

Because Marty had worked for the firm for more than 20 years and a sizable sum was involved, Dan appealed the case to the administrator of the company's benefits plan. As proof of the couple's longtime relationship, Dan produced copies of deeds on the two homes the couple owned jointly with rights of survivorship. The couple also had drawn up wills bequeathing everything to each other. Their wills, designating that their possessions should be left to each other (known as "I love you" wills) have the same effect as what happens automatically when a spouse dies intestate, or without a will. That is, from the court's standpoint, the surviving spouse generally is first in line to receive assets. Dan also argued that Marty had intended to fill out the form and name Dan as the beneficiary.

But Dan's case was a little more complicated. Because the federal Defense of Marriage Act (DOMA), which defines marriage as the union between a man and a woman, preempts the Employee Retirement Income Security Act (ERISA), which lays down federal requirements governing pension eligibility, Dan lost his appeal.

The moral of the story: If your unmarried partner's employer extends domestic partner benefits, including pensions, make sure all the necessary paperwork is completed as soon as possible and filed with the appropriate department—usually the company's benefits office. You have no assurance that you—or the benefit—will be around tomorrow. Your age and health don't matter. Just do it.

In another cautionary tale, the surviving partner not only was left without her partner and out in the cold but given an extra kick in the pants as well. Nora and Jennifer had lived together as domestic partners for 15 years and were raising Nora's granddaughter when Nora died. Because Social Security doesn't recognize same-sex partners, Nora's survivor's benefits went to her ex-husband, an active substance abuser who she despised. Jennifer, who continues to care for Nora's granddaughter, was left with nothing but the knowledge that Nora's sizable benefits were being squandered on drugs.

Nora should have purchased life insurance and designated Jennifer as the beneficiary. She also should have made provisions in her will naming Jennifer as guardian and establishing a trust for the care of her granddaughter with Jennifer as trustee.

The case of another unmarried couple, however, although surrounded by tragedy, offers some hope for domestic partnership recognition. A same-sex couple had been together 13 years when one partner was killed on 9/11. She was a passenger aboard United Flight 11, which crashed into one of the World Trade Center towers in New York. Her partner was denied survivor's benefits from the 9/11 Victims' Fund because she wasn't next of kin. The surviving partner sued the fund and subsequently won. Acknowledged as the legal survivor of her partner, she now receives survivor's benefits.

No Spousal Rollover

Laws stacked against unmarried couples don't stop there. Unmarried partners also are ineligible to take advantage of the spousal rollover of Individual Retirement Accounts and qualified retirement plans. Typically, when one married partner dies, an IRA or qualified retirement plan can be rolled over to the surviving spouse without any immediate tax liability. The name on the account is changed, and the surviving spouse is not required to withdraw any funds until he or she turns 70½.

Unmarried couples, however, have no such luck. When a partner dies and a partner is named beneficiary of his or her IRA or 401(k), the beneficiary immediately must begin withdrawing funds and paying the subsequent taxes. For an IRA, the amount of money to be withdrawn annually is based on the life expectancy of the surviving partner. But in the case of a 401(k), the entire amount may need to be taken as a taxable lump-sum distribution. Or, if the plan allows, withdrawals may be taken annually based on the life expectancy of the beneficiary.

Of course, additional funds may be withdrawn from an inherited IRA at any time, but they might be subject to a 10 percent premature-distribution penalty and income taxes.

Adam's will stipulated that his partner, Stephanie, should receive his $500,000 IRA. The couple had had no long-term commitment to each other, but Adam wanted to ensure that Stephanie would be taken care of in the event that anything happened to him. Adam overlooked, however, the extra tax liability that he'd handed Stephanie. Those taxes included federal and state income taxes on the IRA money as it is withdrawn—and Stephanie, no matter her age, would have to begin drawing down the money immediately over her life expectancy. The couple also happened to live in Indiana, which is among the handful of states that assess inheritance taxes. So, due within nine months of Adam's death would be $70,000 in state inheritance tax on the $500,000 IRA. Indiana law says that, because of the value of the property, the amount due is $10,000 plus 15 percent of the net taxable value over $100,000. Stephanie may have to borrow money, cash in a chunk of the IRA and pay taxes and penalties, or sell other assets just to pay the inheritance tax. As mentioned earlier, inheritance tax rates may vary depending on the size of the inheritance and by state.

PROTECTING A PARTNER

The correct documents written the right way and in their proper place will protect unmarried partners in the event of serious illness or disability. In the event one partner dies, the surviving partner generally needs that protection, too. He or she often runs head on into inequities in the legal system, bickering among the deceased partner's family, animosity, and the taxing wrath of federal and state governments.

Do you have a will or any kind of estate plan? If your answer is no, think again. Even if you haven't made contingency plans for serious disability or prepared in any way for your eventual demise, you *do* have a plan, courtesy of Uncle Sam and the state that's your legal residence. (Each state has its own rules for people who die intestate—without a will.) They have based your estate plan on laws biased against unmarried couples. If you don't make plans to circumvent those laws, Uncle Sam and your state of residence will control your future and that of your intended heirs. If you don't dictate your own estate plan, they dictate it for you.

And beware: Unmarried couples aren't likely to think much of Uncle Sam's ideas of fair and equitable. In Uncle Sam's by-default estate plan, biological family takes precedence, period.

Even if a deceased partner's family acts kindly and caring toward the surviving partner, that partner still could end up out of luck. Arnold and Thelma had been together about eight years and just recently had moved into a huge, upscale apartment in the middle of the city. The rent was exorbitant, but Arnold made the move because Thelma truly loved the place. She deserved it, too, he often pointed out to friends and family. After all, she had spent the past three years caring for him through a very tough illness. About a month after the move, Arnold had a heart attack and died.

Although his will was difficult to locate, it finally surfaced. The only problem: The will was 30 years old. Arnold had been in the process of updating it, but the attorney handling the revisions was in the U.S. Army Reserves and had been called to active duty in Iraq. The paperwork simply had not been completed. Arnold's original will left all his substantial assets to his three surviving siblings. Adding to the problems for Thelma, the lease on the apartment she had shared with Arnold was in his name only. The family couldn't afford to pay the rent for Thelma, so she found herself kicked out of her home. Fortunately for her, Arnold's brothers volunteered to help her financially until she could get back on her feet. But not all partners' families are as caring and generous.

Throughout this book we have cited several examples of unmarried partners being shown the door of their own home after the death of a partner, because, unfortunately, this scenario is all too common. It is not at all unusual for relatives to boot the former partner out the door because the partner's name isn't on the deed, and, therefore, he or she has no legal rights to the home. Hopefully these stories will help you understand some of the risks and possible consequences and, in turn, serve as a catalyst for you to build a financial plan.

Jordan and Betsy shared a home that Jordan initially owned individually. When the couple moved in together, though, they split everything 50-50 and always talked about "their" home and their future together. Betsy just assumed that Jordan had changed the deed on the house to include her. It never occurred to either of them, in fact, that the home didn't belong to both of them. Two years into their relationship, Jordan popped the big question, asking Betsy to marry him. She said yes, but no date was set for the wedding. Jordan's family still hadn't warmed to Betsy, so the couple thought it best to wait a while before tying the knot.

Not long after proposing to Betsy, Jordan died in an automobile accident. Naturally, Betsy was upset and distraught. After the funeral and reception, friends of the couple took her out to dinner. When Betsy finally arrived back at her home, Jordan's older brother and father were in the process of moving Betsy's belongings out of the house and into a rented van. Betsy was horrified to learn that her partner had left the house to his brother, according to terms of his will drafted six years earlier—long before she and Jordan had met. Betsy buried her partner and lost her home in the same day, and she had no recourse.

The biggest tragedy in this scenario is that it easily could have been avoided if Jordan simply had changed his will or altered the title on the home to joint tenants with rights of survivorship. The latter on the deed would have taken precedence over the will.

WARNING *If both partners' names are not on the deed to their home or condo, or if the property is not owned in a trust or some type of partnership that names the surviving partner as heir, or if that partner is not named in the will, or if Transfer on Death/Payable on Death is not available, the surviving partner has no ownership rights when the home's legal owner dies.*

JOINT OWNERSHIP

Joint ownership of a home or other large asset, as we discussed previously, is one way that unmarried partners can protect each other in the event that one or the other dies. From a psychological standpoint, owning assets jointly also can serve as a testament to unmarried partners' commitment to each other. But, as with most financial strategies, joint ownership has its share of drawbacks, too, and isn't always the best answer for everyone.

On the positive side of joint ownership, if Betsy and Jordan had owned their house jointly with rights of survivorship, Betsy would not have been turned out of her home, because a deed takes precedence over a will.

On the negative side, joint ownership carries risks and other drawbacks. If Jordan had put Betsy's name on the deed to the home, that's tantamount to giving her 50 percent equity in the home, plain and simple. He might not want to do that for personal or liability reasons (if Betsy is in an occupation with a high risk of lawsuits, for instance). Or, as we also discussed in earlier chapters, gift tax liabilities could be a concern if Jordan's equity "gift" wasn't set up properly—either spread out over time or given in exchange for cash or a cash equivalent, such as paying the mortgage for a specified time. (We discussed gifts of real estate in detail in Chapter 5.)

At death, joint ownership also can be a way to minimize capital gains on a joint asset for the surviving partner. Remember that the IRS assumes that, if an asset like a home is owned jointly with rights of survivorship by two nonspouses, when the first owner passes away, 100 percent of the value of the house is in the estate of the first-to-die. The value of the asset in the estate is transferred to the heirs, and that becomes the home's new cost basis going forward. It's all about something called the step-up basis that generally occurs with inherited assets. For tax purposes, the new owner or heir calculates taxable gain based on the asset's fair market value at the time of death, not on the price paid by the deceased person who bequeathed the asset.

Chris and Alex bought a home jointly with rights of survivorship eight years ago for $150,000. Unfortunately, Alex died after a long battle with breast cancer. Chris was named executor of the estate and had the home reappraised for estate tax purposes. Its value came in at a whopping $600,000.

If Chris could not prove that Alex contributed equally to the purchase and maintenance of the home, then 100 percent of the value of the house—$600,000—would be included in Alex's estate. Chris's new cost basis, or her cost for tax purposes, would be $600,000. The benefit to her is that no tax has to be paid on the first $450,000 of appreciation (that's the new appraised price, $600,000, minus $150,000, the home's purchase price). In essence, because Alex did not own enough assets to have a federal taxable estate, the potential capital gain has been minimized by titling the asset jointly.

Liability Issues

By sharing ownership jointly, partners open themselves to tremendous liability risks. If Betsy had poor credit, for example, and creditors came after her for payment, they could have slapped a lien on the home if she and Jordan had owned it jointly.

Joint ownership turned into a liability nightmare for another couple. Remember Ed and Esther, the unmarried couple in their 70s in Chapter 2? Ed thought he was doing the right thing by putting his son's name on the account he had set aside for his retirement. But, instead, he ended up losing his retirement account as the result of a lawsuit filed against his son.

In another classic example of liability risk, Saul, a divorced orthopedic surgeon, decided to buy a home for his unmarried daughter and her partner. The house looked like a good investment, so Saul deeded the home in joint ownership with his daughter. Why not pick up an additional mortgage interest deduction for himself, he reasoned. Investment or not, deduction or not, Saul should have thought through possible repercussions of joint ownership, and he should have consulted his financial or legal advisor. As a doctor, he has a higher-than-average probability of being sued. In a worst-case scenario, Saul's daughter and her partner could lose their house, too.

Benefits in Jeopardy

Older couples may not want to own things jointly, either. If, for example, one partner is receiving a social service benefit that's contingent on income and assets—such as assisted living or even Medicaid—joint ownership can create too many assets for that partner. In turn, he or she could lose eligibility for the benefit.

After Janet was diagnosed with multiple sclerosis, her partner, Larry, decided to add her name to the deed on their home. He was concerned that if something should happen to him and they didn't have joint ownership, Janet wouldn't be able to stay in the couple's home. Wisely, he thought to check first with his financial planner. Good thing. The planner told him to reconsider adding Janet's name to the deed, because if her disease progressed to the point that she needed to enter a nursing home, part ownership in the house could affect her eligibility for Medicaid. Worse yet, Medicaid could force Larry to buy out Janet's share for her to be eligible for benefits.

Also worth noting is that Medicaid has the "look back rule." The state will check records over the past three years—and in some cases five years—to determine if any gifts have been made or assets divested to allow an individual to be eligible for coverage. (There are certain exceptions.) If such an asset transfer has occurred, Medicaid slaps a penalty period on that individual during which time he or she is not eligible for Medicaid. The length of the penalty depends on the amount of the asset transfer.

One way Larry could help Janet be eligible for Medicaid and stay in their house if something happens to him would be to place the home's ownership in a trust and name Janet as beneficiary. However, if Larry dies before Janet, she would not be eligible for Medicaid benefits because of that asset until that asset was exhausted. His planner, however, suggested that Larry leave a life insurance policy in a special needs trust designed so that Janet would not become ineligible for Medicaid.

Proving Home Ownership

Mortgage interest and real estate taxes present another difficulty when an unmarried couple owns a home jointly and one partner dies. As we mentioned earlier, the IRS assumes that 100 percent of the value of the home lies in the estate of the first to die. The burden of proof to show otherwise is on the surviving partner.

The best tool the surviving partner has in their arsenal may be a tax return showing that real estate mortgage expense and taxes were split. Canceled checks also will document the money flow. But even that can be a catch-22. If a couple bunches deductions and one takes the standard deduction, he or she gains from the income tax breaks but could be in worse shape if the other partner dies.

One way to handle the issue is for the higher-income partner to claim the deductions. That means he or she writes the property tax and mortgage checks from a personal or joint account, then takes those deductions. Meanwhile, the other partner takes the standard deduction, and the couple buys life insurance to pay the estate taxes due if either partner dies. Couples must weigh the pros and cons of various strategies—including a

FIGURE 6.1 Ownership Strategies

Here's a look at a few of the ramifications of various asset ownership strategies.

	Escape Probate	Avoid Inheritance Tax	Avoid Estate Tax	Avoid Income Tax	Privacy	Dispute Avoidance*
Tenants in Common	No	No	No	No	No	If willed to each other
Joint Tenants with Right of Survivorship	Yes	No	No	No	No	Yes
Revocable Trust	Yes	No	No	No	Yes	Yes
Irrevocable Trust	Yes	Yes	Yes	Taxed at Trust level	Yes	Yes

* May help minimize potential for dispute.

reality check as to who is eligible for and can afford the cost of life insurance—then decide what works best for them.

TRUSTS

Most people automatically think of trusts as tools to minimize estate or transfer taxes. Married couples often use revocable living trusts or irrevocable trusts to do that. Unmarried people look to irrevocable trusts to accomplish the same thing.

Even more important, a trust of any kind enables you to dictate your wishes beyond the grave, which gives you greater influence after your death than a will provides, as well as stipulates what happens in the event of your incapacity. A will simply states what you want done with your assets and belongings and who you would like to care for your minor children at your death. After the will is executed, your influence ends.

Basically, a trust is an entity that holds assets or property for the benefit of another or others. There are many, many different kinds of trusts, each with its own benefits and drawbacks. For purposes of this book and our discussions on unmarried couples, we will look at only a few of the basics. First, let's consider some trust terminology.

Someone who creates a trust is known as the creator, grantor, or donor. If the trust is created while he or she is alive, it's called a living trust or an *inter vivos* trust. If the trust is created by a will, therefore going into effect after death, it's a testamentary trust. Trusts can be either irrevocable, so that they can't be changed, or living and revocable. With the latter, you or your appointed trustee can change it anytime during your lifetime, and maintain control over its assets. A revocable trust, however, cannot be changed after its grantor's death. All trusts bypass probate—the process in which the courts monitor the reading of the will, selection of the estate's executor (that person responsible for carrying out the will and settling the estate), distribution of assets, and settlement of the estate. If the trust is irrevocable, its assets are excluded from the grantor's estate.

If your goal is to ensure that your partner is taken care of in the event of your death or incapacitation, a trust is part of an effective estate plan. A trust also can provide for your children and their future. If a goal is to avoid the costly, time-consuming, and very public probate process, a trust can do that, too. If you want to minimize the possibility of someone contesting your will, a trust will do that. An irrevocable trust also allows an estate to avoid crippling estate taxes. However, keep in mind that with an irrevocable trust, the grantor—you—give up all ownership and control of the assets in that trust.

The Privacy Issue

Another advantage of trusts is that they keep affairs private. Probate, on the other hand, is public record. If your nosy neighbor wants to know who got the car or the big-screen TV or if you really did support those political causes, all they need do is head down to the courthouse and check out the probate records. Do you really want anyone to have access to the details of your private life?

Same-sex couples especially may not want such a public record of their lifestyle. A person also might not wish to subject heirs to any ridicule or harassment that could result from John Q. Public discovering what he or she owned, who got what assets, and what causes he or she supported. Probate makes the details of your life an open book. A trust doesn't.

Probate also makes an estate more vulnerable to challenge. Anyone who is an heir or a creditor—or thinks he or she should be—has the opportunity to challenge the will and argue why he or she deserves the assets and someone else doesn't. The situation can get ugly easily—especially if various biological family members didn't approve of an unmarried couple's lifestyle or living arrangements and don't condone a will that leaves out or "shorts" them of your hard-earned assets or a coveted family heirloom.

Revocable Living Trust

A revocable living trust, as the name implies, can be changed anytime while you are alive. You own the assets in your trust and maintain all control as long as you are cognizant. But if you become unable to act on your own behalf, your named successor trustee can step in and manage your affairs.

In many instances, a living trust makes more sense than other types of asset ownership for unmarried partners. With joint ownership with right of survivorship, for example, partners are exposed to each other's liabilities. In the case of liquid or easily accessed assets, one partner could clean out the account if he or she became upset with the other. That happens all the time in divorce situations, and joint owners have the opportunity to do so.

With a revocable living trust, the details are spelled out. The grantor retains ownership and control of the trust, and any earnings on trust assets flow through to his or her tax return. Assets held in one's trust are treated in every way as a personal asset, including being subject to estate taxes on its owner's death. If the owner of the trust becomes incapacitated, the successor trustee steps in and manages the trust.

Even unmarried partners who take financial planning very seriously all too often overlook contingency plans in case of disability.

Remember April and Jim, the partners in Chapter 1? Jim, the couple's primary breadwinner who owned the couple's home, became incapacitated; the couple lost their home, and Jim's parents took him away forever. April had no legal recourse despite the fact that she and Jim had made long-term plans together. If Jim had held his home in a revocable living trust, he still could have retained individual ownership of the home and any other assets in the trust. But he also could have stipulated that April, as successor trustee, control the home in the event of his death or incapacitation. If April also had gotten health care and financial powers of attorney for Jim, she would have decided how and where to care for Jim, and she would not necessarily have lost her home. (See page 141 for more on such documents.)

Testamentary Trust

These are trusts set up by a will to be created after you die. A testamentary trust is a convenient, income tax–free way for you or your partner to dictate what should be done with your money and assets after you die. (Estate taxes may be due, however.)

A testamentary trust is an ideal way to guarantee income for a child. The trust's grantor leaves money in the trust for a child's designated guardian to use to support that child. A grantor also could leave money or assets in trust for a child stipulating that the child receive the assets over time beginning at a certain age, perhaps when you anticipate that child will reach financial maturity.

Additionally, parents use this kind of trust to help children learn how to manage assets. The assets are left in the trust, and ownership is turned over to the child gradually. For example, the trust could turn over one-quarter of ownership of an asset when a child reaches age 21, another one-quarter at age 25, and the remainder of the asset ownership at age 35.

Irrevocable Life Insurance Trust

This trust is a vehicle to own life insurance so that the amount of its death benefit is removed from your estate and, therefore, not subject to estate taxes. But it involves a big trade-off. In setting up such a trust, the grantor also surrenders all control and ownership of the assets in the trust, the life insurance policy. It can make sense, however, to set up an irrevocable trust to hold a large life insurance policy, perhaps for a child or partner, or both. Removing the value of the insurance from an individual's estate could affect whether the estate faces crippling taxes.

A bit of advice: Over the long haul, it's cheaper to set up an irrevocable life insurance trust than to buy the amount of life insurance needed to cover estate taxes on a large life insurance policy.

Note, too, that these kinds of trusts come with annual maintenance fees—approximately $300 a year. Plus, other details and strict stipulations on handling and funding the trust are involved. The grantor who set up the trust gives the trust a check annually equal to the amount necessary to pay the policy premium and trust maintenance fees. In essence, the grantor gifts the premium to the trust. The trustee, usually a bank or trust company, then must send out what's known as Crummey letters to the named beneficiaries. Those letters notify them that the trust is the recipient of money and asks the beneficiaries if they want their share of the money. With this strategy, the beneficiaries say no, the money remains in the trust, and the trustee pays the premium on the life insurance policy in the trust. Be cautious that the amount of the premium or cost of the contributions to the trust is under the $11,000 annual gift tax exclusion per beneficiary so that you can reduce the taxable value of your estate at the same time without reducing your personal exemption.

If you decide to transfer an existing life insurance policy into an irrevocable life insurance trust, keep in mind that you, the grantor, must survive the establishment of such a trust by at least three years for it not to be included in your estate.

Grantor Remainder Income Trust

A Grantor Remainder Income Trust, or GRIT, is an irrevocable trust in which the grantor creates the trust for a certain time frame, funds it, and then receives income for life from the trust.

On the death of the grantor, the balance of the assets in the trust goes to another individual, often a surviving partner. Beneficiaries of this kind of trust cannot be a related party or family member, so it can be an excellent planning technique for unmarried couples. The advantage of this type of trust is that if the grantor survives the trust term, the trust assets will not be included in his or her gross estate. Note, however, that the grantor is subject to gift tax on the fair market value of all assets placed in a GRIT.

Why Doesn't Everyone Have One?

If trusts are so great, why doesn't everyone have one? First of all, trusts are expensive to establish—around $1,500 a person and up, which is generally more than twice the price of simple wills. And, just like wills, trusts must be updated every few years or when circumstances change. That includes irrevocable trusts.

Unless someone thinks he or she needs the benefits and security of a trust, that's a lot of money to pay. Our society's tendency toward instant gratification also comes into play: Unless someone believes he or she is going to die, there is no instant payback in a trust—and no perceived need for one. However, we strongly recommend trusts for many unmarried clients.

That brings up the second reason why many people don't establish trusts or wills. Most younger and even many middle-aged people fall prey to the invincibility syndrome. They don't see themselves as ever in danger of dying or becoming disabled. Often, that mistaken outlook doesn't change until they see friends become ill or die or they head off to Cancun, Kyoto, or Casablanca. Vacationing out of the country, it seems, often serves as impetus to get one's affairs in order, just in case something should happen.

Among many couples, including males who may be at high risk of AIDS, there could be the mind-set that, "I'm going to die anyway, so let's live it up today and forget tomorrow." Too many such couples see their premature mortality as a given. That might have been true 15 years ago, but huge strides have been made in the prevention and treatment of AIDS. Tomorrow most likely *will* come, so you better prepare for it.

Avoiding Double Taxation

Double taxation of assets is a huge issue in estate planning for unmarried partners. And it's one that usually can be addressed by setting up a revocable or irrevocable trust.

Lacking eligibility for the silent, seamless property transfer in the form of unlimited marital deduction, unmarried couples potentially are taxed twice on the same assets held in one's estate at death. As we talked about earlier, for tax purposes the government considers that a jointly owned asset is wholly owned by the first partner to die, unless you can prove otherwise, and therefore is included in his or her estate. If the asset is bequeathed to a partner, when that surviving partner dies, the asset falls into his or her estate and is subject to estate tax again!

Margie owns a fabulous home that she shares with her partner, Rick. Her will stipulates that the home will go to Rick when she dies. But if Margie's estate exceeds the $1.5 million threshold—which is likely because of the home's value—Margie's estate will have to pay estate taxes on any amount over that $1.5 million. Then, when Rick dies, the house—which, it is hoped, will have appreciated even more by that time—will be included in his estate, too, and subject to taxation.

By placing the house in an irrevocable trust for the benefit of Rick, the asset avoids double taxation. At the same time, however, she may lose the residential exemption on real estate taxes. Once again, it's a legal document soft-shoe that unmarried couples need to dance to get similar tax benefits as their married counterparts.

WHAT OTHER DOCUMENTS ARE NEEDED AND WHY

A Will

Plain and simple: A will allows an unmarried partner to help provide for a partner, other loved ones, and/or charitable causes. Without a will, your heirs can be thrust into a living nightmare. As we've discussed earlier, dying without a will is called dying intestate, and an estate is subject to the government's by-default estate plan.

If you opt not to set up trusts, at the very least have a current will in place.

Don't choose a do-it-yourself will. Work with an estate lawyer experienced in drafting wills for unmarried partners that will hold up in court if challenged. No matter how amicable or frosty the relationship with an unmarried partner's family, it's often all about the money after the partner's death. And it gets even worse if minor children are involved. The propensity for trouble is high. A surviving partner from a same-sex relationship or a partner whose deceased partner was wealthy may run a higher risk of legal challenges from relatives of the deceased.

Many cases involving an older and a younger person bring up the issue of what the surviving younger partner brought to the relationship. When the older partner dies, he or she may choose to leave considerable assets to the younger partner—much to the consternation of biological family members. These cases often end up in court because family members, and often judges, question what this younger partner brought to the table. Sex? If that's all there was—big problem: it's against the law! If the left-out heirs argue their case well, the courts often rule against the surviving partner.

That's just one more reason to have a domestic partnership agreement. If the partners' ages differ vastly and/or one party has no income, the document could state that the younger partner or the one with no income provides support and loving care, tends to the house, prepares the meals, and generally provides companionship. In exchange, the older partner will provide support and other financial considerations either during the partnership or after his or her death.

Health Care Directive

A durable power of attorney for health care or a health care proxy is one of the most important documents that anyone, especially unmarried partners, can have. It's not about death or dying; it's about taking care of you while you're living but unable to care for or make decisions for yourself.

A health care directive states, in a legally binding document, that a specific individual or individuals will make health care decisions for you if you can't make them for yourself.

Without a power of attorney, if you're in a car accident and end up in critical condition in intensive care, your partner cannot sign any documentation or paperwork at the hospital on your behalf or even visit you, because he or she is not next of kin. It matters little if the two of you have been together 30 years or 3 days. Your next of kin have the legal right and responsibility to make decisions for you. Even if you haven't spoken to your father in decades, unless you specify otherwise, that same father may decide your fate should you become incapacitated. If you're hospitalized, your father will decide who may visit you, unless you have a health care directive stating otherwise. By the same token, if you do have a health care directive and it designates your longtime partner as the person responsible for making health-related decisions, he or she can make the decisions and decide which of your next of kin may visit. As the individual making decisions, your partner actually can throw out your next of kin, instead of the other way around—as often happens with unmarried partners. What an empowering concept!

Jill hadn't felt well for the past several weeks, but she still insisted that Sandy, her partner of seven years, go to Montreal on her business trip. Unfortunately, shortly after Sandy left, Jill collapsed and was rushed to the hospital, where doctors discovered she had a ruptured brain tumor. The couple had taken care of all the necessary documentation in the event of death of either partner, but they had no health care directive in place, so Jill's parents, as next of kin, were notified immediately. Adding to the problems, Jill's parents weren't too pleased with their daughter's relationship with Sandy.

Sandy didn't learn anything was wrong with Jill until several days later, when she returned from her business trip. Meanwhile, Jill's parents had arranged for their daughter, still in a coma, to be cared for in an exclusive nursing home. Jill's parents barred Sandy from ever again seeing her longtime partner, who died several months later. Sandy had no closure to the relationship. The parents wouldn't allow it. Jill was an adult woman with definite ideas about her own life. Yet that didn't matter in the end.

When you're incapacitated and don't have someone with power of attorney to act as your agent, your parents, if still living, are the bosses. If your parents are dead, the responsibility falls to your next of kin: adult children, then siblings, and so on. If your parents are dead and that deadbeat brother is alive, he could be in control of you and your dependents. That goes for whether you're 25 or 75, whether your partner is the opposite sex or same sex.

When putting together your health care proxy, some things to consider include:

- *Designating a backup agent.* If you and your partner are in an accident together, this person would make the decisions for you. Unmarried partners might choose each other to handle health care decisions, then name a parent, sibling, or close friend as backup. If your partner is distraught or injured, he or she may have trouble making level-headed decisions. Sometimes it helps to name a trusted person with a medical or social work background as a backup designee. That person may be able to function better under this situation.
- *Life support decisions.* In some states, this document also spells out living-will type details related to life support, so make sure that your designee knows your wishes and is comfortable carrying them out.
- *Coagents.* Consider naming your partner and a biological family member as coagents. That way, both must agree on health care decisions.
- *Communication.* If a health care designee is not next of kin, they should communicate decisions with family members.
- *Power of attorney.* Be sure that your health care designee and your doctor have valid copies of your power of attorney.

Living Will

Along with a health care directive, you also should have a living will, which documents the circumstances under which you do or do not want your life prolonged. For example, if you lapse into a coma and death is imminent, it could direct doctors not to place you on a respirator indefinitely.

A 78-year-old woman with moderate to severe Alzheimer's disease who was, therefore, incompetent to make her own health care decisions, was diagnosed with breast cancer. To the despair of her longtime partner, she did not have a living will. Her partner's fears became reality. Because the woman was not of sound mind and didn't have the living will, her biological family made the health care decisions for her. They decided that she should have surgery followed by radiation treatments. A number of complications ensued, and the woman eventually died but not before she had been subjected to severe pain and suffering. If she had put a living will in place, perhaps the situation would have been very different.

However, be aware that drawing up and signing a living will isn't always enough to ensure your wishes will be carried out. Whatever you do, don't relegate a living will to the safe deposit box. Be sure your doctor has a copy, your partner has a copy, and that another copy is readily available at a moment's notice—take it with you when you travel, too.

Lou and Peggy, a wealthy Florida couple in their 80s, lived in a retirement home and meticulously put together all the documents necessary—including living wills—for the perfect estate plan. One Sunday evening, Lou, who hadn't been well for a long time, suffered a massive heart attack. He was rushed to the hospital, where doctors promptly put him on life support. Both Peggy and her daughter were horrified that the doctors were trying to prolong Lou's life. He obviously was in a vegetative state, and he had a living will that specifically stated he did not want any heroic measures taken on his behalf. Only after months of legal wrangling could Peggy and her daughter persuade the doctors to remove the life support. In the interim, Lou lay in a coma—the one thing he had hoped to prevent with a living will. The problem, it seems, was that Lou's living will was in the safe deposit box at the bank when he was rushed to the emergency room. He didn't have it with him when he was admitted, nor did Peggy or his doctor have access to it. Therefore, it became a legal issue for the hospital to remove the life-support system.

These are tough decisions to make and difficult steps to take. It's not easy to confront your mortality, let alone the prospect of what will happen to your loved ones if something happens to you. But it's much better to be in control of your future and that of your loved ones than to have something happen to you and wind up with a stranger or someone not of your choosing suddenly making major decisions.

Financial Power of Attorney

Like a durable power of attorney for health care, a financial power of attorney stipulates how another person is to make decisions for you if you can't. In this case, the person or persons you designate manage your financial affairs on your behalf.

This individual will determine what happens to you and your finances while you're still alive and unable to make decisions for yourself, so choose this individual carefully. He or she will hold your financial future and possibly that of your partner and other heirs in his or her hands. Once the power of attorney is signed, it goes into effect immediately if it's a *durable* power of attorney. A *springing* power of attorney "springs" into action only when and if you become incapacitated. In almost every case, a springing power of attorney is more appropriate. Again, be sure to pick this person or these people carefully.

Just because you have designated a power of attorney doesn't mean that it covers both health care and financial decisions unless the document stipulates such. Of course, if you and your partner were legally married, you, as spouses, automatically have the right to make some decisions for each other in accordance with state law.

Funeral Directive

No one likes to confront their mortality, least of all spell out what they wish to have happen to their body after death. But doing so can be the ultimate gift to your loved ones, especially a partner.

Do you want a funeral? What kind of ceremony would you like and where? What should be done with your remains? It all needs to be written down in a funeral directive. At the very least, unmarried partners should indicate what they want done with their remains. Family members (remember, legally an unmarried partner is not family) may make decisions that are a far cry from your wishes.

Roger had a strict Roman Catholic upbringing but left the church in his early 20s, shortly before he met Mike. Eventually the two moved in together. The couple spent 11 years together before Roger died of AIDS. Roger long had refused to face his mortality, and even as he lay dying in hospice, he refused to draft any kind of will. After his death, his mother and father made the funeral arrangements, which they had the legal right to do. The service was held in a Roman Catholic church, despite the fact that Roger had despised the Church and had been very vocal about his feelings. His longtime partner, Mike, was allowed to attend the service but was relegated to a back pew.

In yet another unfortunate situation, Ed died of AIDS, and his out-of-town parents, on advice from the hospital chaplain, elected to have his funeral in a local church. In his eulogy, the pastor (who hadn't known Ed) preached not only that AIDS was God's curse against homosexuals but that Ed himself was to blame for his own death and that he would burn in hell. What a horrible situation for all those involved, especially the parents who had had no prior knowledge of the pastor's feelings.

What kind of service do you—not someone else—truly want to celebrate your life? Clearly spelling out your wishes makes the situation so much easier for your loved ones. Putting a funeral directive in writing, so that it's legally binding, prevents family members from bulldozing your wishes. Roger had wanted a quiet beachside gathering of friends to honor him and then spread his ashes across the water. Reality was a far cry from that. Both he and Ed failed to write down their wishes in a legally binding document.

Two wealthy women, both philanthropists, lived together for many years as a devoted couple. Both were pilots and flew their own plane regularly. During a trip around the world, the couple's plane crashed and both women died. Sadly, because neither had documented her wishes regarding disposition of her remains, each woman's family ended up taking the remains and burying them hundreds of miles apart. Anyone who had known the women knew the longtime couple would have wanted to be buried together.

Ensuring your wishes are carried out takes just a few simple sentences in a funeral directive. The families of unmarried couples—whatever the couple's sexual orientation or age—often have other ideas.

Caveats

In addition to working with a well-qualified attorney, unmarried couples need to share their estate plans, thoughts, and wishes with their biological families. Let them know up front what you want to happen to you, your partner, your belongings, and assets. Include them in your decision so that if something happens, they're prepared. They are in on it. It's much harder psychologically, emotionally, and anecdotally for relatives to contest something that a family member thoroughly discussed and made very clear to them when of sound mind.

If you balk at talking with parents or family about your personal living situation and also think it's none of their business, you might want to reconsider. If something happens to you, even if you have a will, your affairs might not go as you had hoped. However, remember that you can avoid the probate process altogether with an effectively designed and executed estate plan that utilizes trusts.

Shelf Life and Relevancy of Documents

A good estate plan doesn't remain "good" forever. It should be fluid and easy to update while your life, the world around you, and circumstances change. If you move out of the county, state, or country where your original estate-planning documents were drafted, recheck your documents to ensure they're valid in your new place of residence. That's especially important for same-sex couples. A move might negate an agreement because of local laws against homosexuality. Other unmarried couples also must be alert for legal prohibitions. Many antiquated laws still are on the books in many jurisdictions.

It's also a good idea to double-check documents with experienced attorneys in your new locale. They are familiar with local and regional nuances affecting estate and property transfer laws.

By the same token, a legal document between partners may not be necessary in one locale while it might be in another. In California, for example, as we mentioned earlier, registered domestic partners—as of January 2005—qualify for the same inheritance rights as do their married counterparts if the partners are the same sex, or if one of the partners is at least age 62. Pay attention to the relevancy of bequests, too. If you made out your will 20 years ago and left your prized heirloom to Jane Doe—remember that friend who lived in Suffolk County?—you might want to ascertain if she still lives there or if she's even alive. Lost or deceased beneficiaries of wills are a very common occurrence.

BOTTOM LINES

Once it's over, it's over. Hindsight is of little help as your heirs and loved ones struggle through the nightmares that ensue without proper estate planning. Again, as with most aspects of financial planning, be proactive with your estate planning, too. Determine which documents your state requires. Take the steps necessary to ensure that you and your loved ones will be taken care of in the event of your incapacity or death.

As a couple and as an individual, if you do nothing else, at minimum do the following:

- Put down all your wishes in writing.
- Consult with an estate-planning attorney or financial planner who is well versed in estate planning for unmarried couples.
- Be sure that you and your partner have in place a living will, health care and financial powers of attorney, a funeral directive, and a will or trust or pour-over will (which "pours over" any untitled assets into a trust).

- Consider setting up a trust, because it enables you to dictate your wishes beyond the grave and, in turn, gives you greater influence after your death than a will provides.
- Look closely at how your home is deeded. Make sure the title fits into your estate plan. If it is not deeded correctly, one partner could find themselves homeless in the event the other partner dies or becomes incapacitated.
- Make sure that all the appropriate parties have valid copies of your documents.

CHAPTER 7

Retirement Planning

A MIXED BAG

Everyone deserves his or her golden years. An individual's marital status shouldn't determine whether retirement is spent in relative financial comfort or struggling to get by. But for unmarried couples, the golden years too often are tarnished by a society geared toward married couples.

As we've discussed in earlier chapters, some seniors are reluctant to commit to or marry a partner for fear of losing pension and survivor's benefits, including health insurance. Many older unmarried couples nearing retirement—as well as younger unmarried partners looking to the future—sweat over whether they can save enough money or whether their company's pension plan will evaporate tomorrow. Same-sex couples, no matter their age, worry about both of the above and wonder if they even stand a chance at a comfortable retirement in a system stacked against them. However, statistically, same-sex couples have significantly more discretionary income, with unmarried opposite-sex couples not far behind, than their married counterparts. That, of course, likely is due primarily to the fact many of these couples are DINKs—dual income, no kids.

The fact of the matter is that no one in America today is guaranteed golden years without advance planning. If you and your partner, individually or as a couple, want a financially sound retirement, possibly with something left for your heirs, you must take the right steps today. For unmarried couples particularly, it's simply not enough to fund and forget a 401(k) retirement plan through an employer or, if self-employed, a Keogh, SIMPLE, one-person 401(k), or SEP-IRA. (See page 161 for more information on these retirement plans.) Collecting CDs and U.S. savings bonds and amassing a stock portfolio or any other investment vehicle likely isn't enough to protect you and your partner, either.

As we've emphasized again and again throughout this book, unmarried couples generally do not have the same benefits or protections available to their married counterparts. That disparity extends to the realm of retirement benefits, too. If an unmarried couple splits up, qualified retirement benefits aren't transferable. If a partner dies, his or her retirement benefits don't automatically go to the surviving partner without proper planning, either.

One notable exception to the latter is the state of California. After January 1, 2005, registered domestic partners who are same-sex partners of any age or who are heterosexual partners with at least one partner age 62 or over, will be treated the same as married partners with regard to the California state retirement system. These unmarried couples automatically will be eligible for a partner's retirement benefits should they elect for a joint and survivor pension payout option, or should the state employee die before they retire. In essence, the new domestic partner bill states that, if the retirement benefit is a spousal benefit only, a domestic partner now qualifies as the spouse.

New Jersey also offers domestic partnership benefits, many similar to California's. Registered domestic partners also are exempt from paying New Jersey inheritance taxes. Additionally Maine, Hawaii, and the District of Columbia provide certain benefits to registered domestic partners. Vermont allows civil unions that grant certain rights ranging from inheritance to coparenting as well as pension benefits for state employees.

Only the state of Hawaii entirely excludes heterosexual couples from domestic partnership laws. Laws in California and New Jersey include heterosexual couples only if one partner is at least age 62.

In all these states, however, in the event a relationship dissolves, the partners will *not* be able to split retirement accounts. A Qualified Domestic Relations Order, or QDRO (pronounced *quadro*), is a federal mandate that allows divorcing couples to split retirement plan assets without incurring early withdrawal or tax penalties. Basically, however, because the federal government doesn't recognize domestic partnerships, civil unions, or Massachusetts's same-sex marriage, the QDRO rule cannot apply to anyone other than heterosexual married couples.

Although recent positive changes in the legal landscape have occurred in several states, including Massachusetts, New Jersey, and California, the federal versus state distinctions prevail. Hence, to plan properly necessitates the dance around marriage-centric laws and practices if unmarried couples want to create a sound financial retirement for both partners. Later in this chapter, we'll look at the challenges faced by unmarried couples who want to save for the future. But first, let's consider why any couple or individual should think about retirement planning. After all, we have plenty of time, and, of course, Social Security will take care of us. Won't it?

WHY BOTHER?

First and foremost, no one should count on Social Security alone to fund retirement. The Social Security Administration makes that clear up front. Even to be eligible for Social Security retirement benefits, an individual needs a minimum of 40 Social Security credits. Workers can earn up to four credits a year, depending on their income, so that's a minimum of ten years of paying into the system. In 2005, for example, it takes $920 in earnings during one calendar quarter for one credit.

Most retirees need at least 80 percent to 100 percent of their preretirement earnings to maintain the same lifestyle in retirement. Social Security provides about only 30 percent of a person's preretirement income—for now. That leaves a minimum 50 percent shortfall, *if* Social Security even exists when you are ready to retire and *if* you need only 80 percent of your preretirement earnings to live on. Those are big ifs.

Add to that the fact that, in the early years of retirement, people often spend as much or more a year than they did before they retired, especially if they have the money to do so. That's often because they now have the time and flexibility to do some of those things they would have enjoyed doing prior to retirement—traveling, golfing, taking flying lessons, visiting the grandchildren, and more—all of which take money. Also, don't overlook added expenses like buying health insurance and even long-term care insurance. So, instead of requiring less income, retirement actually can require more.

Without drastic changes to the Social Security system—even as we all continue to pay into it—the Social Security "trust fund" may be empty, broke, finished, kaput in fewer than 40 years. Some experts estimate that it won't even last that long. There could be nothing left. So much for Social Security.

Few Savers Out There

More sad news on the retirement horizon: Less than 1 percent of all Americans will be able to retire at age 65 and maintain their standard of living. Beyond the insecurity of Social Security, here are some other reasons:

- *People live longer.* When our nation's Social Security system was founded in 1935, the average lifespan of a male was about 60 years, that of a female almost 64 years, according to Centers for Disease Control and Prevention statistics. Basically, Social Security was designed to help out those people who lived beyond the norm for the last few years of their lives. It wasn't designed for what it's been doing over the past generations—helping to fund decades of a person's life. Today, the average life expectancy of a male is just over 74 years, that of a female almost 80 years. That's a major difference in lifespan. It's not unusual for people to spend more time in "retirement" than they did in the workforce. No wonder the Social Security system is in financial trouble.

- *Not everyone takes advantage of retirement plans offered through their employers, and today most employers do not offer traditional pension plans.* Only about half of all private businesses offer workers some type of retirement plan. Within those companies, only about three-quarters of workers participate in those plans, according to Department of Labor numbers. If you have access to a 401(k) or 403(b) plan and your employer makes matching contributions, it makes sense, under most circumstances, to participate at least up to the level of the matching contribution. Not taking advantage of such opportunities basically means you're thumbing your nose at free money. Even if an employer agrees to match contributions up to only $100 a year, that's still free money that grows tax-deferred. If you saw a $1 bill lying on the sidewalk, wouldn't you bend over and pick it up? Or, if the local radio station or video store, grocery store, or department store were giving away $100 with absolutely no strings attached and all you needed to do was sign on the dotted line, wouldn't you jump at the chance?

Why then do so few people fail to take advantage of tax-deferred retirement plans? The oft-uttered excuse is, "I can't afford it." Well, folks, if we can't afford to save for our futures, who's going to? If we can't afford to save now, what makes us think saving will be easier in the future? Time is one of the most powerful concepts when it comes to saving. It can work for or against us. Get started now! There is no better time.

■ *Most Americans have accumulated only a fraction of the amount they will need to retire.* Many don't even bother to figure out how much they'll need. The instant-gratification, credit-crazy, live-beyond-your-means, not-me mentality that's rampant in our society has its repercussions.

HOW MUCH DO YOU REALLY NEED?

As with almost every other aspect of financial planning, the process of figuring out just how much an individual or unmarried couple needs to retire comfortably starts with asking yourself and your partner some questions such as the following:

- Are the two of you committed as a couple for the long haul?
- Do either of you hope to provide for the other should something happen to one of you?
- Do either of you have children, from this relationship or a previous one, who will necessitate your having additional money in retirement?
- How much money will you need annually in retirement to support your standard of living?
- Who will pay for your health care? What should you plan for when it comes to additional out-of-pocket expenses?
- Where will your retirement income come from?
- Does your company offer a pension plan that allows you to name anyone, including a nonspouse, as beneficiary?

The answers to these questions figure into your retirement-planning strategies. If your employer has a sound retirement health care option, you may not need to allocate as much retirement cash to health care as a self-employed person who foots the bill for his or her own health care and faces even greater costs in retirement. But watch out. A number of formerly very strong companies recently have been changing or discontinuing their retiree health insurance benefits. So, it's safer not to count on receiving health insurance benefits paid for or subsidized by your current employer for the duration of your retirement years.

If you're concerned only about your own future and not that of a partner or heirs or leaving money to charity, you won't need much life insurance except, perhaps, to cover the cost of burial and final expenses. If no dependents are involved, that alleviates added costs, as well. (See Chapter 4 for more information on life insurance. We'll address the beneficiary issue on page 171.)

How much money will you really need? To begin with, how long will you live? No one wants to outlive his or her money, and no one knows for certain when he or she will die. Therefore, figure you'll need more money than the life expectancy charts say you'll need. In case you think you won't live longer than the "average" person, how many women do you know older than 79? How many men older than 74? That could be you! "Average" life expectancy means that about half the people will live longer than the average. Life expectancy has more to do with heredity and improvements in medical science than anything else. Play if safe. Assume you'll outlive the current life expectancy tables. One of the last things any of us wants is to wake up one morning broke. No one wants to outlive his or her money. Many advisors suggest a minimum life expectancy assumption of 95 to 100 years—which is well beyond what current life expectancy tables indicate. But is even that enough? Only time will tell. Plan conservatively.

WARNING *When making projections about how much money you and your partner will need in retirement, always figure using ten or more years longer than the life expectancy charts indicate.*

Consider some rather sobering numbers on how much capital it takes to generate monthly income based on a sustainable 4 percent a year withdrawal rate, no matter the time period (numbers courtesy of The Garrett Planning Network, Inc.).

It takes $300,000 in capital to generate just $1,000 a month, $600,000 to provide $2,000 a month, $900,000 for $3,000 a month, and $1.2 million in capital to provide $4,000 a month. (Those numbers assume a balanced portfolio of equities and fixed-income investments over the long term and a 3 percent annual rate of inflation.)

What's the total monthly income for you and your partner? Do the two of you currently save enough to accumulate the funds needed to sustain your standard of living in retirement? Chances are the answer to that question is no.

Again, let's look at some numbers from The Garrett Planning Network, Inc., also shown in Figure 7.1. If you're age 18 and start saving today, you will need to save $48 a month—every month, every year—until retirement at age 65 in order to get only $1,000 a month in retirement income. You will need to save $193 a month to generate $4,000 a month. If you're age 30 today, under the same circumstances, it will take savings of $131 a month to generate $1,000 a month in retirement, or $523 a month to produce $4,000 a month. Even scarier is the fact that, if you and your partner are 50 years old today, you will need to save $867 a month to get only $1,000 a month in retirement, or $3,468 a month to get $4,000 a month. If you are 60 years old and need $1,000 a month in retirement just

---

FIGURE 7.1 Increase Savings

The following illustrates how much money a person, depending on his or her current age, must save monthly to receive the monthly retirement income as indicated.*

To fund $1,000/month in retirement:

Age	$/Month Savings
18	$ 48
25	86
30	131
35	201
40	315
45	509
50	867
55	1,640
60	4,083

To fund $2,000/month in retirement:

Age	$/Month Savings
18	$ 97
25	172
30	262
35	403
40	631
45	1,019
50	1,734
55	3,280
60	8,166

To fund $3,000/month in retirement:

Age	$/Month Savings
18	$ 145
25	258
30	392
35	604
40	946
45	1,528
50	2,601
55	4,919
60	12,249

To fund $4,000/month in retirement:

Age	$/Month Savings
18	$ 193
25	344
30	523
35	805
40	1,262
45	2,037
50	3,468
55	6,559
60	16,332

*Assumes a balanced portfolio of equities and fixed-income investments over the long term and a 3% annual rate of inflation.

Source: The Garrett Planning Network, Inc.

5 years from now, you will have to put away an extra $4,083 a month—or $16,332 a month to get $4,000 a month. Pretty eye-opening numbers. (Those numbers assume no other retirement savings, an 8 percent rate of return, and retirement at age 65.)

In other words, if you're 50 today, you will need to save 87 percent of your current gross income to maintain your standard of living in retirement, presuming that you want to retire at age 65 and haven't yet started saving. That's impossible. You would have to save more than you bring in after taxes. If you couldn't save 4 percent of your income up until now, how can you expect to save 20 percent, 40 percent, or even more at this point?

Only a few variables exist in retirement planning: save more, spend less, work longer, or die earlier. However, dying earlier isn't really a planning strategy. Therefore, beyond saving more and spending less, and avoiding being too conservative in your investment strategies, the only other variable is working longer.

HOW MUCH DO YOU NEED TO SAVE?

The following table shows the percent of income an individual needs to save to maintain his or her current standard of living in retirement, depending on his or her age at the onset of saving.

Age	Savings as a Percent of Income (%)
18	5%
25	9
30	13
35	20
40	32
45	51
50	87

Work Longer

Instead of panicking because you've buried your head in the proverbial sand all these years and failed to save seriously for retirement, forget the preconceived notion that age 65 automatically means you retire. Let go of the unhealthy notion of "retirement" in your 60s or before as the ultimate definition of success. The concept of "traditional retirement age" is only about three generations old. People throughout the ages and long before Social Security worked in some capacity all their lives.

It's human nature to want to be involved and a productive member of society, regardless or your age. Most of us, therefore, need to rethink the notion of retirement. Perhaps the healthiest and most attainable goal may be to work part-time in your current career or reinvent yourself in another field. If you love what you do, you can do what you love for a very long time.

WARNING *Times have changed. We all need to adjust to the fact that retirement is not cut-and-dried at 65.*

Many older couples today already have accepted the inevitability of a deferred retirement—either by default or out of necessity. The necessity is the result of soaring costs of living, exorbitant health care costs, and an unwillingness to cut back.

A recent AARP study, in fact, showed that more than 80 percent of older Americans plan to work in retirement, either out of financial necessity (one-third of those responding yes) or by choice (two-thirds). The "retirement crisis," it seems, is what you make of it. Maybe it really isn't a crisis but a wake-up call to reality. Age 65 isn't old anymore. Today's workforce doesn't engage in manual labor so much as mental labor. It's healthy to continue participating in culture and in society. How many older people do you know who have faded or wasted away after they "retired"? Perhaps instead of viewing age 65 as a preordained retirement age, Americans might want to consider this as the next chapter in their working lives.

Increase Savings

You've already seen the shocking reality of just how much saving it takes today to generate retirement income for tomorrow. Instead of throwing up your hands, consider some of the things you can do easily, which, when combined with other strategies, will boost retirement income.

Foremost, individuals and couples need to take full advantage of all the retirement savings vehicles available. Some of them include:

- *Traditional IRA.* If you're not covered by a qualified retirement plan or if you earn less than $55,000 a year, you're eligible for a tax deduction for contributions up to $3,000 for qualified individuals ($3,500 for those age 50 and over) for 2004, $4,000 and $4,500 respectively for 2005. Earnings grow tax-deferred until withdrawn and then are taxed at personal income tax rates. A 10 percent penalty is assessed on early withdrawals before age $59\frac{1}{2}$, with some exceptions; mandatory withdrawals begin at age $70\frac{1}{2}$ with no additional contributions allowed.
- *Roth IRA.* All contributions are made with after-tax dollars. The entire amount grows tax-deferred with no tax due at withdrawal as long as contributions satisfy the five-year holding period and you don't withdraw the money until you're at least age $59\frac{1}{2}$. A 10 percent early withdrawal penalty applies with income tax due only on earnings. There is no mandatory age for withdrawal, and you may contribute as long as you have earned income and your modified adjusted gross income does not exceed $110,000 (in 2004). The 2005 maximum contribution limit is $4,000 ($4,500 for people age 50 and older).
- *401(k) and other qualified retirement plans.* This is a defined-contribution employee benefits plan in which employee contributions are deducted pretax from an employee's paycheck. Earnings grow tax-deferred until withdrawn, then are taxed at individual income tax rates. Employers may match a portion of the employee's contribution. Beware of maximum annual contribution limits: in 2004, they were $13,000 for people up to age 50 and $16,000 for people 50 and

up; in 2005, limits were $14,000 for people up to age 50, $18,000 for people 50 and over.

■ *Small business/self-employed retirement plans.* SEP-IRA (Simplified Employee Pension Plan), SIMPLE IRA (Savings Incentive Match Plan for Employees), and one-person 401(k) plans allow business owners to save pretax dollars for retirement. These plans have the same advantages of 401(k) plans, except most offer no matching funds (the SIMPLE obviously does call for a match). The maximum contribution limits are as follows:

■ *SIMPLE.* 2004: $9,000 under age 50, $10,500 for age 50 and up. 2005: $10,000 and $12,000, respectively.

■ *SEP.* 2004: 25 percent of net income or $41,000, whichever is less. 2005: the $41,000 maximum is subject to cost-of-living adjustments.

■ *One-person 401(k).* 2004: 100 percent of compensation up to $41,000. 2005: the $41,000 maximum is subject to cost-of-living adjustments.

Reduce Expenses

One of the quickest and easiest ways to save is simply to cut back. That's right. Want to save a fast 12 percent of your net income? Stop squandering your money. It's estimated that Americans fritter away about 12 percent of their net income. That money just disappears, and no one can account for where or how it's been spent. It's the little things such as the latté you buy every day on the way to work or the extra soda you buy at lunch. All that adds up. You and your partner don't have to pinch pennies, but if both of you simply pay attention to what you spend and how you spend it, you could save 12 percent. That certainly can add a sizable chunk to your retirement savings.

A wealth of products is available to help you keep track of your spending. One of the best is a computerized version of the old-fashioned envelope cash flow management system. Many of our parents or grandparents managed their money with a bundle of envelopes and a shoebox. Each category of expenses had its own envelope, and the cash budgeted for each category was placed into the corresponding envelope or box every month. Mvelopes.com from Utah-based In2M Corporation (http://www.mvelopes.com) does the same thing, except it does so with a sophisticated software tool. Another alternative is to use a cash management program like Quicken or Microsoft Money. These software packages can either duplicate your existing checkbook or replace it entirely. Couples, especially, may want to check out these tools as simple ways to manage their money with savings in mind.

YOURS, MINE, AND/OR OURS

Retirement planning for unmarried couples is an extension of the retirement planning each individual already has in place with one big caveat: Pay close attention to ownership of assets and beneficiary designations. Protecting your assets is just as important as getting the most bang for your retirement savings buck.

Inequities Magnified

No matter how committed partners are to each other or how long they've been together, if a couple splits up or something happens to one partner, the other could be out of luck if he or she doesn't have individual retirement savings. That's because retirement savings issues magnify any financial inequities among unmarried couples.

For starters, unmarried couples are not eligible for a Qualified Domestic Relations Order, or QDRO. Remember, that's the federal mandate that enables divorcing couples to split retirement plan options without penalties. If an unmarried couple saves the majority of their retirement funds in one partner's qualified plan, that partner takes it all if the couple breaks up. The only way to split these assets between the partners is if the plan has a very generous hardship provision and the partner is willing to pay huge tax and early withdrawal penalties. A domestic partnership agreement also could stipulate that assets be shared.

A married couple, John, 42, and Mary, 39, have saved the equivalent of $500,000 in John's retirement plan. Mary's employer offers a lousy retirement plan, so she puts nothing in it, opting instead to help increase John's retirement contribution. But the couple decides to divorce. Because of QDRO rules, they immediately split the assets from John's plan tax- and penalty-free, no sweat. John rolls over $250,000 into a retirement account for Mary; the dollars continue to grow tax-deferred, and both continue to save in their individual accounts until they reach 70½, the mandatory age to start withdrawing the money. Of course, taxes are due after that based on the amount withdrawn at the time. If the couple hadn't divorced and John died before reaching retirement age, that would be no problem, either. Mary automatically would roll the entire amount into an IRA and would start taking distributions at age 70½, or sooner if necessary. Once again, assets of married and divorcing partners are transferred seamlessly.

On the other hand, if John and Mary were not married and saved the same amount of money in the same manner, their options would be far less rosy should they decide to split up:

- John can't withdraw any of the money if he still is employed by the company where he has his retirement account, unless the company has a very generous hardship provision.
- If John no longer works at the company and he and Mary want to split equally that $500,000, he can withdraw Mary's $250,000 share from his account. He immediately owes a 10 percent early withdrawal penalty on that money, or $25,000, plus income taxes on that amount, added to his regular income. (The early withdrawal penalty does not apply if a person is at least age 59½ at the time of the withdrawal and in other special circumstances.) Mary does not receive the money in a tax-deferred retirement plan. It's cash instead. One caveat: This strategy may require that John roll over the money into an IRA first before withdrawing Mary's share.
- If the couple wants to access the funds, they have another possible course of action. John can borrow from his retirement account if his employer offers that option. He will have to repay the funds with

interest, according to the terms of the loan, which usually calls for quarterly payments made with after-tax dollars over a period of five years. If he doesn't pay the money back, he faces the early withdrawal penalty and income taxes due on the withdrawal.

- John flatly rejects the notion of sharing any retirement plan funds with Mary. After all, he then would face tax and withdrawal penalties and lose the tax-deferred growth on the money. Mary walks away with absolutely no retirement savings and has no legal recourse or claim to that money if the couple didn't have a domestic partnership agreement that stipulated otherwise.

- In a worst-case scenario, if the couple is near retirement age—and Mary never has worked and therefore doesn't meet the minimum qualifications for Social Security—she will not be eligible for Social Security retirement benefits, either.

- Without the proper planning, Mary gets nothing from the retirement plan if John dies, no matter what his age, unless it's a defined-contribution plan and she's the named beneficiary.

If two partners insist on overfunding one partner's retirement plan, the couple also should have a domestic partnership agreement that stipulates how the other partner will be compensated in the event the relationship ends. How will the partner with the big retirement fund pay off his or her partner? Tapping the retirement fund early may not be possible. At a minimum, it will result in penalties and tax liabilities, not to mention the loss of continued tax-deferred growth on that money. It's not a very sensible option. So what else is there?

The solution to the dilemma that unmarried couples face is two-pronged, involving individual savings and naming the proper beneficiaries.

Individual Savings

Each partner needs to save individually for retirement. Even if an employer offers no retirement plan or the retirement plan has poor investment options and/or no employer matching contribution, that's still no reason not to save. Without individual retirement assets, partners in an unmarried relationship could end up with nothing. From an investment standpoint, it may be advantageous to take full advantage of one partner's retirement plan while not contributing to the other's plan. If one partner has an excellent 401(k) profit-sharing plan with great employer matching contributions and the other doesn't, the couple may be inclined to direct all their money into the better retirement account. But if they split up or fail to plan properly, one partner could come up with empty pockets. Remember, solid financial planning is about covering all your bases in the event of unforeseen problems. It's preparing for the unexpected.

Gregg and Pat, both 62, had been together 12 years. Gregg has a great 401(k) through his employer that includes matching contributions. He had hoped to begin tapping into the money in 3 years, when he hits age 65.

In the early years of the couple's relationship, Pat worked as a waitress part-time to supplement their income. But she stopped working when her parents became ill, and her mom eventually died. Not long after that, her dad died, too. That was five years ago. Her dad had worked for energy giant Enron and had accumulated a sizable amount of company stock in his personal portfolio and in an IRA account. He always had encouraged Pat to hold on to the stock, which had been so good to him. Pat, as the sole beneficiary of her father's estate, contacted the brokerage holding both her father's personal and IRA accounts, and had them retitle the accounts. The IRA became an "inherited IRA," and the personal account was retitled into Pat's name. Unfortunately, Pat should have diversified the portfolios at the same time. But she didn't and continued to hold almost all her assets in the stock of one company, Enron.

Occasionally Pat would sell some of the Enron shares from her personal account to supplement her income. She didn't like to do that, though, because then she also had to pay capital gains taxes on a big chunk of the proceeds. It bothered her to pay out her dad's hard-earned money. Like it or not, Pat should have sold all the stock, paid all the capital gains taxes, then reinvested the money in a diversified portfolio of tax-efficient investments. At the very least, Pat should have sold 100 percent of the stock in the IRA immediately upon receiving the inheritance, because the income and capital gains are tax deferred.

Then came the Enron scandal. Overnight, the stock crashed. Suddenly Pat had nothing to supplement her cash flow needs or for retirement. Fortunately, Gregg still had his retirement account, even though Pat hadn't contributed to it.

Should Gregg and Pat break up, though, Pat would be in even more dire financial straits. Gregg pays most of the household expenses and has a sizable retirement plan. But the couple isn't legally married, and they have no domestic partnership agreement.

Pat has no choice but to return to the workforce to help supplement the couple's current cash flow needs and try to save as much as possible for her retirement. Pat's financial crisis also brought to light the importance of the couple putting in place a domestic partnership agreement and estate-planning documents immediately. All their beneficiary designations should be confirmed, too. Marriage, both agree, might be an option. Pat then would qualify for survivor's benefits should something happen to Gregg. Should the couple divorce after ten years of marriage, she also then would share in Gregg's Social Security retirement benefits.

Would you be willing to go to those lengths for your partner? Would you want that kind of protection for yourself? At least Pat and Gregg had the option of marriage. Many unmarried couples don't. Talk to your partner. How and under what circumstances do you want to help out each other financially? What kind of compromises are you willing to make? These all are issues you and your financial planner, if applicable, and your estate-planning attorney need to address to help you achieve complete financial security.

Leslie and Carolyn both were nearing "traditional" retirement age. Leslie had worked for the same company for almost 30 years. She had participated in its 401(k) plan, which offered mediocre investment options, since its inception 15 years earlier. She received a 25 percent employer match annually on the first 6 percent of her compensation, and she contributed 6 percent when she first enrolled so she could get all the available "free money" from her employer. Every time she got a raise, Leslie used half of the wage increase to boost her 401(k) contribution.

After a few years, Leslie was making the maximum allowable contribution by law. Carolyn, on the other hand, didn't feel comfortable invest-

FIGURE 7.2 Two Approaches to Retirement Savings

Here's a simplified look at two different approaches to annual retirement savings—contributing to an employer-sponsored 401(k) with a 25% employer match on the first 6%, and regular investing in certificates of deposit. Assumptions include: $100,000/year salary with no raises, annual contribution is equivalent of 6% of salary, 28% marginal tax rate.

	Approach	
	401(k)	**CD**
Starting Amount	$ 0	$ 0
1990 Year-End Value	8,025	4,428
Assumed Rate of Return	7.0%	2.5%
Total Employee Contributions Over 15 Years	90,000	64,800
Total Employer Contributions Over 15 Years	22,500	0
Total Earnings	89,160	14,603
Account Total after 15 Years	**$201,660***	**$79,403**

* Taxes due as regular income on money as it is withdrawn.

ing in her employer's 401(k) plan. She was concerned because the account was not insured by the Federal Deposit Insurance Corporation, and she feared that if, somehow, the company went out of business, she would lose all her money. Besides, her employer matched only 25 percent of the first 3 percent of compensation anyway, and, as usual, the match was tied to a vesting schedule. Carolyn didn't know how long she would stay with the employer, either, so she opted out of the 401(k) plan. Instead, she put aside 15 percent of her after-tax income and invested it in certificates of deposit with her local bank.

Figure 7.2 takes a simplified look at the contrast between these two approaches to retirement savings.

Money never had been an issue for the couple before. However, as they approached their targeted retirement dates, they consulted with a financial planner and discovered that Carolyn's ultraconservative investment strategies had cost them dearly. Leslie had saved just over $342,800. Her 401(k) had earned just 6.5 percent. Meanwhile, Carolyn had saved just over $228,000 and pays taxes on her earnings every year. The couple can't count on Social Security to fund their retirement financial needs, either. According to some estimates, Social Security only picks up one-third of the average cost of retirement.

The result is that the couple can't afford to retire and maintain their lifestyle. Instead, they'll both have to keep working and try to save as much as possible, while cutting back, and pray neither is laid off, forced into retirement, or tires of the other.

The way around the retirement dilemmas faced by both of these couples is to make equal contributions to each other's respective company-sponsored retirement plans, if available. If not, at least contribute a like amount to the personal portfolio of the partner who does not have the retirement plan. Also, allocate the assets of the portfolios in accordance with the couple's risk tolerance instead of each individual's risk tolerance. (Carolyn and Leslie failed to do that.) If the couple splits up, then it may be necessary to reallocate one or both portfolios.

Plan for the worst. Remember, you don't *plan* to win the lottery. You plan if you *don't* win the lottery.

WARNING *Plan for the worst-case scenario, because planning for the best-case scenario almost always falls short.*

STEPS TO SECURITY

No matter their financial circumstances, age, or sexual orientation, unmarried couples should take the following four steps to save for their retirement, in this order:

1. Both partners should contribute to their own retirement plans, up to the matching amount, if there is one.
2. Each partner, if eligible, should contribute the maximum allowable to Roth IRAs.

3. If any money is left over beyond the first two steps, each partner then should contribute additional money to his or her retirement plan. Ideally the accounts will be fully funded.
4. If any more money is left, fund other investments.

This strategy doesn't necessarily minimize a couple's current income taxes, but it does help to equalize retirement savings. And don't fret that you're overfunding your and your partner's retirement, either. Virtually everyone needs to save that much, but most people won't have that much money to save. If you don't have a retirement plan at work, maximize contributions to a Roth IRA if eligible for it, then look for other tax-efficient ways to save. And make sure that each partner saves in his or her own name.

Some possible low-cost, tax-efficient investment options include index funds and exchange-traded funds (ETFs). An index fund is a mutual fund with a portfolio that mirrors a stock index such as the Standard & Poor's 500 Index, for example. An exchange-traded fund is a pool of stocks that tracks an index but can be bought or sold anytime during the trading day—unlike an ordinary mutual fund, which trades at the close of each trading session. An investor gets the benefits of owning a group of individual stocks without the expense of buying each one separately. They're extremely low cost and tax efficient, because the list of stocks in the pool doesn't change very often and can be purchased through a discount broker online or in person. Some examples of ETFs include Barclay's iShares (http://www.ishares.com); Nasdaq-100 Index, known as a QQQ; Standard & Poor's Depositary Receipt (SPDR), known as a Spider or Spyder; and Vanguard's VPRs. Good sources of information about ETFs include MSN's Microsoft Money Central (http://msn.moneycentral.com) and Barclay's (http://www.ishares.com).

Unmarried partners also should consider using annuities to supplement each other's income in retirement, especially when one partner is not eligible for Social Security benefits. An annuity is a vehicle in which an individual invests either a lump sum or makes periodic payments for a specified time to a tax-deferred account. The account then grows at either a fixed rate (fixed annuity) or a rate that varies with its underlying investments (variable annuity). At any given time, the account can be annuitized—it's paid out as a steady income stream over a specified period of time. An individual can tap the equity or assets in the account to be paid out in regular amounts over time.

Scott and Fintan knew that, as a same-sex couple, they wouldn't be eligible for each other's Social Security survivor benefits. That worried Fintan, who was an artist and had only a small IRA as retirement savings. The solution, Scott realized, was to fund a fixed annuity that would provide Fintan with his Social Security benefit equivalent of $1,000 a month for 30 years (Fintan's life expectancy at retirement). By using an online annuity calculator (http://www.immediateannuities.com and http://www .annuity.com are two of the dozens out there), Scott determined that he would need approximately $209,000 to fund Fintan's retirement income stream.

WARNING *Couples with a stay-at-home partner who doesn't qualify for Social Security benefits may want to consider marriage, if that's an option. It automatically qualifies that individual for immediate Social Security benefits, if necessary.*

Strategies for Your Situation

Say one partner has a good retirement plan through his or her employer, but the other partner doesn't qualify for a Roth IRA because he or she made too much money and has no 401(k). The couple might consider funding a traditional IRA account and a personal retirement investment account in the name of the partner who doesn't qualify for the Roth. The couple also should fund equally the other partner's qualified retirement plan and Roth IRA, if eligible.

In another scenario, if one partner doesn't work outside the home and isn't eligible for Social Security, you may want to rethink the idea of marriage, if it's an option for you, solely for benefits' reasons. As an unmarried partner ineligible for Social Security (without 40 credits or 40 quarters—ten years—of paying into the Social Security system), he or she will not qualify to receive Social Security benefits but can receive a portion of a spouse's benefits. (For information on Social Security benefits, eligibility, and more, check out the Social Security Administration's Web site, http://www.socialsecurity.gov.)

BENEFICIARY DESIGNATIONS

Without the benefit of laws pertaining to married couples, it's important that unmarried couples take the time and make the effort to name their designated beneficiaries of tax-deferred retirement accounts, life insurance policies, personal investment portfolios, and other retirement vehicles. A surviving partner of an unmarried couple is not the automatically designated beneficiary. (Beneficiary designations take precedence over wills or trusts.)

That means if a partner wants a surviving partner as the beneficiary of his or her 401(k), it does no good simply to talk about it. A formal beneficiary designation must be on file with the administrator of the 401(k). It's also a good idea to keep a copy of the document.

WARNING *Periodically check to make sure all your beneficiary designations are current with your wishes.*

Stay Up-to-Date

Partners in newer or casual relationships generally designate family members or friends as beneficiaries of retirement plans. These people remain constant in their lives as opposed to partners, who may come and go. If a person does want a current partner to be a beneficiary of a retirement plan, here's a note of caution: If you split up with that partner and no longer want him or her to be your beneficiary, don't forget to change the official beneficiary designation.

The same is true for long-term, committed couples. Pay attention to beneficiary designations. That sounds simple enough, but partners often forget to do so.

Lou and Marion ended their relationship on a bitter note. One day, Marion walked through the door of the couple's condo and announced she was leaving. That was it. No warning. One day she was just gone. The couple had comingled assets but had no domestic partnership agreement. As a result, they battled over the assets for two years. In the end, not surprisingly, they were sworn enemies. Fast-forward ten years. Lou receives a certified letter from Marion's former employer. Lou discovers he's the designated beneficiary of Marion's retirement plan. Marion, who died unexpectedly, had forgotten to change the plan's beneficiary. While she was alive, she often declared that she wouldn't give Lou a plugged nickel if he was the last man on earth. Now, he's inheriting her hard-earned money.

Kelly had been married previously to a man who physically abused her. Then she met Liza, and the two committed to each other. That was six years ago. Kelly, an Army reservist on active duty in Iraq, was killed in action. Unfortunately, she had neglected to remove her ex-husband as designated beneficiary of her retirement plan at work. He got her money. Liza lost her partner and got stuck with the bills.

If you are serially monogamous and make each successive partner the new beneficiary of your retirement plan, you'll need to update your wills or trusts and change beneficiaries on all your documents when you change partners. (Remember: Beneficiary designations take precedence over wills.)

Don't forget, too, that changing beneficiaries is more than a one-stop job. Potentially, you may have to change the beneficiary designations on various IRAs, life insurance policies, 401(k) plans, pension plans, and TOD/POD accounts. Otherwise, ten years down the road, that ex may end up with your hard-earned cash.

The Right Beneficiary

For unmarried couples, choosing the right beneficiary isn't a matter of automatically naming your partner. Instead, you should take into account the financial self-sufficiency of the person or people you're considering. You could designate your partner, or someone else, as your beneficiary. For example, Ben's partner, Max, was independently wealthy. But Ben's widowed sister, Stella, 37, was raising two kids on her own and had trouble making ends meet. Ben decided to leave his IRA to Stella, because that made financial and emotional sense to him, and Max supported Ben's decision.

Lisa and Tina, on the other hand, decided to designate each other as beneficiaries of their 401(k) plans, because they both had saved a lot but at the expense of life's luxuries. That solution didn't come easily to the couple. They discussed at length several other possible beneficiaries before deciding on each other. If you are a committed couple, take the time and make the effort to discuss the matter with each other and your families. It's much better for all involved to be aware of your wishes than to be blindsided after you're dead. There's also less chance that someone will challenge your wishes if they know about them up front.

Michael and Jane were comfortable financially and set for their retirement when Michael's dad died, leaving him significant assets. The couple talked at length about what Michael should do with the inheritance. Because he and Jane didn't need the money, and because he wanted to keep the assets in the family, Michael decided to designate his two nephews—both just starting out in business—as beneficiaries of the inherited assets.

MORE ISSUES AND CONCERNS

Another Catch-22

If you no longer work at a company or institution and have your old 401(k) or 403(b) money sitting there, don't assume that your former employer will allow your partner (nonspouse beneficiary) to roll over the money into an IRA if you pass away unexpectedly. Many retirement plans discriminate against unmarried couples by forcing a nonspouse beneficiary to take a taxable lump-sum distribution for the entire balance. On the other hand, a surviving spouse can roll over the entire balance into an IRA that doesn't have to be tapped until age 70½.

It is imperative that you check with your plan's administrator to find out its policy on nonspouse beneficiaries. If the plan forces a nonspouse beneficiary to take a taxable lump-sum distribution, you may want to roll the money over into an IRA instead. But if you do that, keep in mind that the IRA may not offer the same creditor protection as the 401(k), so you may need to weigh its pros and cons.

Erin quit her job for a better one elsewhere. She had significant savings in her 401(k) and was concerned how to handle it, especially because the plan's beneficiary was her long-time partner, Jeff. After talking with her CFP®, Erin called her ex-company's 401(k) plan administrator to find out the plan's rules on nonspouse beneficiaries. To her surprise, plan rules stipulate that if she were to die, Jeff, as a nonspouse beneficiary, would have to take the entire balance as a taxable lump-sum distribution, so she decided to roll the money over into an IRA and designate Jeff the beneficiary. The laws governing IRA distribution would allow him to stretch withdrawals out over his life expectancy.

Do It Yourself

Retirement is one area of financial planning where you definitely can get a head start by doing everything you can to educate yourself. Plenty of good retirement planning calculators, information resources, and more are available at various Internet sites from all kinds of companies. A few of those sites include:

- http://www.quicken.com
- http://www.financecenter.com
- http://www.smartmoney.com
- http://www.troweprice.com
- http://money.cnn.com
- http://moneycentral.msn.com
- http://finance.yahoo.com

- http://www.nasdaq.com
- http://www.nyse.com

More informative sites are listed in Chapter 10 and the Addendum.

But a word to the wise as far as calculators and planning and investing software are concerned: It's all only as good as its built-in assumptions—garbage in, garbage out. Some people use these calculators without thinking about the assumptions. For example, a proposed investment plan may count on a 10 percent average annual return for the rest of your life, when in reality your actual return may amount to only 4 percent. The projections then stray far from reality and are essentially useless. Also, pay attention to life expectancies factored into calculators and programs. As we've discussed, many of us will live much longer than the "average." You had better count on potentially living a very long time.

Consider visiting with a qualified Certified Financial Planner™ and confirming your retirement plans and projections. The last thing you want to happen is to base all of your plans on faulty assumptions or inadequate information. This is your future we're talking about. Invest in yourself! For a list of personal financial advisors who provide advice on an hourly, as-needed basis, visit http://www.GarrettPlanningNetwork .com, and for advisors serving nontraditional couples and families, visit http://www.PridePlanners.org.

BOTTOM LINES

Retirement planning, whether done individually or as a couple, is really a trade-off. Do you want to see the money in your paycheck today or invest it in your future? It's now versus later. It's very tempting for us to say now and neglect later. But we must find a healthy compromise. More planning now leads to a more secure tomorrow.

For every couple, of every age and sexuality, almost any financial situation can be improved.

As a couple and as an individual, if you do nothing else, at a minimum do the following:

- *Social Security.* Don't plan your retirement cash needs around Social Security. Chances are it won't be there for you, or it won't be nearly enough.
- *Life expectancy.* Figure you'll live much longer than the current life-expectancy charts indicate. Those numbers are averages, and you wouldn't want to outlive your money.
- *Retirement age.* Get over thinking of age 65 as time for retirement. That's an unhealthy notion—and one most Americans can't afford, anyway.
- *Roth IRAs.* Don't overlook Roth IRAs if you qualify. Earnings are tax deferred, and better yet, withdrawals in retirement are *tax free.* You can't beat that!
- *Tax-advantaged retirement plans.* Maximize funding of all tax-advantaged retirement plans available to you, including those from your employer. The plan doesn't need to have the "greatest" investment options. Put the money in it anyway. It's automatic, the contributions are tax deductible, the earnings grow tax deferred, and there might even be an employer match. Do it!
- *QDROs.* Pay attention to and maintain individual and equal retirement-asset ownership, because partners don't qualify for a QDRO, which allows spouses to divide and roll over pension assets in the event of divorce.
- *Beneficiaries.* Unmarried couples also must pay attention to beneficiary designations as they relate to pension and retirement benefits. Wills and trusts do not take precedence over beneficiary designations for IRAs and other retirement accounts.

CHAPTER | **8**

Other Legal and Personal Issues

When two people say, "I do," as in getting married, they in essence sign a legal contract and agree to abide by the rules implicit in that marriage contract. Those rules cover everything from ownership and division of property while both are living and when either dies, to financial support in the event a relationship ends through separation or divorce.

Unmarried couples, on the other hand, don't share their relationship within the context of an automatic legal contract. Instead, they must build their own framework, using legal documentation, financial strategies, and personal commitments. To create their own contract, unmarried couples may initiate certain legal agreements that clarify and iron out differences and lay down ground rules. It all needs to be spelled out on paper—signed, witnessed, and preferably notarized.

Agreements between unmarried partners may face court challenges at some point, so it's a good idea to work with an attorney experienced with such documents and situations. Do-it-yourself resources like http://www.Nolo.com and http://www.LawDepot.com are excellent ways to familiarize yourself with the issues and view samples of various documents, but it's important to finalize any documents with an attorney who is an expert in these matters. Check out http://www.PridePlanners.org

for a list of member attorneys who specialize in working with nontraditional couples and families.

In this chapter we will look more closely at some of the issues and agreements that unmarried couples would be wise to consider.

DOMESTIC PARTNERSHIP AGREEMENTS

Whenever two individuals of any age or sexual orientation commit to each other as a couple, the partners should establish up front each others' rights, obligations, and responsibilities to their relationship and living situation. As we've mentioned in earlier chapters, that's done with the help of a domestic partnership agreement, also known as a living-together or cohabitation agreement or contract. A sample agreement is provided in Figure 8.1.

This agreement goes far beyond discussing what each partner would like to see happen in the relationship, and it isn't about sex or undying love. A domestic partnership agreement details in writing the rights, responsibilities, and obligations of each partner in the relationship, and in the event of dissolution of the partnership. It's a legal contract.

Think of a domestic partnership agreement as a contract similar to that of marriage—but for unmarried couples. It's designed to protect both you and your partner as well as your and your partner's loved ones.

Chapter 1 discussed the rather unromantic but very necessary *business* of coupling. Consider a domestic partnership agreement your employment contract for that business. It provides a job description and lays the foundation for success. After all, if you're an employee of a company, you can't do an adequate job—let alone excel at it—unless you are aware of what's expected of you. A domestic partnership agreement is an unemotional, detailed contract that spells out what's required of each partner as it relates to financial issues and how those obligations will be carried out. If a couple also would like to write down their personal obligations and expectations for the relationship, they can do so in a separate document, perhaps an addendum to the main partnership agreement. If a domestic partnership agreement ever does end up in court, personal details possibly could overshadow the real issues in the dispute.

Some solid advice for unmarried partners of any age or sexual orientation: Don't share any kind of commitment, don't merge any assets, don't share parenting or a household operating account or even buy a chair together, until you have a domestic partnership agreement in place. That may sound unrealistic, but it's the best way to protect yourself. In reality, most people explore living together before spending a lot of money on lawyers drafting living-together agreements. But consider keeping your finances and financial commitments separate until after you have the proper documents in place.

Below, we briefly examine some of the many issues a couple may want to address in their domestic partnership agreement. The following seems like a lot to think about, but it's not—especially considering that married couples have hundreds of laws that apply to them and govern how situations will be resolved.

FIGURE 8.1 Domestic Partnership Agreement

DOMESTIC PARTNERSHIP AGREEMENT
(EXAMPLE ONLY)

We, the undersigned, Mary Hendricks ("Hendricks") of Kansas and Samantha Gavin ("Gavin") of Kansas agree to share living quarters indefinitely for the following reasons and with the following conditions:

I. **Representations**
   A. Each of the parties hereby represents to the other:
      1. that she is not married and has no other domestic partner;
      2. that she is at least 18 years of age and has the capacity to enter into a contract; and
      3. that they share their residence and intend to do so indefinitely.

II. **Independent Persons**
    The parties enter their domestic partnership as independent persons. Each of the parties has achieved a measure of material independence, and each party agrees not to claim any interest in the property accumulated by the other party before or after the effective date of this Agreement, or in any of the income or appreciation derived from it, except as provided in this Agreement.

(continued)

FIGURE 8.1 Domestic Partnership Agreement, continued

III. Property Rights; No Support

A. The parties hereby define and clarify their respective rights in the property each owned prior to the effective date of this Agreement and in any property they might accumulate after the effective date of this agreement.

1. The parties agree that, except as specifically set forth herein, all property owned by either of them prior to the effective date of this Agreement, all property acquired after the date of this Agreement, and all income derived from it and all increases in the value of it shall remain their respective separate property. Each party may acquire other separate property in the future as a result of income or proceeds from or increase in the value of existing separate property or by income, earnings, gift, or inheritance. The parties agree that any transmutation of any of their separate property interests into shared property shall be by their express written agreement.

2. The parties currently cohabit real property commonly known as [1127 Plains Drive, Emerald City, Kansas] (the "Residence"). The Residence is owned solely by Hendricks. The parties will contribute equal amounts to mortgage payments and all other costs and expenses related to the Residence, including but not limited to taxes, insurance, utilities, upgrades, and maintenance.

3. In the event the parties jointly acquire any real or personal property (the "Shared Property"), they shall list a full description of such property on a schedule entitled Schedule A, which shall be maintained with this Agreement. They shall record on such Schedule the method of acquisition and any amounts contributed by each party to the purchase and to the maintenance, repair, and improvement of such property. Ownership in such Shared Property shall be in proportion to each party's contribution to the purchase and maintenance, unless otherwise agreed in writing.

4. In the event of the death of either party, the ownership of the Residence and all Shared Property shall be vested in the survivor. Each party agrees to execute a will or other estate planning documents that comply with the provisions of this section. Life insurance will also be secured and maintained on both parties to cover any remaining mortgage, and possible estate and inheritance taxes.

5. In the event of the termination of this Agreement as provided herein, Hendricks shall retain title to and possession of the Residence in exchange for payment to Gavin of the greater of (a) the amount of actual contributions paid by Gavin for costs and expenses related to the Residence, or (b) fifty percent (50%) of the appraised value of the Residence and a $2,000 relocation reimbursement allowance. For purposes hereof, the "appraised value" shall be the value as determined by a qualified appraiser selected by mutual agreement of the parties less the remaining amount of any mortgage on the Residence. In the event the parties cannot agree on an appraiser, each

FIGURE 8.1 Domestic Partnership Agreement, continued

shall select an appraiser and the two appraisers shall select a third appraiser who shall conduct the appraisal. Payment is due within 90 days of the date of written notice of termination of this agreement.

6. In the event of the termination of this Agreement as provided herein, the parties shall determine which items of Shared Property each party shall continue to hold. In the event the parties are unable to reach agreement, the Shared Property shall be sold and the proceeds divided among the parties in proportion to their contributions to such Shared Property as set forth on Schedule A.

B. Neither party has any right to support or other compensation from the other party in consequence of cohabitation or this Agreement. No agreement for support by one party of the other shall be effective unless in writing signed by both parties.

IV. **Effective Date**
The effective date of this agreement is March 1, 2004.

V. **Miscellaneous**

A. Except as otherwise herein contained, the parties hereto may give, devise, or bequeath any of their property to the survivor or to third parties and may make gifts or other conveyances to each other or to third parties at any time.

B. Each party hereby acknowledges the following:

1. She has had a full opportunity to examine this Agreement and to confer with her separate counsel concerning the same and is satisfied that she has been adequately represented and has had all rights and obligations fully explained to her.

2. She has ascertained and weighed all of the facts, conditions, and circumstances likely to influence her judgment herein and she clearly understands and freely and voluntarily consents to all of the provisions hereof.

3. She has entered into this Agreement freely and voluntarily after taking into account the advice of her own legal counsel.

4. This Agreement contains the entire understanding of the parties. There are no representations, warranties, promises, covenants, or undertakings, oral or otherwise, other than those expressly set forth herein.

C. This Agreement shall inure to the benefit of and shall be binding upon the parties hereto and their respective heirs, personal representatives, and assigns.

D. This Agreement is made and executed in the State of Kansas, and this agreement shall be construed under the laws of the State of Kansas.

E. This Agreement may be amended if both parties so agree in writing. It may not be modified orally.

(continued)

FIGURE 8.1 Domestic Partnership Agreement, continued

F. Either party may dissolve the parties' domestic partnership and terminate this Agreement by giving notice to the effect to the other party (which notice may be verbal or in writing), or by moving out of their shared Residence and establishing a new primary residence that the parties do not share, or if either party enters into another such agreement with another person, or marries. Upon such dissolution/termination, the Residence or Shared Property of the parties shall be divided as set forth herein.

G. If Hendricks initiates dissolution/termination, Gavin will have 60 days to secure alternative residency and fully vacate the property. If Gavin initiates dissolution/termination of partnership, she will have 15 days to fully vacate the property.

IN WITNESS WHEREOF, the parties hereto have executed and delivered this agreement as of the date first above written.

Dated: _____   _____

Dated: _____   _____

WITNESSES:

Dated: _____   _____

Dated: _____   _____

Domestic partnership agreements can be as basic or as detailed as a couple decide. Whatever the choice, however, it's always a good idea to include a provision that lays out a mechanism for resolving disputes and differences of opinion, especially when money is involved. It's also wise to sign and date the document in the presence of a witness, or preferably a notary public, in case it ever makes its way to court.

Paying the Mortgage or Rent and Household Bills

One of the first matters a couple must discuss is how to pay housing costs. We've talked about some of the options and their ramifications in earlier chapters. Will they split the monthly mortgage or rent 50-50 or, perhaps, alternate who writes the check each month? Will the partner with the larger income pay the entire mortgage or rent, or will partners share in the expenses some other way? Remember, don't automatically assume that the mortgage or rent should be split 50-50, because doing so could cause financial hardships and ultimately harm the relationship.

Remember the stories of couples we've talked about throughout this book who decided to split household expenses 50-50 despite what, in some cases, were vast differences in the partners' incomes. The couples' relationships suffered, because they hadn't thought through the division of expenses—including saving and investing—up front. If each couple had set up a domestic partnership agreement based on an honest assessment of their situation, they undoubtedly could have avoided many headaches—and heartaches.

More contingencies. When couples draft their domestic partnership agreements, they also should consider what will happen if one partner can't meet his or her monthly obligation or, in a worse scenario, is laid off or becomes unable to work due to health problems. If he or she had been contributing to the mortgage or rent, how will the shortfall be handled? Will the other partner pick up the financial slack, or will the couple tap into an emergency fund set up for just such a contingency? If they do draw on the emergency fund, how will that money be replaced?

Who will be responsible for paying the utilities, which include power, sewer, cable, Internet connection, phone bills, and more? Whose name will be on the accounts? Will partners divide the bills and pay them individually? Will they each contribute 50-50 into a joint household account? Many of the same issues regarding paying the mortgage apply to household bills, too. What happens if the phone bill is exorbitant one month? Will the perpetrator be responsible for picking up the above-normal costs? Who will pay for food? Picking up the tab for one trip to 7-Eleven won't break a budget, but the cost of a year's worth of quick trips can add up to quite a chunk. Who will foot the bill for the couple's entertainment?

Also, include a clause on how a difference of opinion or protest will be handled.

Detailed or not. However you and your partner decide to answer these questions and subsequently meet the mortgage or rent, the important thing is to define the obligation so clearly in your domestic partnership agreement that it is indisputable. Be as detailed or as simple as you and your partner like. These financial details, if addressed up front and early in a relationship, can make a big difference over the long haul. Far too many relationships, unmarried and married alike, unravel because of lack of communication and inability to compromise over money.

Emergency Funds

Do you and your partner want to set up a joint emergency stash to handle the unexpected or to supplement any shortfall in cash to pay household expenses? If so, how will that stash be funded? Again, will it be divided 50-50, or based on the percentage of household income each partner contributes, or funded by one partner only? Will you stuff the money under the mattress, deposit it in the bank, or invest it? If banked or invested, will the money be placed in a joint or individual account?

Note that emergency funds are just that: for an emergency. They should be readily accessible, or liquid, and as risk free as possible. Check out http://www.Bankrate.com for information on competitive rates on money market accounts. Think twice before investing emergency funds in a stock, stock mutual fund, or commodity. Such vehicles usually are associated with higher risks, and rarely are they as appropriate as a money market account, for example.

Possessions

Will partners keep their individual possessions separate or contribute some or all of them to the relationship? What happens if a partner receives an inheritance during the relationship? Will those assets remain separate? If you have strong preferences, spell out the details in your agreement.

Consider labeling or inventorying your belongings when entering any domestic relationship. That way, if the relationship ends, you'll at least bring out of the relationship the possessions you went into it with.

In Sickness and in Health?

What are each partner's expectations or responsibilities should one of them contract a debilitating disease like cancer, or Alzheimer's, or osteo-arthritis? A disease or accident can befall anyone, young or old, and leave both partners feeling helpless and desperate. The marriage contract says, ". . . for better or worse, in sickness and in health . . ." Do you want the same contractual obligations in your domestic partnership agreement? The answer isn't a simple yes or no. Unmarried partners need to discuss the reality of these potential situations and weigh the ramifications of their decisions

Debt

The issue of who will be responsible for paying current and prior debt needs to be ironed out very carefully. We talked about the pros and cons of various liabilities, including debt, in Chapter 3. Before any partner agrees magnanimously to share every burden with his or her partner, consider all the options and ramifications. It may be fine to pitch in some cash to pick up an occasional bill, but making a commitment in a legal contract to shoulder half the burden is quite another thing.

Kids

Do you or your partner have or want children—either biological or adopted—now or in the future? Partners should be brutally honest with themselves and each other. If your opinions differ, listen respectfully to each other's viewpoints.

Keep in mind, too, that there's nothing wrong with not wanting or having children. Many couples don't. There's nothing wrong with adopting or having children for any adult of any age, either. Whatever a couple decides, the decision should be the conscious decision of both partners, not a situation by default that a partner may regret terribly later on.

If you and your partner decide against children, how will you handle potential parental pressure to have children and heirs? That goes for same-sex couples, too. Are you and your partner open to changing your minds about having children in your lives?

Other Dependents

What happens if, by default or tragedy, one partner must care for his or her parents, a niece or nephew, a best friend's child, or a grandchild? With today's extended and blended families, caring for dependents may be in your future whether you planned for it or not. What would be your partner's responsibilities and obligations, if any, in such a scenario? At the very least, talk about it. Planning, after all, involves considering contingencies.

Breaking-up Provision

Many couples resent the idea of the legal system mucking about in their relationship, but unless couples have some sort of settlement agreement in the event they break up, they're asking for trouble. A breaking-up provision is similar to a prenuptial agreement, without the nuptials. It's become almost standard operating procedure for couples involving wealthy or high-profile partners. But other couples need it, too.

Even if a couple opts for bare-bones detail in their domestic partnership agreement, the details need to be fleshed out in the breaking-up provision. Doing so will make your life and that of your partner much easier in the event the two of you go your separate ways. From a legal standpoint, a detailed breaking-up agreement could keep you out of court.

About possessions. No one likes to broach the "what if this doesn't work out" aspect of a relationship, especially in the beginning, when you're excited, having fun, and in love. But what happens if one partner gets fed up and walks out or falls in love with someone else? That's when fighting, bickering, and downright meanness can make your estranged partner seem like a total stranger. Who will get the house, the car, the pets, the lawn and garden equipment, or the jet skis? One couple had two dogs, and when they split up, each partner took one. Initially both parties felt very strongly about keeping both dogs together no matter what. But reality became something else entirely for this couple, as it does for many others.

What about the contents of the kitchen and the music collection? What will happen to the items you purchased jointly? One young couple lived happily and comfortably together for several years. They had a beautiful, large, waterfront home, a boat, and just about everything else they wanted. They didn't bother to get married or draw up a domestic partnership agreement with breaking-up details because, the duo bragged, "We don't need one." But then Lauren met someone else, fell in love, and decided to marry that person. One evening Bob came home to discover that the house had been emptied completely—down to the drawers and cabinets. All that was left intact was the couple's boat. At least, Bob reasoned, he still had a few pots and pans and some silverware and dishes aboard the boat. Bob's partner also left him with another surprise—all the couple's bills.

More about debt. Any breaking-up provision absolutely needs to address what happens to all the bills. Who will be responsible for picking up the tab? Often the answer isn't as simple as one partner or the other, and then the bickering takes off in earnest. But acrimony is less likely if a couple has a legal and binding document that spells out the responsibilities of each partner. It's back to the *business* of coupling again.

By default, Bob had to pay the couple's debts because his former partner just disappeared and his name was on the accounts. If he hadn't paid off the creditors, his own credit would have been jeopardized. If only the couple had kept their debts separate and laid out contingencies in the event of a breakup, Bob could have avoided his own personal hell. Saddled with debts, Bob had to sell the boat and live in the cavernous house—he closed off half of it—for almost two years before he could afford to move.

Unmarried couples don't have divorce court or legal precedents. They don't have the benefits of a legal marriage contract that spells out asset and liability distribution in the event of dissolution of the relationship. It's up to unmarried couples to provide the legal framework for themselves. And, it's worth repeating, sign it when you're in love, because money takes center stage in a breakup. The letter of the law makes an acrimonious situation emotionally more bearable and less stressful if the terms of a breakup are clearly drawn.

When it comes to partnership agreements, unmarried couples do have one advantage over married ones. They can include anything at all in these agreements. Married couples must accept cut-and-dried, one-size-fits-all marriage laws. An unmarried couple, on the other hand, may have better success at realizing a partner's unusual contribution in the event of dissolution of the relationship.

Geoff and Michael decided to buy a real fixer-upper property. It was cheap because it needed significant updates and repairs. Geoff, a stockbroker, easily made the down payment and agreed to pay the mortgage. Michael, on the other hand, was a construction worker with a much more modest income. And, because of the nature of the construction business, Michael and his fellow workers often were without work and a paycheck. Consequently, he often had considerable extra time, and he had the skills and patience to remodel the house. When the couple drew up their domestic partnership agreement, its breaking-up provision took into account the sweat equity Michael planned to invest in the couple's home. Even though Michael would make no capital contribution to the home, he would receive 50 percent ownership in the property in exchange for refurbishing it.

Housing provisions. A breaking-up agreement also must address what happens to the couple's house in the event of breakup. Will one partner keep it? Who has first right to buy the property and at what price? A sensible way to value the house might be to call for two independent market appraisals and take the average as the buyout price. Where will the money come from to buy out the departing partner? When must this buyout be completed? By what date will the property have to be retitled and the mortgage refinanced, if necessary?

Any agreement also should specify time frames for different eventualities. It's not enough to state, "If we break up, I get the house." Consider the domestic chaos if your partner falls in love with someone else, decides to leave you, but refuses to leave the home that the two of you shared in a respectful fashion.

How soon must a partner move out? When must all of his or her stuff be out? If a couple rent and have a long-term lease, what, if any, financial obligation will the departing partner have toward that lease?

Spell out in your agreement, for instance, that the departing partner and all his or her property must be out within 30 days of receipt of notification of dissolution of the partnership and that the other partner has 90 days to transfer title on the home, 30 days to come up with a written plan to buy out the other partner, and 6 months to come up with the money to do so. Specify when the money will change hands and when the liability, ownership titles, and actual cohabitation cease. In other words, everything that a divorce decree or a separation agreement would include should be spelled out in a domestic partnership agreement.

Dump your hang-ups. It's healthy for all of us to consider these issues. If a relationship doesn't last, how do we want to proceed? We need to overcome the fallacy that laying out a plan in case of a breakup indicates a lack of love or commitment. It's a planning concept that, if not put it in place while times are good, can lead to a legal and emotional nightmare if a relationship sours. A stranger, the judge, then will be the one to untangle what once was a happy couple.

Having a safety net of documents in place doesn't say to a partner, "I love you or trust you less." It means that, as a couple, both partners desire to take care of themselves and each other in the event the unthinkable happens. More importantly, the documents proclaim to you, your partner, your family, your community, and the legal system that, though you choose not to marry or cannot legally marry, your relationship is important and valid enough that you're willing to put in writing your rights, responsibilities, and obligations to that relationship.

LEASE AGREEMENT

Before an unmarried same-sex couple ever starts the house/apartment/condo hunt, they should investigate the cohabitation and partnering laws in their area. Is cohabitation illegal? What are the laws pertaining to same-sex couples? Do any regulations prohibit or restrict leasing by unmarried couples? If you know the law before dealing with potential landlords, you're more likely to avoid possible problems.

Don't sign any property lease or rental agreement without *reading the fine print.* Look for any clauses or language in the contract that mention "cohabitation" or "immoral" or "illegal" actions or behavior. Remember, in many states homosexual activity still is against the law. Pay attention to the details; otherwise, you could find yourselves booted out of a house, condo, or apartment on the whim of a landlord.

Be sure you understand the landlord's policies on tenancy. How long can you have a houseguest? How do they feel about having another tenant move in after the lease is signed? Does a new lease agreement have to be signed by both tenants? Can the terms of the lease be changed in a way that could hurt you and your partner? Remember that both parties to a lease are wholly liable for its terms and payments.

A landlord may allow joint occupancy but allow only one name on the lease. In that situation, the couple also should draw up their own separate agreement regarding each other's obligations and responsibilities toward the lease. Just as with partnering agreements, this one should address matters such as who pays what, when, and how; what happens in the event of dissolution; and so on. Whether or not both partners' names are on the actual lease, it's a good idea for both partners to draw up a lease agreement between themselves.

BOTTOM LINES

You wouldn't buy a house or a car, join a CD club, or sign on any dotted line without reading the fine print first. A football game has its rules, so does a tennis match, golf, a spelling bee, or a game of gin rummy. Why then do so many people move in together and buy things jointly or borrow money jointly without ever bothering to lay down any ground rules?

Unmarried partners simply don't have the benefit of the ground rules provided married couples in the form of the marriage covenants, which set expectations for financial support while married, and divorce laws governing everything from custody of children to division of assets and debts and the terms of distribution should a marriage end. If unmarried couples don't draft their own set of rules, one partner often walks away from the relationship with much less than his or her fair share. Or, if the partners want to fight it out in court, they're subjecting themselves to the whims of a judge and the cost and potential publicity of a court battle.

As a couple and as an individual, if you do nothing else, at a minimum do the following:

- Talk with your partner about the logistical issues of your living arrangement up front, while the two of you are in love. Issues to discuss include: who pays what and when, and what happens if one or the other of you can't meet an obligation.
- Talk about, draft, sign, and have notarized a domestic partnership agreement up front. It lays down on paper the rights, obligations, and responsibilities of each partner. Include a breaking-up provision that details what will happen in the event of dissolution of the relationship.
- Consult with an attorney who has experience drafting domestic partnership agreements.
- Be sure that any agreements you put together with your partner address the "for better" or "for worse" and "in sickness and in health" contingencies. After all, these agreements are an unmarried

couple's version of prenuptial agreements, marriage laws, and divorce decrees.

- The more issues you and your partner hash out ahead of time and address in writing, the better things will be in the long run.

CHAPTER 9

Children

ISSUES AND ANSWERS

Years ago, parenting options were limited. Society ostracized single parents. Children born to unmarried parents were considered "illegitimate" and second-class citizens. Adoption was a quiet secret. Few kids knew about or admitted to being adopted. Even those who knew they were adopted knew very little about their birth parents, who often seemed mysteriously to have "died in a car accident." Single-parent adoption was almost unheard of. Same-sex couples had no chance of adopting unless they hid their relationship and broke the law. A surrogate mother would have been thrown in jail. And, of course, the general populace relegated to science fiction or blasphemy the notion of sperm donation or artificial insemination. Unmarried couples faced a pretty grim outlook or, at the least, a steep uphill road if they wanted to become parents, or even if they ended up being parents by accident or chance.

TIMES CHANGE

Fortunately, a lot has changed considerably in the past few years—including living situations, laws, technology, and opinions. All of the above parenting options and more have entered the mainstream. Families today are extended and blended. Nearly 1.7 million unmarried couples have children in their households today, according to U.S. census data. The actual numbers probably are higher. The National Adoption Clearinghouse reports that more than 100,000 children are adopted each year in the United States, thousands of them from foreign countries. The treatment of infertility has become big business. Like adoption, advances in infertility treatments also have enabled many couples to become parents. Some health insurance companies pay for infertility treatments. Some states require insurance companies doing business in their states to provide coverage for infertility treatments. Marital status is not considered.

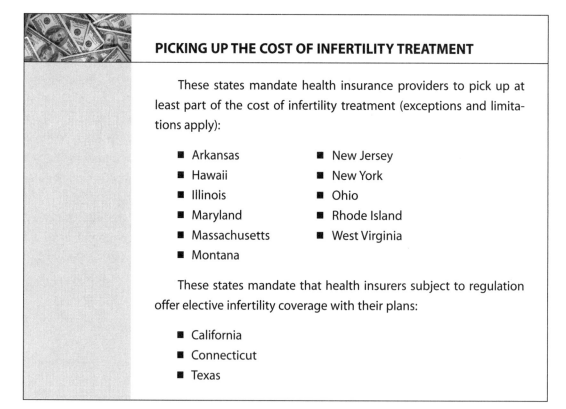

PICKING UP THE COST OF INFERTILITY TREATMENT

These states mandate health insurance providers to pick up at least part of the cost of infertility treatment (exceptions and limitations apply):

- Arkansas
- Hawaii
- Illinois
- Maryland
- Massachusetts
- Montana
- New Jersey
- New York
- Ohio
- Rhode Island
- West Virginia

These states mandate that health insurers subject to regulation offer elective infertility coverage with their plans:

- California
- Connecticut
- Texas

PROTECT YOUR CHILD AND YOURSELF

With all these options and opportunities, it's become absolutely essential that a parent—biological, adoptive, or nontraditional—address the issues head on and, where necessary, establish contracts and legal documentation to spell out clearly their responsibilities and obligations toward the child. Mom and Dad no longer represent the sole parenting model. It could be Mom and Mom, Dad and Dad, Mom and Partner, Dad and Partner, Grandma and Partner, Grandpa and Partner, and so on.

Each situation is different. As with domestic partner agreements, plain vanilla, off-the-shelf versions of agreements may not fit your circumstances. Agreements on basic parenting, guardianship, custody, financial support, or adoption need to be tailored to your situation. If you, as a parent, don't take care of the issues, the courts will take care of them for you. Judges, by statute, rule for what they believe to be "the child's best interests." Make the child's best interests yours, too.

Keep in mind that if children are in your life plan, they also need to be in your financial plans. After all, raising a child is one of the biggest expenses that you'll have in your lifetime. Those costs soar even before you have a child if fertility issues or adoption are involved.

Legal Assistance

It's generally a good guideline to avoid the do-it-yourself approach to agreements, especially those involving children. Such documents easily could wind up in court, where they could be subject to close scrutiny and fierce attack. Nolo.com (http://www.nolo.com), LawDepot™ (http://www.lawdepot.com), and many other resources are good starting points for research on a particular issue. They also help parents and partners understand some of the complexities involved. But always, always bring in a competent lawyer experienced in your specific area of concern. It's not enough that John or Jane Doe is your next-door neighbor, a good friend, or a well-respected attorney. If he or she is inexperienced in the details of adoption and you and your partner are trying to adopt, particularly same-sex partner adoption or single-parent adoption, find someone who is well versed in this area.

Losing a child-custody battle, being refused an adoption, or getting saddled with a crippling financial burden because of a loophole in a legal document is hardly worth the money you might have saved by forgoing an experienced attorney. No matter the cost of legal advice, use it. It's in the best interests of you and your child or potential child.

Paternity Issues

The old practice of classifying children of unmarried couples as "illegitimate" has no standing in today's legal system. Yet, in practice, a child born to unmarried parents could run into stumbling blocks later in life, especially concerning disability or death benefits and inheritance from an estranged biological parent. A potentially sticky situation is exacerbated if an estranged father dies intestate (without a will) and the child has no proof of paternity.

Also, without proof of paternity, the mother has little recourse if a father decides not to provide support for his child. That's why it's in the best interests of the child if a father signs a declaration of paternity, like the one in Figure 9.1, at birth or shortly afterward. All states must offer unmarried parents the opportunity to do so. Simply listing a father's name on the birth certificate doesn't necessarily obligate the father to provide any financial support to the child. A declaration of paternity or acknowledgment of paternity signed by both parents does. (With married couples, paternity of the husband is presumed.) Keep in mind that a declaration of paternity doesn't automatically come with visitation rights and that the rules and regulations may vary by state.

Another note of caution to male partners in unmarried relationships who are not the biological father of the child in question: Think twice before declaring paternity. By doing so, you become liable for child support until that child turns 18. Be as certain as you can be that you are deeply committed for the long term. Otherwise, your partner could be long gone, while you would be legally responsible to support her child.

FIGURE 9.1 Declaration of Paternity (Sample Only)

Child	Complete name	FIRST _____ MIDDLE ___ LAST _____
	Date of birth	MONTH _____ DAY ____ YEAR _____
	Sex	MALE _____ FEMALE _____
	Place of birth	HOSPITAL NAME _____
		COUNTY _____ CITY _____ STATE ____

Father	Complete name & SSN	FIRST _____ MIDDLE ___ LAST _____
		_____-____-_____
	Place & date of birth	PLACE OF BIRTH: CITY _____ STATE ____
		DATE OF BIRTH: MONTH _____ DAY ___ YEAR ____
	Current address	STREET _____
		CITY_____ STATE ____

Mother	Complete name & SSN	FIRST _____ MIDDLE ___ LAST _____
		_____-____-_____
	Place and date of birth	PLACE OF BIRTH: CITY _____ STATE ____
		DATE OF BIRTH: MONTH _____ DAY ___ YEAR ____
	Current address	STREET _____
		CITY_____ STATE ____

FATHER:

I declare under penalty of perjury under the laws of my state that I am the biological father of the child listed above and that the information provided about me is true. By signing this form I understand the rights and responsibilities of paternity and I consent to the establishment of paternity. I wish to be named as the father on the child's birth certificate.

Signature of Father _____ Date Signed _____

MOTHER:

I declare under penalty of perjury under the laws of my state that I am the biological mother of the child listed above and that the information provided about me and the child is true. I certify that the man signing this form is the only possible father of this child. By signing this form I consent to the establishment of paternity.

Signature of Mother _____ Date Signed _____

(Signatures must be signed and notarized)

Amanda and Joseph have been together about six months. New to the family is Sarah, Amanda's infant with her former boyfriend, who vanished shortly after Amanda became pregnant. Despite the newness of his casual relationship with Amanda, Joseph signed a declaration of paternity for Sarah, because he doesn't want the little girl to grow up without a father. Shortly after he signed the papers, however, doctors discovered that Sarah has a congenital condition that likely will require extensive treatment—possibly for the rest of her life. Suddenly, a gesture that seemed like the right thing to do at the time has turned into possibly a significant financial burden. Because Joseph signed the papers, he's considered the legal father and responsible for Sarah's care and support until she turns 18. Marital status has nothing to do with his situation. If he splits, he's technically a deadbeat dad and could have his wages garnished for child support.

In the case of couples who have chosen to become parents utilizing a known sperm donor or a surrogate mother, it's important that the donor or surrogate's parental rights—if any—be spelled out in a legal document drafted by a competent attorney before the baby is conceived.

In other cases where a gay male couple or individual, or a lesbian couple or individual, opt to conceive children together and share parenting, it's advisable to spell out coparenting rights, duties, and responsibilities of all the parties involved prior to conception.

PARENTING AND COPARENTING AGREEMENTS

As Joseph learned the hard way, first and foremost, both parents are responsible for supporting their child. It makes no difference if the parents are married or not. That's the law. That's not, however, always the practice, especially in cases involving unmarried parents. Although rules and regulations abound for parental support, where are the rules and regulations addressing child care and support after the dissolution of an unmarried relationship, if the absent partner never signed a declaration of paternity or never formally adopted the child? Without going to court, no such rules exist for unmarried parents, unless you make them part of your own contractual agreement. A parenting agreement can do just that.

The Basics

A parenting agreement can be as detailed or as simple as partners and participants choose, as long as it covers certain issues. It doesn't matter if a child is adopted or biological, or if the couple is same-sex, older, or younger. In the case of a same-sex or infertile couple, a parenting agreement also could involve a surrogate mother, sperm donor, or birth parents, as in an open adoption. The important thing is that the agreement addresses your unique situation and the rights and responsibilities of the parties involved. Don't overlook that overriding concern of the courts: "the best interests of the child."

As with the business of coupling, the parenting contract should address the business of the child's welfare and rearing. As dispassionate as it may sound, the reality is that parenting and coparenting agreements are very similar to those addressing joint home ownership. The specifics are different, but many of the issues are the same. Who is responsible for what? Who pays for what, how much, when, and how? What happens in the event of change or disagreement? If the situation or relationship deteriorates, who is responsible for what and in what time frame? Raising a child requires flexibility on the part of parents. Any parenting agreement requires flexibility, too, as circumstances change.

A few of the specifics include:

- Will parents share custody, or will one have sole custody?
- If sole custody, will the other partner have visitation rights?
- How about their parents—the child's grandparents? If so, how will their rights be structured?
- Will any other relatives of that parent have visitation rights?

As unmarried partners, the answers to all these questions are up to you and your partner. Lay it all out clearly.

Who will claim the child as a dependent for tax purposes? How will the child's education be funded? What about the child's health care and medical insurance? What about day care responsibilities—not only financially, but the physical delivery and pickup of the child? Should disagreement arise, how will it be resolved? Will an arbitrator or mediator step in? If one partner doesn't live up to his or her obligations and responsibilities, what will be the consequences? All this and more needs to be spelled out in writing in this legal document.

Coparenting Details

If the agreement involves coparenting—as may be the case with a same-sex couple (more on that later)—be sure, as we mentioned earlier, that it specifically addresses each partner's rights in terms of the child. Don't forget to include details such as the last name that the child will take. Partners also should closely consider what will happen to the child and the partners' obligations and responsibilities if their relationship ends. For example, the agreement could stipulate: "In the event of the ending of this relationship, we as coparents of this child or children intend to coparent."

Even if the same-sex coparents live in a state that allows them to be named as coparents on a child's birth certificate, establish your own documentation. (At least a half-dozen states don't allow both same-sex coparents to be named on a child's birth certificate.) You may want to consider crosspartner adoption to legalize both parent-child relationships and to protect your child and your parenting rights. Realistically, two men or two women still are not widely accepted as coparents or afforded the same treatment as their heterosexual counterparts. Coparents also don't have the same rights and protections afforded biological parents who are partners or married couples and their children without going to court to battle it out. Even then, there's no guarantee. The court will do whatever it believes is in the best interests of a child, which may not coincide with what the coparents think is best. The courts often are unsympathetic to same-sex parents and may rule against them.

Coparenting isn't just a same-sex couple issue, either. With today's blended, extended, and nontraditional families, extended family members as well as close friends may end up intricately involved in raising a child.

Same-sex partners always should work with an attorney specializing in family law and experienced in same-sex parenting issues. It's just not worth it to do otherwise.

ADOPTION

Adoption today has become mainstream. All kinds of couples adopt all kinds of kids from all over the world. To make it all work, however, requires meticulous attention to the details, both legal and personal, between partners and other involved parties.

Here are some of the essentials to keep in mind if you and your partner are considering adoption:

- Private adoption agencies can create their own rules, as long as they don't violate any laws in their individual states.
- State laws on adoption vary.
- Both parents of a child must give their consent for the child to be eligible for adoption. The exception is if a parent has abandoned the child or has no relationship with the child.
- If your partner has a biological child and you don't adopt that child, you have no legal right to custody of or visitation with the child or financial responsibility for the child if you and your partner break up.
- The adoption process—international and domestic—has plenty of room for fraud. Before dealing with any agency or individual, get references, and contact those references.
- Costs vary widely by type of adoption, agency, parties involved, and more. It's often wise to decide ahead of time approximately how much money you and your partner can afford and/or are willing to spend in the process. That amount may help you decide the type of adoption that's best for you.

Know the Lingo

First, consider a few semantics:

- *Birth mother/father.* The biological parent/parents of a child
- *Closed/confidential adoption.* Adoption in which a child's birth parent and adoptive parents do not meet and don't even know each other's names
- *Coparenting.* When an individual who is not a biological or adoptive parent shares the responsibility of raising a child
- *Domestic adoption.* Adoption of a child born in the United States
- *Home study.* A process in which a licensed agency helps the courts determine, in accordance with state requirements, whether or not a couple or individual are considered "fit"—medically, emotionally, and otherwise—to adopt a child. As part of the process, a social worker from the agency will meet with and interview prospective parents, or parent, several times in the home. Some words to the wise: Despite the fact these licensed experts are looking for compliance with specific state requirements (ranging from fire extinguishers in the home to good health and sound finances), the process also can be subjective and intimidating.
- *International adoption.* Adoption of a child born outside the United States, generally involving a private agency, though it can be facilitated by individuals. A note of caution: This process involves an incredible number of legal hoops and roadblocks involving the FBI, U.S. Citizenship and Immigration Services, and other organizations. It's best to work with an experienced adoption agency and attorneys to facilitate the process.
- *Interstate Compact for Placement of Children.* Monitors movement of foster and adoptive children across state lines
- *Open adoption.* Adoption in which birth parents/parent meet and know the adoptive parents, sometimes including a contract for continued contact and visitation with adopted child
- *Private/independent adoption.* Adoption arranged between a facilitator, usually a private attorney, and a birth mother or birth parents

■ *Special needs adoption.* Adoption that involves a child who is developmentally, physically, or emotionally disabled

Obstacles for Unmarried Couples

Generally, in theory and by law, unmarried couples can adopt, although in reality, they may face more difficulties than their married counterparts. Some agencies frown on and even ban outright adoption by single people or unmarried couples.

Same-sex couples face even more difficult obstacles to adoption. Several states—Mississippi, Florida, and Utah—ban adoption by same-sex couples. Other states allow single-parent adoptions, and some allow coadoption. About half the states allow second-parent adoption. Many same-sex couples also look to international adoption instead, but even that can be trying and difficult. (A great state-by-state overview of adoption laws is available online, courtesy of the Lambda Legal Defense and Education Fund: http://www.lambdalegal.com, click on "Resources/Family.")

Because same-sex couples may not be able to adopt a child as a couple, one partner may adopt the child initially; then, in those states that allow it, the other partner in turn will do a second-parent adoption. The second partner becomes a legal parent of the child without the "first parent" giving up any parental rights. This gives the child two legal parents and typically gives the adoptive parents the same rights as biological parents in custody and visitation matters.

If an unmarried couple is committed to coparenting but one of the partners can't or chooses not to adopt the child involved, it's important to draft, sign, and have notarized a coparenting agreement. That agreement spells out both partners' intentions, commitment, and responsibilities (including financial). It also should address contingencies in the event of dissolution of the partnership. A custodial parent, for example, and his or her partner may be committed to raising a child jointly, but the partner may be unable to adopt the child because a birth parent doesn't want to relinquish parental rights to the child.

! **WARNING** *Plenty of information about adoption is available on the Web and elsewhere. However, all of it may not be accurate or up-to-date, so don't base your decisions on what you read. Work with reputable, qualified experts before making any final adoption decisions.*

Defer to Lawyers

As with other issues involving children, unmarried couples should defer to lawyers who specialize in adoption and know and understand its nuances, rules, and regulations. Adoption is a legal process involving forms, filings, affidavits, character witnesses, and court-approved measures. As mentioned above, international adoption is even more complicated. A single slipup and would-be parents could lose the opportunity to realize their dream of parenting. Worse yet, without the proper documentation and procedures, adoptive parents could face a child being taken from them after placement. That's definitely not worth the cash savings of doing it yourself.

It's absolutely essential that prospective adoptive parents find the right attorney or agency that specializes not only in adoption but in the adoption niche they're considering. For example, if a same-sex couple wants to adopt a child domestically, they should find a lawyer specializing in working with same-sex couples on domestic adoption. If an older couple wants to adopt a child from Russia, the partners need to find a reputable adoption agency and attorney that know the ins and outs of Russian adoption.

No matter what kind of adoption, always, always check out the reputation of these agencies, attorneys, and purported "experts." Talk to them in detail, and make sure that you are prepared to sign a contract before ever exchanging any money.

Even with the best legal advice, be very cautious about what you sign. Don't hesitate to ask questions and get second opinions. If you have the slightest question about any document or any procedure, demand a thorough explanation. Get references, talk to those references, and make sure that you are getting the expertise and legal skills you really want and need as well as the client services, communication, and interaction you desire. If your gut says no, don't do it! That's especially important with international adoptions. And don't quit probing until you are satisfied with the answer.

CHILD CUSTODY

Battles for child custody can get pretty nasty, especially if either parent—or both—is living with someone else and the children are in that home. It doesn't necessarily matter if the widowed grandma, Martha, is living with her longtime partner, Ben, or Mom left Dad for her same-sex partner, Elizabeth. If a married couple's child-custody battle makes its way to court and Mom or Dad is cohabitating with another partner, the court takes note. A judge does take living arrangements into account when weighing a decision, and not all judges are open-minded or embrace cohabitation outside of marriage.

Even if an unmarried couple with children breaks up without a custody battle, the situation can be extremely tough on the outgoing partner if he or she grew very attached to their partner's child. Without documentation, the departing partner has no legal recourse or relationship with the child. If a child is adopted by both parents or if they are in a coparenting relationship, the couple should have a parenting agreement that spells out visitation or joint custody rights. Remember, however, that the courts always rule on what they consider to be the best interests of the children.

Kevin and Sally had been together 11 years when their partnership began to fall apart. Though the two never had married—either traditionally or by common law—Kevin had raised Sally's son, Shawn, 11, as if he were his own. Kevin was the only father Shawn had ever known. For the first three years of Shawn's life, Kevin was a stay-at-home parent. Then the couple split up. They had no partnership agreement in place, no visitation agreement, no custody plan. Kevin also had recently lost his job. He simply was out—out of the house, out of work, and out of a family. He had no formal recourse. Fortunately, Sally informally granted Kevin minimal, but meaningful, visitation rights with Shawn. Hopefully, the privilege will work out satisfactorily for all parties. Sally also asked for, and receives, child support payments from Kevin.

If the custodial parent dies without a will or any guardianship provisions, then next of kin will be entrusted with the child. That's Uncle Sam's default plan. Of course, it can be challenged in court, but it's a tough road.

If Sally had died before she and Kevin ended their relationship, Shawn's care automatically would have fallen to Sally's next of kin, if the biological father couldn't be found. What if the next of kin was Sally's deadbeat uncle? Without documentation stating otherwise, Kevin has no legal standing as a parent or caregiver. Don't let this happen to your family.

Financial Considerations

Unmarried partners with children may have an advantage over their married counterparts when it comes to qualifying for financial aid to fund their child's college education. Typically, a student and his or her family are required to fill out a standard document, the Department of Education's Free Application for Federal Student Aid, known as a FAFSA form. The form seeks extensive financial information on the student as well as on the spouse or parents as in "mother" and "father." If, for example, the child lives with his or her legal parent and that parent's partner, he or she would be required to provide financial information on the legal parent only, presuming that the child has only one legal parent. If only one adult's income and assets figure into a person's eligibility for financial aid, that child likely has a better chance of qualifying for aid.

Of course, one may wonder about the legal or ethical responsibility of unmarried partners to divulge that one of them is a de facto parent. The partner who is not the legal parent may want to fill out the "other parent" part of the form in keeping with the spirit of the application. But would doing so be considered perjury because that partner is not the mother or father?

ESTATE PLANNING WITH YOUR CHILDREN IN MIND

Whenever children are involved in a relationship, a parent or guardian needs to protect them with a will with a guardianship provision and a testamentary trust. The trust, created by your will after you die, tells the world—and, most importantly, the courts—who you want to care for your children and what you want to occur in terms of monetary support, education, and more. If you spell out your wishes with the right written documentation, the courts will see they are carried out, unless others can prove to the judge that your wishes are not in the best interests of the child. A judge who doesn't know you, your child, or your family may decide your child's future. Same-sex couples with children especially run the risk of losing custody or visitation rights with an unsympathetic judge.

A testamentary trust also instills accountability to whoever will handle the assets you have left to your minor children. Trust laws dictate certain fiduciary responsibilities of trustees regarding the management of assets for trust beneficiaries. The designee in charge of the purse strings is required by law to act with the care, skill, prudence, and diligence of a knowledgeable person under the same circumstances. Your dishonest brother-in-law can't siphon off money from a trust intended for your children without breaking the law. It's not common to separate the management of assets from the guardianship of a child. Yet it may make a lot of sense, because naming one or more people as caretakers of your child and a different person or people as custodians of your child's money provides some additional accountability.

It's not good enough to assume that "of course" your partner will be able to take over the responsibility of raising the child because, after all, he or she is a coparent now. Not so fast! Unless your partner has coadopted that child, he or she has no legal rights or responsibilities. An unmarried partner is *not* family as defined by law.

The fact that the courts could get involved should send up a red flag for same-sex partners. Unless you're guaranteed a sympathetic judge (and you're not), without guardianship set up or crosspartner adoption (both partners named as parents), your child—and your partner's child, even if in spirit only—could end up in a foster home.

Drawing up guardianship directives or any other legal document regarding children or assets is not for do-it-yourselfers, either. Work with an attorney who specializes in parenting issues for unmarried couples.

The Right Guardian

Choosing who you would like to step in and take care of your child, should anything happen to you, is a tough decision. You should select someone you know and trust explicitly—perhaps someone who shares your values, cultural background, and spiritual or religious beliefs, and who already has a relationship with the child.

Be careful not to assume that your domestic partner is willing to take on the sole parenting responsibilities should something happen to you. He or she may go along with having the child in the family only because of feelings for you. As mentioned earlier, if you aren't married and your partner has not adopted your child or entered into any legally binding parenting agreement, no implicit contract exists.

Use common sense in your choices. If your relationship with your partner is marked by any kind of abuse—emotional, verbal, or physical—don't name that partner as a guardian. An ex-husband and father or ex-wife and mother with whom you no longer have a relationship may not be the best choice as guardian, either. Understand, however, that the courts may not agree with you. If one biological parent dies, the court will award custody of a child to the other biological parent, unless he or she is unwilling to accept the responsibility or the court considers that individual unfit to parent.

Financial Protections

You may not want that estranged ex-partner or biological parent to handle the money for your child. Often, it's better to designate an independent third party, such as a trusted friend or bank trust department, to monitor the purse strings and serve as watchdog.

Consider appointing a guardian to look after the child's care and someone else to look after the child's money. Separation of personal care and finances is practical, and it makes good business sense. A person who is good with money may not be the ideal person to take care of your child should anything happen to you. Separating the jobs also serves as a check and balance to ensure that money decisions are made with the child's best interests in mind.

BOTTOM LINES

Keep in mind that the law differentiates between assets and children. Assets go directly to whomever a will or similar document dictates. What happens to a child in the event of his or her parent's death, despite legal documentation, ultimately is up to the courts. The courts will always rule in what they believe to be "the best interests of the child." You may or may not agree with a court's decision, but it doesn't matter.

As a couple and as an individual, if you do nothing else, at a minimum when kids are involved, do the following:

- Don't sign anything, make any agreements, or proceed without the advice of a reputable and reliable attorney who is well versed in family law *and* the specific laws pertaining to your situation.
- Unmarried couples need to draft, sign, and have notarized parenting agreements. Like domestic partnership agreements, these documents lay down on paper the rights and obligations of both partners. Be sure to include visitation privileges if other individuals—such as birth parents, surrogate parents, or other family members—are involved.
- Don't overlook including provisions in the parenting agreement for who has what responsibilities and obligations in the event of dissolution of the partnership. That includes visitation rights for nonparent partners in the event of a breakup.

- When choosing a guardian and financial custodian for a child, first and foremost consider what's best for the child. Often, it's unwise to name the same person as the keeper of the child and the money. By separating responsibilities, you build in checks and balances.

CHAPTER | **10**

Putting It All Together

Solid financial planning for unmarried couples begins with partners—no matter their age or sexual orientation—"coming out" about their relationships, feelings, and wishes. Although traditionally the term has meant same-sex couples revealing their sexual orientation, *coming out* applies to couples of all ages and sexual orientation who are open with loved ones, family, and friends about a lifestyle that breaks with outdated taboos. Unmarried is how we spend more than half of our lives. Coupling is natural at any age.

Seniors often are afraid or reluctant to remarry or cohabitate because their adult children have difficulty accepting the fact that they are dating—let alone coupling with—someone other than mom or dad. Whether divorced or widowed, senior partners also may face resentment from children worried about the financial repercussions of their parent's unmarried relationship.

Same-sex partners often must deal with the irrational behavior and attitude of family members who don't understand their relationship. Sometimes, out of sheer confusion, those same family members will reject the same-sex partners, or vice versa. Sadly, family rifts and alienation are not unusual in these situations.

Heterosexual couples often endure a seemingly endless water torture of the same questions over and over: When are you getting married?, What's wrong with you?, and You'll get married if you get pregnant, won't you? Why can't everyone just accept and understand that a couple simply may not be ready or doesn't want to get married?

All these couples and situations cry out for openness, honesty, and understanding. If an adult child and his wife are distraught because dad has moved in with another woman—and mom has been dead *only* seven years—dad needs to discuss the situation with them. Conversely, if parents disapprove of a son's or daughter's choice of partner or unmarried lifestyle, the family needs to talk about it. Instead of both sides rejecting or turning away from each other, they need to come out with their thoughts and feelings and work toward mutual understanding. Family counseling could be an option, too.

A warning to unmarried partners: Sneaking around doesn't resolve anything, and isolating or closing yourself off from family and loved ones only alienates them all the more. At the same time, family members need to come clean about why they're upset by a parent's or child's domestic situation. Are children worried about their inheritance? That's a legitimate concern. It doesn't have to be, though. Be open about your concerns. Many financial-planning and estate-planning strategies can be put into place to ease your worries.

Are parents worried about their child's health, welfare, and finances? Those, too, are reasonable concerns. But until both sides talk, little is resolved. Unless understanding and some degree of acceptance or tolerance are reached, distrust, animosity, and even court battles can rip a family apart. That's certainly not the legacy any parent wants to leave their children. And that's not how children want to remember their parents.

WARNING *Financial planning can help you prepare for all kinds of potential outcomes.*

CONTINGENCY PLANNING

Why, you may ask, are topics related to family counseling and life planning in a book on financial planning? Remember, as we've discussed throughout this book, financial planning is not about planning for the best. It's about planning and being prepared for various possible what-ifs we all experience in our financial lives.

What if life doesn't turn out as you have dreamed it would? No need to worry about that; we can guarantee right now that it won't. Life just doesn't work that way, no matter how much we would like to dream otherwise. That's why, as individuals and couples, we all need to think about contingencies. We must have a Plan B.

What if you or your partner suffers a significant illness? What if you or your partner gets laid off? What if you die and the mortgage isn't paid off? What if you die and your partner can't keep the house? What if you and your partner split up and you can't handle the bills by yourself? What if you don't want your family to get your assets? What if you're disabled suddenly?

Sound financial planning allows unmarried couples to address all these issues and more up front. Then they are as well prepared and protected as possible. The fulfillment of your life's objectives is far more probable if family and loved ones are on your side, instead of squared off to do battle, should something happen to you.

Uncle Sam couldn't care less that you haven't talked to your dad ever since he moved in with *that* woman seven years after Mom died. If Dad's will stipulates that the other woman gets everything, she's going to get it. If you end up in court trying to get it back, that's your problem. And what about Jim and April, the couple who never saw each other again after Jim became gravely ill? His mom and dad waltzed in and whisked away their incapacitated son forever. Emotionally, that's an issue between the parties involved. Legally, Mom and Dad have the right to do what they did, unless proper legal documents are in place to stop them. But maybe if Mom and Dad and Jim and April had taken the time and made the effort to sit down, listen to each other, and strive for understanding, the ending would have been far different.

In these pages, we've discussed many situations and offered strategies to help unmarried couples successfully deal with them. But no strategy will work unless you make the effort to put it into place. When planning for tomorrow, complacency just doesn't cut it. "Unforeseen circumstances" are precisely why we plan.

WHY BOTHER WITH THE HEADACHES?

If unmarried couples don't pay attention to financial planning, Uncle Sam and his government gang are likely to walk away with more of their hard-earned assets than necessary, today as well as tomorrow.

Should something happen to you, without proper planning ahead of time, your partner likely won't be able to visit you in the hospital, make decisions for you, plan your funeral, or inherit anything. Your next of kin will. That's the law, unless you plan ahead to ensure otherwise.

That goes for casual and newer partners, too. If you share responsibilities and liabilities, if you buy or own anything together, you need to communicate with each other about those obligations and assets. If you don't, what happens if you split up? Who will get stuck paying the rent or the mortgage? How will the bills be paid? Who will walk away with the big-screen TV, the massage chair from Sharper Image, or the Spode china? Did you buy them jointly or separately, or does that matter? Can you even remember who bought them? Do you know where you stand? Do you want to argue with your ex about all these details? Are you prepared to fight in court if that becomes necessary?

Wouldn't it be nice if, when a couple breaks up, the property was divided and the bills are paid off in a civilized manner? Well, as you've discovered in this book, that's exactly how a breakup can be for unmarried couples who plan for contingencies. That planning includes drafting a domestic partnership agreement with a detailed breaking-up provision. Such an agreement is not a declaration of distrust. It's a matter-of-fact business contract drawn up when partners like and love each other.

Thanks to divorce laws and decrees, married couples already have the benefit of automatic and unequivocal division of property and disposition of debts. There are rules about these kinds of things. But unmarried couples don't have that clarity without creating it themselves in the form of their own executed written agreements.

Remember, economically, an unmarried couple's relationship is a business partnership. It's not so different from the legal commitment of marriage, which also is a legal partnership. When both partners sign the marriage license, they sign a legal pact to abide by the rules and regulations that govern married partners. As unmarried partners, though, whatever your age or sexual orientation, you and your partner must write your own rules and regulations to govern your financial relationship.

Even casual partners who don't comingle assets and plan only short-term coupling need contingency plans for what will happen to their joint obligations and commitments if they break up. If both names are on the condo or apartment lease, for example, how will they handle that financial obligation? Who will pay the utilities? Who gets the damage deposit? If both partners move out, who picks up the tab for the cleaning crew that comes in to clean up the condo? Even though the couple isn't currently planning a life together, both partners still have joint issues that need to be considered.

Settle the issues up front, when you both like each other. Read this book together so you'll both be motivated and empowered to start planning to take care of yourselves and each other. You will be much kinder to each other, and that will make compromise easier. That's across-the-board advice for all couples.

DO IT YOURSELF OR JOIN THE TEAM?

Attention, do-it-yourselfers. Are you a gambler and a risk taker?

Can, and do, you and your partner talk openly about money, your relationship, your families, and the future—whether or not it includes each other? How do both of you see the relationship playing out?

Are you willing to assume that you are aware of all the proper documents you and your partner need to sign and that any one of them will hold up to a court challenge? What happens if you and your partner adopt a child and the child's birth parents decide a year later that they want the baby back? Are you sure all your legal bases are covered?

What if you die? Even though you and your partner both are listed on the mortgage, if your partner's name is not also on the home's deed as a joint owner with rights of survivorship or as beneficiary of your trust that owns the house, too bad. Your partner is out of luck and out of a home.

What happens if, after you die, irate family members challenge your do-it-yourself, off-the-Internet, or off-the-shelf will leaving all your worldly possessions to your longtime partner? Will the documents be valid in your state? Did you remember to get those documents signed and notarized? Does your county require domestic partners to register first to receive certain benefits?

Are you willing to gamble that even though you and your partner "forgot" the breaking-up provision in your domestic partnership agreement, he or she will be so loving and kind as to split everything fairly—including the bills—after they're kicked out?

Are you willing to base your retirement funding and savings on an Internet calculator? What if some of the built-in assumptions change? Are you confident enough in preparing your taxes that you are willing to take on the IRS or your state's department of revenue?

You get the picture. Plenty of reasons demonstrate why it takes more than just you and your partner to fashion a solid financial plan that will work for both of you.

Yes, you can do parts of your financial planning yourself. You must, in fact, to create a plan that's right for you as an individual and that works for your partner, too. Financial planning takes introspection and analysis—personal and objective—of goals, thoughts, and ideas about life, relationships, resources, and loved ones. This book will help you start putting in place a solid foundation on which to build your own plans.

Hiring experts and getting needed advice don't have to cost an arm and a leg plus your life savings. You do, however, need to choose wisely and be diligent in working with those experts whether they offer legal, financial, psychological, or tax advice.

How do you get competent, objective expertise at a reasonable cost? Let's examine some of the options.

Financial Planner

Throughout this book, we've provided an overview of most of the primary financial-planning issues that you and your partner should address. It's critical, however, that both your wishes and needs be addressed fully and correctly. Since financial planning for unmarried couples can be very specialized, it often takes professional planning assistance. If you need it, get it! You don't want to waste time, money, or trust on an incompetent advisor or take your chances without professional guidance.

Be sure that any financial advisor has, at minimum, the Certified Financial Planner™ designation, indicated by the initials CFP® after his or her name. That certification, awarded by the nonprofit, Denver-based Certified Financial Planner Board of Standards (http://www.cfp.net), indicates that an individual has met CFP® education, examination, and experience requirements and has agreed to adhere to the organization's code of ethics.

Before you and your partner decide on any financial advisor, it's important to understand clearly who the advisor works for and how he or she is compensated. That can affect your relationship with the planner as well as the advice.

Commissions. The most common method of compensation is via commissions. The planner is paid commissions from insurance and investment companies, the products of which he or she sells. Conflicts of interest may occur, and consciously or subconsciously, they can skew a planner's advice. That's not always the case, nor does it mean that these advisors cannot provide solid advice and direction. They can and do as long as you, the consumer, are aware of and alert to any possible biases.

Salaried. A planner also may be a salaried employee of a financial or investment institution. That removes the commission conflict of interest. But these advisors often have strict sales quotas. Their bonuses and incentives also may be tied to production numbers. As a result, that may affect the advice they offer.

Fee-only wealth managers. Clients pay these fee-only advisors an amount established ahead of time, often based on a percentage of the value of a portfolio. The conflict-of-interest concerns aren't obvious. However, advisors who charge based on the size of an investment portfolio have incentive to manage all of your money—even if that is not in your best interest. Many fee-only wealth managers or advisors also must set minimum portfolio values or annual fees charged. That leaves out the majority of Americans.

Hourly, fee-only. Middle-income Americans do have an alternative tailored specifically for the overwhelming majority of their needs: hourly, fee-only financial planners. These experts are available for hire on an as-needed basis. They're paid directly by the client based on the amount of time the advisor works with and for you.

Looking for someone to help you and your partner decide what to include in your domestic partnership agreement before you show it to a legal expert? A fee-only planner with experience and training in planning strategies for unmarried couples can do that. What about an objective expert to help determine how much life insurance you and your partner need? Or do you need advice on how you and your partner should divide expenses? How should your assets be titled? How, where, and how much do you need to save to meet your financial goals and objectives? What planning strategies are available and most appropriate for your unique situation? An hourly, fee-only planner can help you and your partner find answers to all these questions.

A note of caution when it comes to fees: Be sure any advisor that you work with provides an estimate of the total fees and scope of services to be provided up front and in writing.

Special Needs

No matter how a planner gets paid, make sure he or she has expertise in planning for unmarried couples and, more specifically, working with couples in situations similar to yours. For example, if you need an estate plan for you and your partner, it's not enough to find an advisor specializing in estate plans. Look for one who also has expertise in working with unmarried couples. Seniors need to be even more selective to find an estate specialist with expertise in planning for unmarried seniors, as well. And whatever plan you and your advisor hammer out, always have the final legal documents drafted by an equally well-qualified attorney.

It's important to deal with advisors who are well versed not only in the pertinent financial and legal details but in the nuances of your living situation as well.

Finding a Planner

A number of resources can help couples find the right planner to meet their needs. A good starting point is The Garrett Planning Network (http://www.GarrettPlanningNetwork.com), a nationwide network of hourly, fee-only planners who specialize in helping middle-income Americans and do-it-yourselfers with their financial-planning needs. The Garrett Planning Network was founded by coauthor Sheryl Garrett in 2000. The group's Web site has an easy-to-navigate locator map with direct hot links to individual planners across the country.

The largest organization of fee-only financial advisors is the National Association of Personal Financial Advisors (http://www.napfa.org). Its members agree to submit a comprehensive financial plan for peer review, operate under a strict code of ethics, and take a fiduciary oath.

Be sure to check out PridePlanners™ (http://www.prideplanners.org), a Massachusetts-based organization of financial, tax, insurance, and estate-planning professionals who serve the gay and lesbian community as well as other nontraditional couples and families nationwide. Although the group most often is associated with planning for gays and lesbians, its professional members are experts in issues faced by all types of unmarried couples. Its Web site also is a wealth of resources on pertinent issues for unmarried couples and has a planner locator tool online. Coauthor Debra Neiman is a founder of PridePlanners. Coauthor Garrett also is a member.

The Financial Planning Association (http://www.fpanet.org) is a 30,000-member, nationwide organization of planners and others involved in the financial planning industry. Its PlannerSearch is an online locator of CFP® professionals.

Other good sources of information include The Human Rights Campaign (http://www.hrc.org), a Washington, D.C., lobbying group. Their Web site provides good links to legislative developments and information on marriage, children, and personal and financial issues facing same-sex couples. The Alternatives to Marriage Project Web site (http://www.atmp.org) is another great resource for all unmarried couples.

Wherever you turn, and whoever you choose, make sure your advisor truly understands the issues and is not merely talking a good game. This book, we hope, will help you recognize that difference.

And, of course, before you ever choose a particular planner, interview him or her. You can use the Financial Advisor Interview Questionnaire in Figure 10.1 to get you started. Ask for references—either client or professional—and follow up with them. Find out what the reference liked or did not like about the planner. What are the planner's perceived strengths and weaknesses? Also, check with the Certified Financial Planner Board of Standards to be sure no complaints have been filed against any planner you're considering working with. That group's Web site also has an excellent tool (http://www.cfp.net/learn/knowledgebase.asp?id=7) with hot links to other sites to help you discover whether complaints have been filed with other organizations—including the North American Securities Administrators Association (http://www.nasaa.org), the National Association of Securities Dealers (http://www.nasd.com), and the Securities and Exchange Commission (http://www.sec.gov).

FIGURE 10.1 Financial Advisor Interview Questionnaire*

1. Why did you become a financial planner? What is your educational and experiential background as it relates to personal financial planning?
2. What are your financial planning credentials/designations and affiliations?
   a. Certified Financial Planner™ Professional (CFP®)
   b. CPA/Personal Financial Specialist (CPA/PFS)
   c. NAPFA-Registered Financial Advisor
   d. NAPFA-Provisional Member
   e. Chartered Financial Consultant (ChFC)
   f. Certified Public Accountant (CPA)
   g. Chartered Financial Analyst (CFA)
   h. Other (e.g., MBA, JD, EA, CLU, RFC): _____
4. What are your areas of specialty?
5. Please describe your most common engagement/service provided? And the type of client or client situation you target?
6. Are you a registered representative of any broker/dealer?
   Are you a licensed insurance agent with any company or agency?
   If so, which one(s)?
7. Are you registered as an investment advisor, either with the SEC or with a state or states?
8. Are you a fiduciary?
9. How are you compensated?
   a. *Fee-only.* Please explain how you determine your fees.
   b. *Commissions only.* Please explain how you determine your fees.
   c. *Fee and commissions (fee-based).* Please provide a typical breakdown.
   d. *Other.* Please explain.
10. Do you have minimums for assets, account size, annual fees paid, etc.? And what is your typical fee or charge for an initial engagement?
11. Do you provide a written agreement detailing the total amount of compensation and services that will be provided in advance of an engagement? Please elaborate.
12. Do you provide a thorough written analysis of one's financial situation and recommendations? Please elaborate.
13. Do you offer assistance with implementation with the plan? Please elaborate.
14. Will you provide a second opinion or one-time review? Please elaborate.

Signature of Planner: _____

Date: _____

Firm Name: _____

*A downloadable copy is available at http://www.GarrettPlanningNetwork.com.

Couples' Counselor

You also might consider bringing in a couples' counselor as part of your life-planning team. Couples often are paralyzed by money issues and lack the emotional resources to hash things out. A counselor may be able to help partners communicate their thoughts and feelings about their situation as it relates to money and financial issues. Communication, after all, plays a major role in financial planning for all couples.

Don't feel too bad or inadequate if you and your partner don't or can't talk about money or your goals in life. You're not alone. Few people can discuss their finances and personal aspirations openly. Our parents probably didn't, and we likely don't, either. Often a psychologist or couples' counselor can help. Sometimes an independent intermediary is needed to help couples approach tough topics and then work through their differences.

Invaluable intermediary. It's one thing to write or read about all the "quick and simple" steps unmarried couples can take to ensure a secure financial future. It's quite another thing—and often very difficult—to talk about the issues with a partner, let alone put all those thoughts on paper, sign, and notarize them. The emotions that lie behind topics such as income inequities, morality, children, extended families, and money are deep and often seem unmanageable. Even when a couple is willing to discuss such subjects, they often fail to reach a compromise and could end up parting ways.

However, as stated throughout this book, couples—whether new, casual, or long-term—need to deal with the issues immediately. If they don't, the consequences can be traumatic and even disastrous.

Remember the same-sex couple who had differences of opinion regarding children? If only the couple had met with a counselor early in their discussions, perhaps that counselor could have helped both partners avoid the unnecessary headache and heartache that paved the way to their final decision.

Finding a counselor. Finding a counselor may be easier than you think. Many financial planners are becoming more familiar with the psychological aspects of helping couples communicate about and work through money issues. If your financial planner lacks the expertise you need, ask who he or she would suggest. There's another reason for looking to your financial planner for that advice. The counselor you choose should have an appreciation for the psychology of communicating about money issues. A financial planner is likely to refer you to a couples' counselor with that kind of understanding.

Legal Advice

Lawyers get a bad rap. The majority of them are here to help all of us navigate our nation's complex legal system. As mentioned throughout this book, the laws—especially as they pertain to unmarried partners—can be extremely tricky. Laws also change regularly and vary by state, county, and local jurisdiction. And we are not lawyers! For those reasons and others, it's extremely unwise to tackle the legal system on your own. It's always a good idea to familiarize yourself with the help of organizations like Nolo.com, LawDepot™, and the Human Rights Campaign. But don't go it completely on your own. At minimum, always ask a qualified attorney to review what you and your partner have put together. Ideally, hire a qualified expert to work with you and your partner to draft all your documents to ensure that your wishes will be carried out.

Attorneys, like financial planners, needn't cost an arm and a leg. Choose wisely. Ask your financial advisor, friends, family, or business colleagues to suggest a potential attorney for you. As with other members of your planning team, your attorney should have expertise in working with unmarried couples. Then demand even more expertise in the area of specific concern, such as adoption for same-sex couples, domestic partnership agreements, or estate planning for unmarried senior partners.

The American Bar Association (ABA) (http://www.abanet.org) has a handy online lawyer referral service (http://www.abanet.org/legalservices/

lris/directory.html#). Be sure to check out the ABA's "Consumers' Guide to Legal Help on the Internet and a Little Beyond."

Lawyers.com (http://www.lawyers.com) is another well-qualified source. Don't let the generic name fool you. It's from Martindale-Hubbell, the world's leading source of information for the legal profession. The company publishes the *Martindale-Hubbell Law Directory* and Martindale .com (http://www.martindale.com) with information on more than 1 million lawyers and law firms in 160 countries.

AARP (http://www.aarp.org) also offers a wealth of knowledge available online and in hard copy for consumers. The organization's AARP Legal Services Network lists independent attorneys who have been screened to meet certain standards of experience and customer service but who are not affiliated with AARP.

For more sources of legal advice, check out the Addendum that follows this chapter.

A note of caution when it comes to fees: Be sure any advisor you work with provides in writing and up front an estimate of the total fees and scope of the services.

TIPS TO TAKE WITH YOU

In this book, we've provided unmarried partners a quick look at their unique financial planning issues and concerns. Some of the points to remember and take away include:

- Partners must make the effort to talk to each other and lay out goals, individually and as a couple, so those goals can become reality. You and your partner can achieve your financial goals, *if* you talk about them first.
- No matter what their age, financial situation, or sexual orientation, unmarried couples across the board face virtually the same financial issues and must deal with them in much the same way.

- Life is dynamic. Financial plans should be dynamic, too. The problem with most financial plans is that they never get written down or implemented, and if they do, they become static.

- Talk with your partner about the logistical issues of your living situation up front. Discuss issues such as who pays what and when and what happens if one or the other of you can't meet an obligation.

- Discuss, draft, sign, and have notarized a domestic partnership agreement up front. It spells out on paper the rights, obligations, and responsibilities of each partner. Include as part of that a breaking-up provision that details what happens in the event of dissolution of the relationship.

- Be sure that any agreements you put together with your partner address the "for better," "for worse," and "in sickness and in health" contingencies. After all, these agreements are an unmarried couple's version of prenuptial agreements, marriage laws, and divorce decrees.

- Insurance is about protecting you and your partner. You need to have enough life, health, auto/property, disability, and possibly long-term care insurance to cover the major contingencies. It just doesn't pay not to have the appropriate coverage.

- Pay attention to whether your state recognizes common law marriage and act accordingly.

- Be proactive about your taxes. Sit down with your tax advisor and determine the best strategies to cut down on your taxes *before* the end of the year. Successful tax planning requires proactive thinking. Couples may want to look at lumping tax deductions. Whatever you do, make sure your documentation matches your strategies.

- Be sure you and your partner have in place a living will, health care and financial powers of attorney, a funeral directive, and a will or trust and pour-over will.

- Consider setting up a trust, because it enables you to dictate your wishes beyond the grave and, in turn, gives you greater influence after your death than a will provides. If you don't feel as if you need the provisions provided by a trust, at the very least get a will executed. Otherwise, Uncle Sam dictates what happens to your assets and your dependents.

■ Pay attention to the way in which your home is titled. If your planning is not done properly, one partner could be left homeless if the other partner dies. If both partners' names are not on the deed and no powers of attorney are in place and something happens to the home's sole owner, the other partner would have no legal authority to manage the property and could lose the home.

■ Don't plan your retirement needs around Social Security. Chances are it won't be there for you or any of us. And if it is, it won't be nearly enough to fund retirement.

■ Figure you'll need more retirement savings than the life-expectancy charts indicate. The chart numbers are averages, and you wouldn't want to outlive your money.

■ Get over thinking that you're not successful if you can't retire at age 65. That's an unhealthy notion, and one most Americans can't afford, anyway.

■ Maximize funding on all tax-advantaged retirement plans available to you and your partner, including those from your employer—especially if that employer offers a matching contribution. The match is guaranteed return on investment; the money you contribute is added automatically to your account, and the earnings grow tax-deferred. At least contribute to your plan up to the employer's match limit.

■ Don't overlook Roth IRAs if you qualify. Again, these plans offer tax-deferred earnings, and qualified withdrawals are tax free. Roth IRAs are possibly one of the greatest retirement vehicles available to most people.

■ Unmarried couples need to balance their retirement assets because they don't qualify for a Qualified Domestic Relations Order (QDRO), which allows spouses to divide and roll over pension assets without penalty in the event of divorce.

■ Unmarried couples must pay attention to beneficiary designations as they relate to pension, retirement, and investment accounts and life insurance.

- With proper planning, unmarried couples can minimize their income tax liability.

BOTTOM LINES: THE ULTIMATE QUESTION

Now that you have read this book and, we hope, understand the importance of planning to protect unmarried partners as individuals and as a couple, you might want to rethink the ultimate coupling question: Is it worth getting married if you and your partner have the legal right and the opportunity?

Of course, if partners aren't committed for the long term, marriage isn't the answer or even an option worth considering. Too, for most same-sex couples, it currently remains impossible.

If you and your partner already have decided you want to get married eventually and simply are postponing the inevitable, it may make sense from a financial planning point of view to go ahead and tie the knot. Or you still may change your mind and decide that the best course for you is to stay coupled and unmarried.

Whatever your decision, make sure it's consciously made, knowing the pros and cons of your ultimate choice.

At publication of this book, many questions are yet to be answered with regard to same-sex marriage. A same-sex couple can legally marry in Massachusetts. But what happens if that couple then moves to another state? And what about federal income taxes? Because of the Defense of Marriage Act, the federal government doesn't recognize same-sex marriages, nor are they recognized by many other states.

As of January 1, 2005, although California still bans same-sex marriage, same-sex domestic partners who register as such are eligible to receive comprehensive employer domestic partner benefits, including health care and state employee pension benefits. New Jersey offers similar comprehensive domestic partner benefits. The District of Columbia, Maine, and Hawaii grant certain benefits to qualified registered domestic partners. Vermont allows civil unions between same-sex partners, and while not the same as marriage, a civil union still offers statewide benefits and protections.

Only domestic partner laws in Maine and the District of Columbia include *all* domestic partners, no matter their age or sexual orientation.

Many unknowns eventually will find their way into the courts, where they will be litigated and, we hope, resolved.

And what about older couples with partners who count on Social Security survivor's benefits? Will laws be relaxed to allow them to marry yet still retain those benefits? Only time and the courts will tell.

Whether some unmarried couples admit it or not, all unmarried couples, regardless of sexual orientation, face the same legal and many of the same social hurdles. Two people who, as a couple, share their lives and finances face the same legal and financial issues as any other unmarried partners—whether straight or gay or age 20, 40, 60, or 80.

"Coming out" is only the beginning. It's a first step toward raising awareness and understanding, not only among friends, family, and loved ones but also within our government and public organizations. Unmarried coupling is a huge and growing part of today's lifestyle for Americans of all ages and walks of life. Unmarried couples should not be treated as second-class citizens reduced to dancing around laws that discriminate against them.

Until the laws change, however, unmarried couples armed with knowledge of financial planning and its importance can help and protect themselves. The key is to get started today. Consider the young woman who died on United Flight 11, which plunged into the World Trade Center on 9/11. She hadn't planned. She didn't need too, she reasoned. She wasn't going to die at her age. She put things off, and then she died.

You have the opportunity to think about your partner today. You have the opportunity to consider your future—as an individual and as part of a couple. And you now have the tools and knowledge to get started on your financial planning. What are you waiting for? We never know which tomorrow will be too late.

Smith and Delila had been together for 18 months. They had addressed many financial matters, and both were involved in their financial planning and goal setting. They decided to buy a new home together, turn their individual residences into rental properties, and aggressively pursue early retirement. The couple also began to discuss becoming adoptive parents and realized it was time to consult with experts.

When all of the proper plans, strategies, and documents were in place, Smith and Delila experienced a huge sense of relief and accomplishment. They also felt as if they had much more control over their financial future.

The benefits of having done all this work became starkly apparent shortly after the couple returned to the United States with their newly adopted infant. Smith was diagnosed with a tumor, and the couple anxiously awaited the results of the biopsy. They were comforted somewhat in knowing that they had prepared as best they could. They hadn't predicted the future, but they certainly had planned for it.

To the couple's immense relief, the biopsy showed that the tumor was benign—a happy outcome for a well-prepared partnership. Even if the medical diagnosis hadn't been so positive, however, the couple at least would have been prepared financially. You and your partner, too, can be just as prepared for the unexpected.

As financial advisors, we often ask people what they would do differently in their financial lives if they had the chance to do it all over again. Resoundingly, the response is, "I wish I had started sooner."

Whether you're 27 or 77, you've already taken a huge step toward financial security by reading this book. We urge you to take the next steps and implement all of the plans, strategies, and documents that you now know you need.

Addendum

Books

A Legal Guide for Lesbian and Gay Couples, by attorneys Hayden Curry, Denis Clifford, and Frederick Hertz. This is a legal guide for couples concerned with the legalities behind children, domestic partner benefits, marriage, wills and estate planning, property, and more.

Living Together: A Legal Guide for Unmarried Couples, by attorneys Ralph Warner, Toni Ihara, and Frederick Hertz. This book provides information and forms that unmarried couples need to define and protect their relationship in the eyes of the law. It includes 18 forms such as Agreement of Joint Intent Not to Have a Common Law Marriage, Agreement to Keep Property Separate, Agreement to Protect Property during a Split-up, and more.

Four Steps to Financial Security for Lesbian and Gay Couples, by Harold L. Lustig. This is a good overall source of sound advice on different approaches to titling of assets, tax planning, and estate planning. The concepts apply to all unmarried couples.

Other Resources

Aging with Dignity (888-5WISHES [888-594-7437], http://Agingwithdignity.org). Check out their "Five Wishes" brochure for a nominal price. Provides practical information, advice, and legal tools on health care directive and living will combinations.

AARP (888-687-2277, http://www.aarp.org). Offers a wealth of information, online and off, geared toward people 50 and older. Includes AARP Legal Services Network, a list of independent attorneys screened to meet certain standards of experience and customer service but who are not affiliated with AARP.

American Civil Liberties Union (local phone numbers available on Web site, http://www.aclu.org). Lots of information on rights, parenting, adoption, foster care, and more. There is an article on lesbian and gay parenting, adoption, and foster care.

American Psychological Association (800-374-2721, http://www.apa.org). Scientific and professional organization that represents psychology in the United States. Check out its help center (http://www.apahelpcenter .org/) for articles on topics ranging from insurance and Medicaid to parenting and retirement.

Barclay's iShares (800-ISHARES [800-474-2737], http://www.ishares.com). Learn about exchange traded funds.

Employee Benefit Research Institute (202-659-0670, http://www.ebri.org). Nonprofit, nonpartisan organization committed to data dissemination, policy research, and education on economic security and employee benefits. Check out its domestic partner benefits fact sheet (http:// www.ebri.org/facts/0304fact.pdf).

FirstGov (http://firstgov.gov). U.S. government portal to information. Go to http://www.firstgov.gov/Topics/Seniors.shtml for FirstGov for seniors.

Gay.com (877-269-2775, http://www.gay.com). Check out the site's information on family and parenting (http://www.gay.com/families).

Investopedia.com (http://www.investopedia.com). Information on retirement plans, investing, investment definitions, financial calculators, and more.

Lambda Legal (212-809-8585, http://www.lambdalegal.com). Rights advocate. Check out its wealth of information on domestic partnership laws.

Law Depot.com (866-608-1020, http://www.lawdepot.com). Many of the legal forms you need available online and customizable to individual situations.

Lawyers.com (800-526-4902, http://www.lawyers.com). Lawyer referral service from Martindale-Hubbell has profiles of 440,000 attorneys and firms worldwide, helpful tips on how to select an attorney, an interactive "Ask a Lawyer" forum for submitting questions, consumer-friendly explanations of major areas of law, articles on current legal topics, links to legal resources on the Web, a glossary of 10,000 legal terms, and more.

Marriage Laws (http://www.usmarriagelaws.com). Portal to valuable information on requirements for common law marriage; states recognizing common law marriages; cohabitation and cohabitation agreements; same sex marriages; marriage laws and licensing requirements of each state; plus plenty more.

Martindale-Hubbell (800-526-4902, http://www.martindale.com). The world's leading source of information for the legal profession and publisher of the *Martindale-Hubbell Law Directory* and Martindale.com, with information on more than 1 million lawyers and law firms in 160 countries.

MSN Money (http://moneycentral.msn.com). Resource for information about ETFs, banking, taxes, investing, financial planning, and more.

Mvelopes® (866-367-4626, http://www.mvelopes.com). Mvelopes Personal, easy online home budgeting system. Create a household budget or track your spending.

NOLO (800-728-3555, http://www.nolo.com). Do-it-yourself resource for legal issues. View samples of various documents; find reliable, plain-English books, software, and forms.

PridePlanners™ (888-896-8891, http://www.prideplanners.org). National association dedicated to keeping financial professionals up-to-the-minute about the changing and unique needs of the gay and lesbian community and nontraditional couples and families.

The Alternatives to Marriage Project (518-462-5600, http://www.unmarried .org). Advocates for equality and fairness for unmarried people, including people who choose not to marry, cannot marry, or live together before marriage. Provides support, information, and education.

The Garrett Planning Network (866-260-8400, http://www.garrettplanningnetwork .com). Nationwide organization of more than 240 fee-only, hourly as-needed financial advisors. Find a planner in your area with its online locator tool (http://www.garrettplanningnetwork.com/index .asp?tohome=yes).

The Human Rights Campaign (800-777-4723, http://www.hrc.org). A Washington, D.C., lobbying group. Site provides good links to legislative developments and information on marriage, children, and personal and financial issues facing same-sex couples.

Insurance Information

A.M. Best Company (908-439-2200, http://www.ambest.com). Worldwide insurance-rating and information agency.

Comparison Market, Inc. (877-605-7707, http://www.comparisonmarket.com). Clearinghouse (online and off) that works with a number of automobile insurance providers to link consumers with competitively priced auto insurance.

Independent Insurance Agents and Brokers of America (http://www.iiaa.org). Nation's largest national association of independent insurance agents and brokers with more than 300,000 members. Web site includes insurance agent database.

InsWeb Insurance Services (916-853-3300, http://www.InsWeb.com). Online insurance marketplace offering a variety of insurance products.

Moody's Investors Services (212-553-0300, http://moodys.com). Provides independent credit ratings, research, and financial information to the capital markets.

PrimeQuote (888-600-3600, http://www.primequote.com). Insurance marketplace that provides information, resources, and personalized quotes on insurance products.

Quotesmith and Insure.com (same thing) (800-556-9393, http://www.quotesmith.com or http://www.insure.com). Excellent source of information and comparison tools for all kinds of insurance from many different providers. Instant policy quotes available from more than 200 insurers.

Standard & Poor's (212-438-2400; http://www.2standardandpoors.com). Independent analysts; includes rating service.

United Underwriters Incorporated (http://www.uuinc.com). Exeter, New Hampshire, national organization catering to insurance brokers but providing a wealth of insurance information online to anyone. Check out an insurance company's rating (http://nettrac.ipipeline.com/link.asp?cin=10&npt=14) and more.

Weiss Ratings, Inc. (800-289-9222, http://weissratings.com). Tracks ratings for thousands of insurers as well as banks, savings and loans, stocks, and mutual funds.

Professional and Industry Organizations

American Bar Association (312-988-5000, http://www.abanet.org). Offers an online lawyer referral service.

CFP Board (888-237-6275, http://www.cfp.net). Nonprofit Denver organization that awards Certified Financial Planner™ designation. Find out about this designation and the financial planning process at its Web site.

Financial Planning Association (800-322-4237, http://www.fpanet.org/public). A membership organization for the financial planning community. Check out its National Financial Planning Support Center (http://www.fpanet.org/public) for lots of information and CFP® search tool.

Legal Services Corporation (http://www.rin.lsc.gov/rinboard/rguide/pdir1.htm). National directory of free legal services providers for low-income individuals.

National Association of Personal Financial Advisors (NAPFA) (800-366-2732, http://www.napfa.org). Resource about fee-only financial planners. Check out its consumer tips.

Society of Financial Service Professionals (888-243-2258, http://www.financialpro.org). Membership group of financial services professionals.

Government Agencies and Regulators

Internal Revenue Service (800-829-1040, http://www.irs.gov). Estate tax rules, retirement plan contribution limits, income tax brackets, tax forms, FAQ about filing taxes, etc.

National Association of Insurance Commissioners (816-842-3600, http://www.naic.org). National organization of state insurance regulators. Visit its Consumer Information Source (http://www.naic.org/consumer).

National Association of Securities Dealers (301-590-6500, http://www.nasd.com). Regulates America's securities industry. Find out about a broker via its BrokerCheck or brush up on your investing education online.

North American Securities Administrators Association (202-737-0900, http://www.nasaa.org). Investor protection specialists. Find a regulator in your area (http://www.nasaa.org/nasaa/abtnasaa/find_regulator.asp), tips to identify securities fraud, and more.

Securities and Exchange Commission (202-942-7040, http://www.sec.gov).

Social Security Administration (800-772-1213, http://www.ssa.gov). Find out everything you need to know about you and Social Security. Includes an online benefits calculator.

U.S. Department of Health and Human Services, Administration on Aging (http://www.hhs.gov). List of legal hotlines for seniors (http://www.aoa.gov/eldfam/Elder Rights/Legal Assistance/Legal Hotline.asp).

Glossary

adoption Legal process in which adult(s) become parent(s) to and raise a nonbiological child as their own.

annuity Investment vehicle issued by an insurance company in which an individual invests a lump sum or makes periodic payments into a tax-deferred account for a specified period of time; account grows at a fixed rate (fixed annuity) or a variable rate (variable annuity); and a periodic income stream or lump sum can be received anytime in the future.

birth parent(s) A child's biological parent(s).

charitable remainder unitrust Irrevocable trust that provides financial support to its creator or specific individuals for a specified time. At the end of that time, the assets left in the trust pass to a designated charity.

closed adoption Confidential adoption in which records are sealed so there is no further contact between biological and adoptive parents or families.

coadoption Adoption by two unmarried people.

cohabitation Living together.

common law marriage Legally recognized spousal union between domestic partners if certain conditions are met, including living together for a "significant" time, presenting yourselves as a married couple, and having the intention to be married.

coparenting Situation in which adult, nonlegal parent provides ongoing support and assistance in raising a child.

Crummey letter Name of annual notification in writing to beneficiaries of an irrevocable life insurance trust that a gift has been made to the trust; named after the person, Crummey, who won a related case against the IRS.

Defense of Marriage Act Also referred to as DOMA, this federal law passed in 1996 defines marriage as the union of a man and a woman and mandates that no state has to recognize a same-sex marriage allowed in another state.

defined contribution plan A qualified retirement plan in which the employee's benefit is determined by the amount of contributions made by the employee and the employer; most closely associated with 401(k) and 403(b) plans.

disability insurance Safety net providing income replacement in case of severe illness or disability that affects policyholder's ability to perform his or her job.

domestic adoption Adoption within the United States.

domestic partnership Unmarried couple living together as spousal equivalents.

domestic partnership agreement Legal document between unmarried partners spelling out rights, obligations, and responsibilities of each partner; also may address contingencies in the event of dissolution of the relationship.

donor Same as a creator or grantor, the person who establishes and funds a trust.

Employee Retirement Income Security Act Also known as ERISA, it lays out federal requirements that govern pension eligibility.

financial power of attorney Legal document that stipulates a specific individual to manage financial affairs of someone else in the event that person becomes incapacitated.

funeral directive Document stipulating what an individual wants to happen to his or her body after death, including funeral/memorial plans and disposition of remains.

gifting over time Strategy of giving that limits gift tax liability.

gift tax Assessment levied by the government on a donor who passes assets to another. Anyone can gift up to $11,000 a year to any one person gift tax–free ($1 million lifetime).

grantor Also known as creator or donor, the person who establishes and funds a trust.

grantor remainder income trust Also known as a GRIT, this is an irrevocable trust in which the grantor creates a trust for a certain time frame, funds it, and then receives income for life from it.

health care directive See power of attorney for health care.

"I love you" will Will in which domestic partners designate each other as beneficiaries of all of each others' assets.

insurable interest For purposes of insurance, relationship in which a beneficiary would incur financial hardship at the death of the insured.

international adoption Out-of-country adoption.

inter vivos **trust** Also known as a living trust, a trust created while the grantor or donor is still alive.

intestate Dying without a will.

irrevocable life insurance trust Third-party asset ownership—in this case, of a life insurance policy. Grantor or creator of trust exchanges control of asset for the ability to exclude these assets from his or her estate.

irrevocable trust Trust that, once established, cannot be changed or altered. Assets of trust are removed from grantor's estate and not subject to estate taxes.

joint ownership Method in which more than one person holds title to an asset.

joint tenancy Asset ownership split equally between two or more partners. Generally includes rights of survivorship (JTWROS); after death, that partner's share of ownership automatically transfers to the surviving owner or owners.

Keogh A tax-deferred qualified retirement plan for self-employed individuals and unincorporated businesses, also called a self-employed pension.

living trust Also known as revocable trust, a financial-planning tool enabling its grantor or creator to maintain full control over the assets in the trust while he or she is alive. It can be changed, altered, or even revoked.

living will Legal document put in place that stipulates if an individual becomes incapacitated, if and under what circumstances he or she would want to be kept alive by artificial means.

long-term care insurance Financial safety net to handle cost of extended skilled and custodial nursing home care or, in some cases, in-home care, in the event of extended illness and/or incapacity.

look-back rule Process in which Medicaid goes back three to five years in an individual's financial life to ascertain that he or she has not divested assets solely for the purpose of obtaining Medicaid eligibility.

older/mature couple Older heterosexual man and woman (including seniors, widows, and widowers) eligible for Social Security benefits who are a couple but opt not to marry or remarry for family, financial, or personal reasons.

open adoption Adoption in which child's birth parents and adoptive parents meet and often have an ongoing relationship.

partition A court-ordered separation of the interests in property of joint owners or tenants in common so that each may take possession and control his or her share of the property.

Payable on Death (POD) Asset transfer method in which the individually owned asset passes to a designated beneficiary on the death of its owner.

phantom income For purposes of domestic partner benefits, the cost of the premium paid by the employer that is added to the employee's income for tax purposes.

pour-over will Document stipulating that deceased individual's assets without beneficiary designations will transfer, or pour over, into a trust.

power of attorney for health care Also known as health care proxy or health care directive, this legally binding document states a specific individual or individuals will make health care decisions for another in the event that person cannot make them for themselves.

private/independent adoption Adoption that does not involve licensed agency. Often involves private attorney, birth parent(s), and adoptive parent(s).

probate Legal process of settling deceased person's financial affairs and distributing his or her assets.

Qualified Domestic Relations Order Also known as QDRO, a federal mandate allowing divorcing couples to split retirement plan assets into two separate retirement accounts without incurring early-withdrawal or tax penalties.

revocable living trust Individual places his or her assets in the trust and, as the trustee, continues to control those assets as long as he or she is living and cognizant. Can be changed or revoked. Provides contingencies in the event of disability by naming a successor trustee.

same-sex couple Gay or lesbian domestic partners.

Social Security survivor's benefits Qualified monthly cash assistance from Social Security available to spouses, former spouses, widows, widowers, and some other qualified family members following the death of a person who has worked and paid into Social Security for a certain period of time.

springing power of attorney A power of attorney that goes into effect only if and when a person becomes incapacitated.

step-up in basis On inheriting assets, the recipient receives a new cost figure for tax purposes, which is the value of the asset at the date of death or six months later, depending on the valuation date used by the estate's executor.

successor trustee Individual designated in a living trust to take over management of that trust in the event of the grantor's or creator's incapacity.

tenants in common Asset ownership in which multiple parties hold varying percentages. After death, a partner's share goes to their designated heir(s) via a will, or by state law if intestate.

testamentary trust A trust created by a will after the grantor/donor dies.

tort Intentional or unintentional harm to the person or property of another, as in tort law.

Transfer on Death (TOD) Asset transfer technique designating that the property or asset passes to a specific beneficiary after its owner's death.

trust Method of holding and/or passing assets in which another entity holds title to asset for the benefit of another. Can be "revocable," in which grantor retains control of asset, or "irrevocable," in which grantor relinquishes all control over the assets in return for estate tax savings.

unlimited marital property transfer Ability of spouses to pass any amount of assets to each other while living and at death.

waiting period Also known as elimination period, the period of time before one can collect disability or long-term care benefits.

younger couple Heterosexual man and woman who choose to postpone marriage or not marry at all or who are divorced and choose not to remarry.

Index

Share the message!

Bulk discounts
Discounts start at only 10 copies and range from 30% to 55% off retail price based on quantity.

Custom publishing
Private label a cover with your organization's name and logo. Or, tailor information to your needs with a custom pamphlet that highlights specific chapters.

Ancillaries
Workshop outlines, videos, and other products are available on select titles.

Dynamic speakers
Engaging authors are available to share their expertise and insight at your event.

**Call Dearborn Trade Special Sales at
1-800-621-9621, ext. 4444,
or e-mail trade@dearborn.com**

Dearborn™
Trade Publishing
A **Kaplan Professional** Company